# Cultural Influences and International Students

## Understanding Academic Experiences in US Higher Education

**Kruti S. Chaliawala**

*Boise State University, Boise, ID, US*

Series in Sociology

VERNON PRESS

www.vernonpress.com

| *In the Americas:* | *In the rest of the world:* |
| --- | --- |
| Vernon Press | Vernon Press |
| 1000 N West Street, Suite 1200, | C/Sancti Espiritu 17, |
| Wilmington, Delaware 19801 | Malaga, 29006 |
| United States | Spain |

Series in Sociology

Library of Congress Control Number: 2025947334

ISBN: 979-8-8819-0420-3
Also available: 979-8-8819-0400-5 [Hardback]; 979-8-8819-0416-6 [PDF, E-Book]

# Contents

# List of Abbreviations

**AI (Artificial Intelligence):**
The simulation of human intelligence processes by machines.

**APA (American Psychological Association):**
A widely used style guide for academic writing, particularly in the social and behavioral sciences.

**CPT (Curricular Practical Training):**
A temporary employment authorization for F-1 student visa holders while pursuing education to gain practical experience directly related to their major field of study, which is an essential part of their curriculum.

**F-1 Student:**
A non-immigrant visa status for students pursuing academic studies and language training programs in the United States.

**GPA (Grade Point Average):**
A numerical measure of a student's academic performance, usually calculated by dividing the total number of grade points earned by the total number of credit hours attempted. A grading system native to the US.

**H-1B (Specialty Occupation Visa):**
A non-immigrant visa category that allows US employers to hire foreign workers in specialty occupations temporarily, often three years, with the opportunity to extend. The H-1B visa program is subject to an annual cap, usually requiring a lottery for selection.

**IIE (Institute of International Education):**
A nonprofit organization focused on international education and exchange, known for its Open Doors Report and accurate statistics on international student mobility.

**IELTS (International English Language Testing System):**
A standardized test of English proficiency for non-native speakers, typically taken to gain admission to a college or university in an English-speaking country. IELTS is a must for countries such as the US, Canada, the UK, Australia, and some parts of Europe.

**MLA (Modern Language Association):**
A widely used style guide for academic writing, especially in the humanities.

| **NAFSA (NAFSA Association of International Educators):** | The world's largest nonprofit organization dedicated to international education and exchange. |
| **OPT (Optional Practical Training):** | A temporary employment authorization allowing F-1 student visa holders to gain practical experience directly related to their major, after their academic program is concluded. |
| **PhD (Doctor of Philosophy):** | The highest academic degree awarded in many fields, requiring original research and a dissertation, often referred to as a terminal degree in many fields. |
| **PWIs (Predominantly White Institutions):** | A term referring to higher education institutions in the US where the student demographic composition is mainly white students. |
| **STEM (Science, Technology, Engineering, and Mathematics):** | An umbrella term for these academic disciplines focusing on various science, technology, engineering, and mathematics-related fields. |
| **TOEFL (Test of English as a Foreign Language):** | A standardized exam to assess the English proficiency of non-native speakers aiming to enroll in English-speaking universities. |
| **TPB (Theory of Planned Behavior):** | A social-psychological model linking beliefs and actions, suggesting that a person's intention to perform a behavior is the most immediate predictor. |
| **UIS (UNESCO Institute for Statistics):** | The statistical office of UNESCO and the UN's repository for global data in education, science and technology, culture, and communication. |

# Preface

In 2010, at the age of nineteen, I began a journey from a small town in India to a university in the United States, filled with a mix of excitement and nervousness. My family, unfamiliar with international travel and the ticket booking process, found the system somewhat confusing due to a lack of proper guidance. After a tiring 38-hour flight across three time zones and two long layovers, I arrived in Denver, Colorado. As per the regulations, anyone travelling from outside the US has to go to customs and border patrol with their luggage. Note that this was not only my first flight but also my first experience in an entirely new world.

Instead of a warm welcome, I faced suspicion. At the immigration desk, my slight build and four large suitcases seemed to attract extra scrutiny, and Homeland Security officers questioned me for hours. This initial encounter in this new, unknown, foreign country was far from friendly; it felt like I was being judged. This uncomfortable and isolating experience profoundly influenced my early years in the US, marking my first encounter with being "othered," a silent challenge many international students face but rarely speak about. My undergraduate journey began with a shy approach, yet it was marked by a firm determination, despite the rocky start. However, difficulties continued in several ways. In classes, some instructors showed a lack of understanding of students' diverse accents and dialects. Comments like, "Since English is your second language, you probably do not know how to write a proper paper," chipped away at my confidence and created barriers to success, making it challenging to participate in conversations with faculty members and peers alike.

Outside class, I dealt with complex visa rules, language barriers, racial discrimination, and obstacles most local students may never have faced. Tasks that should have been straightforward often became primary sources of stress due to various barriers, including vague guidelines, discriminatory explanations of education-related questions, and a convoluted system of credit hours that was never part of the education system back home. Still, I pressed on. Despite a plethora of self-doubt and the challenges of finding resolutions to numerous hurdles, I completed a dual bachelor's degree. With dedication and determination, I further gained two master's degrees. The light at the end of the tunnel for me was ultimately earning my PhD in Health Education. Each achievement was hard-won, fueled by resilience, persistence, and unwavering effort.

This book offers a glimpse into my journey, serving as a testament to the resilience of international students navigating the US higher education system. It explores the emotional challenges of cultural adjustment, language barriers, discrimination, and the ever-going search for belonging. Using a mix of personal stories, research, and lived experiences, this work aims to foster understanding and inspire positive change towards the overall health and well-being of international students. By the end of this book, educators, institutions, and readers alike will be encouraged to create a more inclusive and supportive environment for all students, especially those who have traveled thousands of miles to pursue their education.

Regards,

Kruti S. Chaliawala, PhD, CHES

(Note: In my culture, my middle initial, S., honors my father, whose wisdom and unwavering encouragement empowered me to face the world bravely. He passed away in 2020 from non-COVID complications, a profound loss that left me, an international student, unable to return for his funeral due to pressing visa issues and border closures. This book is dedicated to his enduring spirit and the sacrifices, seen and unseen, that international students often make to pursue their goals, demonstrating extraordinary resilience and perseverance in carving out their paths.)

**Disclaimer:** I acknowledge that I have used the AI-based tool Grammarly to assist with grammar checking, language refinement, and paraphrasing during the manuscript preparation process. No AI tools were used to generate original content.

Chapter One
# Introduction
# The Cultural Context of Education

Every year, millions of students undertake a significant life change, moving abroad to pursue higher education. As Shapiro et al. (2014) note, these individuals undertake a significant relocation to engage with colleges or universities in a host nation. In the United States (US), this population is officially recognized by the United States Citizenship and Immigration Services (USCIS) as non-US citizens enrolled in higher education institutions who are neither immigrants (permanent residents) nor refugees (USCIS, 2015). The very designation "international student" is a temporary identity, applicable only while one is actively pursuing education abroad. Once academic pursuit concludes or their visa status shifts, this particular identity ceases to exist (Bista & Foster, 2016). However, despite this widely accepted legal definition, the precise classification of international students can surprisingly change depending on the countries and institutions. For instance, a Malaysian student attending a local branch of an Australian university may be considered both a regional and an international student, depending on the specific institutional context and classification (de Wit, 2016). Indeed, the global education landscape uses a diverse range of terms to describe these individuals, including non-immigrant, foreign, transnational, non-resident alien, and inbound/outbound students (Filomeno & Brown, 2022). These varied classifications underscore the inherent complexity of international student mobility and the continuously evolving nature of global higher education policies, which often shape, and sometimes fundamentally limit, the lived experiences of those they define. This academic framework, however, usually overlooks the profoundly personal and disorienting reality that students like me face.

When I first stepped off the plane in the US in 2010, I was just 19 years old, brimming with hopes to start a new chapter as an international student from India. I had no idea about the term 'alien' that people used in official paperwork, an official label that, even then, felt tinged with an uncomfortable sense of "otherness." The first few days in this new country were riddled with an overwhelming sense of fear. Everything was unfamiliar, new, and confusing, and I constantly felt like I was being watched. Simple errands, like getting a Subway sandwich, became an ordeal where I was too scared to go alone, continually worried about how I would be perceived. Strangers in the community often approached me with curiosity, and sometimes unsettling questions about whether I was from the Middle East or Mexico. Their questions made me feel even more out of place, as if I did not belong anywhere. I was here with one goal: to focus on my studies and build a better future. However, these interactions chipped away at my confidence and deepened my sense of isolation and lack of belonging. I felt incredibly alone, more than I ever had before, in a place that was supposed to be full of opportunities, new experiences, and beginnings.

## 1.1 Global Trends in International Student Mobility

The lasting presence of international students greatly enriches academic, social, political, and cultural discussions across countries (Wang & Sun, 2022). Worldwide, the United States, the United Kingdom, Australia, Canada, and New Zealand consistently emerge as the top destinations for these mobile scholars (UNESCO Institute for Statistics, 2021). A mix of global factors, such as ongoing economic globalization, rapid technological advancements, and the perceived quality of educational systems in host countries, mainly drives the increasing trend of international student mobility. In particular, globalization has fundamentally transformed the academic landscape, as the rising interconnectedness of economies and the expansion of multinational corporations have created a highly competitive global job market.

In this changing landscape, international students emerge as highly valued talent. They gain invaluable cross-cultural skills, develop broad global perspectives, and acquire specialized knowledge, making them highly attractive to employers worldwide. Technological advances have greatly supported this trend by improving communication, making information more accessible, and simplifying the study-abroad application process. At the same time, the exceptional quality of education in top destination countries acts as a strong draw. Reputable institutions known for research excellence and innovation, especially in the United States, Canada, Australia, and parts of Europe, are consistently ranked among the best in the world. Attending these prestigious universities offers more than just respected academic credentials; it also opens doors to vital professional opportunities, enriches internships, and provides invaluable networking within global industries. Moreover, strong economic reasons often drive these educational choices; studying abroad can lead to better job prospects, higher earning potential, and an increased chance of obtaining permanent residency or work opportunities after graduation.

Despite the occasional fluctuations driven by external factors, global trends unequivocally reveal a consistent upward trajectory in international student mobility over recent decades, a phenomenon robustly evidenced by UNESCO

Institute for Statistics (UIS) data. Although traditional strongholds like the United States, the United Kingdom, and Australia remain immensely popular, Asia has rapidly emerged as a pivotal source region for migrating students. China, India, and South Korea are among the top countries known to send the highest number of students abroad, fueled by powerful aspirations for higher-quality education, specialized training, and accelerated global career advancement.

## 1.2 Impact of the COVID-19 Pandemic on International Student Enrollment

The COVID-19 pandemic has significantly impacted international students and disrupted their academic schedules. Many students faced uncertainty about their study plans, with some delays or abandoning their goals due to financial issues, visa problems, and health concerns. Online learning became the main alternative, but it brought challenges such as time zone differences, limited access to campus resources, and difficulties staying engaged academically. The lack of face-to-face interaction also increased feelings of isolation and cultural disconnect among international students. Governments and universities around the world implemented various measures to address these challenges. Some institutions offered tuition discounts, extended application deadlines, and adopted hybrid learning models to accommodate students unable to travel.

Additionally, policy changes like visa relaxations and post-study work options were introduced in several countries to attract and keep international students amid declining enrollments. As pandemic restrictions eased, international student numbers gradually recovered. Many students who had postponed their plans resumed their applications, leading to increased enrollments. The shift back to in-person classes has renewed interest in studying abroad, driven by the desire for immersive academic experiences and global career opportunities.

## 1.3 Comparative Analysis: International Students in the US vs. Other Countries

The experiences of international students vary considerably, heavily influenced by their host country's policies, culture, and institutional systems. In the US, for example, international students often face high financial costs, strict visa regulations, and tough social integration challenges (Bista & Foster, 2016). This differs from countries like Canada and Australia, which have more flexible immigration policies aimed at supporting post-graduation work opportunities and residency (Bozdogan & Comeaux, 2007). Each country's unique approach significantly shapes the international student attitude.

**United States:** The US continues to attract a large number of international students, mainly because of its world-renowned universities and unmatched research opportunities. However, this appeal is often limited by some of the strictest visa and work restrictions in the world. The F-1 visa only allows limited on-campus employment, and even the Optional Practical Training (OPT) program provides only a temporary work permit after graduation. The highly competitive H-1B visa lottery system adds considerable uncertainty for those trying to secure long-term employment (Jiang & Altinyelken, 2021). Additionally, while many US universities excel at offering academic support, comprehensive cultural integration programs are often limited, leaving students to face complex social and cultural challenges with little institutional help.

**Canada:** Canada has quickly become a top choice, mainly because of its very student-friendly immigration policies. The nation's Post-Graduation Work Permit (PGWP) allows international students to work for up to three years after graduation, making it much easier to find meaningful employment and move toward permanent residency. Besides policy, Canadian universities are praised for offering extensive support for international students, including strong mentorship programs, accessible counseling services, and essential language support initiatives (Institute of International Education, 2022).

**United Kingdom:** The UK has a long history of hosting international students, especially at prestigious institutions like Oxford and Cambridge. However, things have changed after Brexit, which introduced new, complicated visa and work restrictions affecting students from EU countries. However, the UK's Graduate Route visa allows eligible students to stay in the UK for two years after graduation (extended to three years for PhD graduates), mainly to seek employment. Though UK universities emphasize academic support, they often fall short in providing dedicated social integration resources, which can make it harder for students to fully integrate into the broader community (Brogden-Ward, 2021).

**Australia:** Australian universities are widely recognized for their proactive focus on inclusivity and their deep engagement with international students. The country's Temporary Graduate Visa (subclass 485) allows international students to stay and work in Australia after completing their studies, providing a clear post-study pathway. Australian institutions invest significantly in comprehensive cultural adaptation programs, strong mental health services, and valuable peer mentoring initiatives, all strategically designed to facilitate both academic and social integration (Erturk & Nguyen Luu, 2022).

**Europe:** The diverse range of European countries offers a spectrum of policies affecting international students. Countries like Germany and the Netherlands stand out by providing low or no tuition fees, along with accessible work opportunities during and after studies. Many European universities have strategically incorporated English-language programs to attract international students, and numerous government-backed initiatives help students adjust to new environments (Domínguez & Cheng, 2022). Despite these benefits, persistent language barriers and complex bureaucratic processes can still present significant challenges for non-EU students navigating these systems.

### 1.4 International Student Enrollment in the United States

International student enrollment in the United States has historically been substantial, significantly impacting the nation's higher education system. The Institute of International Education (IIE) reported that during the 2018/2019 academic year, the number of international students in the US reached 1,075,496, which was the highest in recent years. These students come from various regions, with the most significant numbers from China, India, South Korea, Saudi Arabia, and Canada. However, the COVID-19 pandemic brought unprecedented challenges, leading to a substantial decline in international enrollment. Travel bans, student visa processing delays, embassy closures, health concerns, and financial uncertainties have forced many prospective students to defer or cancel their plans. As a result, many institutions experienced drops in international student enrollment during the 2020/2021 academic year, with a particularly decline in new student enrollments. Despite these setbacks, the 2021/2022 academic year marked a turning point, with international student numbers rebounding as travel restrictions were lifted, universities adapted to remote and hybrid learning models, and the demand for US higher education remained strong.

According to IIE's Open Doors Report, international student enrollment increased by more than 4% in 2021/2022, signaling renewed interest and mobility. The resurgence of international students has significant economic implications. According to the NAFSA Association of International Educators, tuition and other income from international students contributed over $40 billion to the US economy. They supported more than 368,000 jobs during the 2022-2023 academic year. Their financial contributions go beyond tuition and fees, including housing, transportation, food, healthcare, and other personal expenses that benefit local economies. Many universities, especially public institutions, depend on international student tuition to fund academic programs, research projects, and financial aid for domestic students. Beyond their economic impact, international students significantly enrich the educational and cultural fabric of US higher education. Their diverse backgrounds and perspectives promote cross-cultural exchanges, enhance classroom discussions, and boost the global competitiveness of American universities. They also make notable contributions to research and innovation, particularly in STEM fields, where they represent a large share of graduate students and researchers. Their involvement in scientific discoveries, technological progress, and interdisciplinary collaborations strengthens the global reputation of US institutions, attracting further investments and partnerships. As global mobility recovers after the pandemic, universities are continuously refining recruitment strategies and support systems to sustain and expand their international student populations. These efforts include increasing scholarship opportunities, simplifying application and visa procedures, improving support services, and cultivating inclusive campus environments. US institutions aim to remain leading destinations for international education and global talent development by focusing on these initiatives.

### 1.5 Demographic Characteristics of International Students

International students bring a rich and diverse set of backgrounds, identities, and experiences that shape their academic journeys. To understand who these students are and better guide the reader to the central point of this book, it is essential to explore their cultural, national, and racial backgrounds. Their racial and ethnic identities, socioeconomic statuses, and geopolitical influences are vital to their educational experiences and results. The intersectionality of these factors emphasizes the complex reality of international students' integration into higher education institutions worldwide. Language barriers, differing learning styles, and social integration challenges further shape their experiences. As the international student population continues to grow, institutions may need to adapt to meet the needs of this dynamic demographic by fostering culturally competent support systems and creating inclusive learning environments.

International students come from a variety of racial and ethnic backgrounds, shaped by their countries of origin, historical experiences, and cultural traditions. While they all contribute to a diverse global academic community, their experiences differ greatly depending on their racial and ethnic backgrounds. For instance, the largest groups of international students in the US traditionally come from Asia, particularly China and India, followed by South Korea, and increasingly from other regions, such as the Middle East (e.g., Saudi Arabia) and Latin America (e.g., Brazil; IIE, 2022). However, outside of this leading group, there is growing representation from countries like Brazil, Saudi Arabia, and Canada, showing an evolving international student landscape.

Despite this diversity, racial and ethnic minority international students often face distinct challenges. Students from underrepresented racial and ethnic groups, including African, Latino, and Indigenous communities, may encounter added difficulties related to identity, discrimination, and social integration. The intersection of race, ethnicity, and nationality can significantly influence their sense of belonging and academic success. Microaggressions, racial biases, and systemic barriers often reflect the experiences of minority students. Still, they may be intensified for international students due to cultural differences and unfamiliarity with the host country's norms. For example, African students in predominantly white institutions (PWIs) may face implicit biases and stereotypes that influence their academic involvement, interactions with faculty and peers, and success. Latino international students might also experience dual pressures, balancing adaptation to US higher education with navigating racialization within the broader social setting. The effects of racial discrimination on international students go beyond academics, impacting their mental health, social connections, and willingness to participate in need to adopt policies and programs that acknowledge campus life or find a place where they belong. To promote inclusivity, universities and address racial inequalities among international students. Anti-racism training, culturally relevant counseling services, and mentorship programs can offer essential support. Furthermore, promoting diverse faculty representation and inclusive curricula can help create a learning environment that values and affirms everyone's experiences.

Beyond racial and ethnic diversity, international students come from various socioeconomic backgrounds, which greatly affects their educational experiences. Students from low-income families, those with disabilities, and individuals from economically disadvantaged areas face extra obstacles that make adjusting to academic life in the US more difficult. Financial constraints are among the biggest challenges for low-income international students. Unlike domestic students, they often have limited access to scholarships, grants, and financial aid. High tuition fees, combined with expenses for housing, healthcare, and transportation, put significant economic pressure on them. Many students have to work part-time jobs, but even that becomes an obstacle due to visa restrictions and limited job opportunities. This financial stress can cause increased anxiety, lower academic performance, and a higher chance of dropping out (Li, 2020). International students with disabilities also encounter unique challenges when navigating higher education abroad. Although some US universities offer strong disability support services, international students may find it hard to access these resources because of cultural stigmas surrounding disability or unfamiliarity with campus accommodations.

In many cases, students come from educational systems that do not offer the same level of support, making the transition especially challenging. The lack of accessible learning environments can hinder their academic participation and limit their ability to integrate into campus life fully. To better assist students from diverse socioeconomic and ability backgrounds, universities should develop targeted programs that address their unique needs. Offering emergency financial aid, increasing access to disability accommodations, and providing dedicated mentorship for marginalized groups can significantly improve international students' academic experiences and overall well-being.

Geopolitical events play a key role in shaping international student mobility and academic experiences. Political instability, economic crises, global pandemics, and changing immigration policies affect students' ability to study abroad and their experiences in host countries. For instance, the COVID-19 pandemic significantly disrupted international education by imposing travel restrictions, changing visa policies, and raising new health concerns. Many students from countries like China, India, and Brazil faced unforeseen hurdles, such as sudden border closures, challenges with remote learning, and uncertainties regarding their student status (IIE, 2022). Furthermore, some students encountered xenophobia and discrimination, especially those from regions heavily affected by the pandemic. Beyond global health crises, political tensions, and economic downturns, other factors also impact international students. Trade disputes between the US and China, for example, have affected the mobility of Chinese students, with concerns over visa denials and academic restrictions. Similarly, students from politically unstable regions, such as Ukraine or Afghanistan, face heightened uncertainties regarding their legal status, personal safety, and financial stability. These geopolitical factors can create an atmosphere of fear, anxiety, and isolation, further complicating academic and social experiences of these students. The impact of such events extends beyond legal boundaries; they also have psychological and emotional repercussions. International students from conflict-affected areas may suffer from heightened levels of stress, trauma, or face difficulty concentrating on their studies due to concerns for their families back home. Moreover, visa irregularities and restrictions can cause uncertainty about their academic and professional futures, leaving students in a state of constant apprehension.

## 1.6 Challenges & Barriers

Despite their diverse contributions to the American higher education system, international students face numerous challenges when adapting to life in the US. These issues can be very stressful and sometimes overwhelming, especially during the early part of their academic journey. Culture shock and adjustment difficulties are among the most immediate obstacles international students encounter. Moving from one's home country to a foreign environment often involves learning new social norms, values, and expectations, which can cause discomfort and fear. Differences in communication styles, academic standards, and classroom participation expectations can make students feel out of place or unsure about their roles in that environment. The emotional stress of these changes is worsened by homesickness as students are apart from their usual support networks, including family, friends, and familiar cultural outlets. This separation from their home culture and community can make emotional adaptation particularly challenging. Students frequently feel isolated and stressed as they try to integrate into a new environment (Rivas et al., 2019). Academic pressure affects international students, who may already feel intense pressure to succeed in an unfamiliar education system. Variations in teaching styles, such as shifting from rote memorization to critical thinking, and differences in assessment methods often require significant adjustments.

Additionally, striving for academic excellence can lead to feelings of inadequacy, as international students might struggle to meet new educational standards. This pressure is further intensified by their families' expectations, many of whom invest substantial financial and emotional resources into their children's education abroad. For many students, the pressure to fulfill their family's hopes for success adds an extra layer of stress and anxiety, which can result in academic burnout and mental health issues (Forbes-Mewett & Nyland, 2008; Lee & Rice, 2007; Poyrazli & Lopez, 2007).

Language barriers pose a significant challenge, particularly for students whose first language is not English. Limited speaking, listening, reading, and writing ability can interfere with academic performance and social integration. Students may often face challenges grasping complex academic terminology and articulating their thoughts effectively in both class discussions and written work. This communication gap can lead to frustration, self-doubt, and feelings of inferiority, further worsening the academic and social difficulties they encounter. Although US universities usually require international students to demonstrate English proficiency through standardized tests like TOEFL or IELTS for admission, excelling in these exams does not always guarantee full linguistic readiness for the complex academic and social environment of the United States. These tests mainly evaluate basic language skills in artificial, created settings. However, the US university class environment is different and may present significant linguistic challenges that can still impede comprehension and proper integration. For instance, the rapid pace of lectures, the specific academic schedule, and the diverse range of regional and international accents encountered in classrooms and social settings often exceed the demands of these aforementioned tests. Consequently, even students with high test scores may struggle to grasp nuances in active lectures, participate effectively in discussions, and fully integrate into social circles, leading to feelings of "language incompetence" despite being proficient. Social isolation and discrimination are widespread issues that often accompany the academic and cultural challenges faced by international students. Building meaningful friendships and fully engaging in campus life can be intimidating, especially when cultural differences create barriers to social interaction. The majority of international students may experience a sense of exclusion, finding it difficult to relate to others who may not understand or appreciate their cultural backgrounds. Some students also face direct or subtle discrimination, including microaggressions and xenophobic attitudes, which can have a profound impact on their mental health and academic performance. These negative experiences may hinder social integration and can lead to feeling anxious and alienated, affecting the overall well-being of students (Forbes-Mewett & Nyland, 2008; Lee & Rice, 2007; Poyrazli & Lopez, 2007).

Lastly, financial constraints are a primary concern for many international students. These students often face significant financial challenges while studying abroad, including high tuition costs, living expenses, and other educational fees. Visa restrictions often limit their ability to work, making it harder to manage these enormous financial burdens. Financial stress worsens when students cannot work or earn extra income, making it challenging to afford essentials like rent, food, and textbooks. For many, this financial strain can cause anxiety, affect their academic focus, and complicate their adaptation to student life. International students face multiple challenges when adjusting to the American higher education system. These challenges include culture shock, language barriers, financial stress, and social isolation. To succeed academically and feel a sense of belonging in a new environment, international students need comprehensive support from educational institutions. They encounter diverse academic and cultural hurdles, which require institutional awareness and tailored support. These challenges often intertwine, creating a complex web of obstacles that influence students' experiences in US higher education.

International students often face significant challenges and barriers related to housing and food insecurity, in addition to the cultural and language barriers. These barriers may affect the overall well-being of these students and indirectly affect their academic journey. Understanding these issues is crucial for universities to support international students and ensure their academic success.

**Housing Insecurity:** Housing insecurity is a significant issue faced by international students, particularly those unfamiliar with the housing market in their host country. The transition to a new cultural and educational environment often leaves international students vulnerable to exploitation in housing arrangements, resulting in overcrowded living conditions, a lack of affordable housing options, and difficulty navigating lease agreements or landlord expectations. International students may struggle to find housing that aligns with their cultural norms or personal preferences, such as space for communal cooking or a quiet environment conducive to studying (Amoyaw et al., 2022). In addition to these cultural factors, a majority of international students face financial constraints that make it difficult to secure stable housing. They may not have the same access to credit or economic resources as domestic students, further limiting their housing options. As a result, international students may resort to substandard housing conditions, leading to increased stress and anxiety, directly impacting their academic performance.

These stress factors associated with housing insecurity often lead to depression and anxiety, which can hinder students' ability to focus on their studies and engage in academic activities (NAFSA, 2019).

**Food Insecurity:** This is another prevalent issue among international students, with many facing difficulty accessing affordable, culturally appropriate food. International students often struggle to manage food costs due to unfamiliarity with local grocery stores, high prices, and a lack of cooking facilities. Cultural differences in food preferences and dietary restrictions further complicate their ability to find suitable food options on or near campus. Additionally, international students may face the challenge of cooking in shared or inadequate kitchen spaces, leading to food scarcity or the consumption of nutritionally inadequate meals (Amoyaw et al., 2022). The experience of food insecurity can have significant implications for international students' mental and physical health. A lack of access to basic and nutritious food can lead to fatigue, reduced cognitive function, and overall diminished physical health, effectively undermining academic performance. Furthermore, food insecurity often leads to heightened stress and anxiety as students get worried about their ability to meet basic needs. As outlined by NAFSA (2019), food insecurity can also contribute to feelings of isolation, as students may feel ashamed or reluctant to seek help due to cultural stigmas associated with poverty or needing assistance.

**Impact on Academia:** Cultural differences may have a compounding effect on the housing and food insecurity issues for international students. Many international students come from countries where housing and food systems differ significantly from those in their host country. They may not be familiar with the local norms surrounding shared housing, rental agreements, or the expectations of landlords, which can lead to confusion and miscommunication. Additionally, cultural differences in food practices, dietary preferences, and cooking styles can make it challenging for international students to adapt to the local food environment (NAFSA, 2019). The inability to access culturally familiar foods or the struggle to find appropriate food alternatives can impact students' emotional well-being and sense of belonging, further complicating their adjustment to academic life. The stress associated with housing and food insecurity can result in significant educational challenges. International students facing housing instability may find it difficult to concentrate on their studies or participate fully in campus life due to the distractions and anxiety caused by their living situation. Similarly, food insecurity can lead to physical and mental exhaustion, impairing cognitive function and reducing academic performance. In addition, the stigma associated with food insecurity and poor housing conditions may prevent international students from seeking help, leading to increased feelings of isolation and disconnection from their peers (UWS-Promethean, 2019).

**Support Strategies and Recommendations:** A culturally and economically sensitive approach needs to be undertaken by the institutions in order to provide the basic needs of food and housing security to international students who are often sent to the foreign countries by their parents and family members in a hope that institutions will take care of their child/family member when they arrive. When I first arrived in the US, due to delays in visa appointments, I was unable to secure housing on campus and as a result, I had to live in a motel nearby for few days which made me feel insecure. Due to lack of knowledge about where to get food or things to eat, I survived on some snacks that my mom packed. Once, the housing on campus was available after 15 days, I was able to eat a meal and take a breath of relief. Hence, it is imperative that universities provide resources such as emergency food programs, affordable housing options, and culturally appropriate food services that can help relieve some of the pressures international students face. Moreover, universities should establish clear communication channels to inform international students about available resources and support systems, ensuring they feel comfortable seeking help. Peer mentoring programs can also be beneficial, as they allow international students to connect with domestic students or other international students who are familiar with local housing and food systems. These programs allow students to share experiences, offer advice, and provide practical support, fostering a sense of community and reducing the isolation associated with housing and food insecurity (NAFSA, 2019). Faculty and staff training on the specific needs of international students is another important step in ensuring that students receive the support they need. Universities should offer intercultural training to staff, informing them of international students' challenges and how to best support them. Creating a welcoming and inclusive environment for students to discuss housing and food concerns without fear of judgment is essential for improving academic success and overall well-being. Housing and food insecurity are significant issues that can severely impact international students' academic success and well-being. Cultural differences, financial limitations, and unfamiliarity with the local housing and food systems can contribute to these challenges. To lessen these issues, universities must take a holistic approach by offering targeted support services, providing culturally sensitive resources, and fostering an inclusive campus environment.

Another pressing challenge for international students is comprehending the language in their host countries. For most of these students, particularly those from non-English-speaking countries, difficulties in speaking, reading, listening, and writing in English can impede their ability to engage in academic life fully. These challenges are not confined to classroom communication but also extend to social interactions, where misunderstandings may arise due to differing accents, idiomatic expressions, or cultural references. The inability to express oneself clearly can lead to isolation, academic frustration, and alienation (Gartman, 2016; Leong, 2015; Taş, 2013). For example, students may struggle with specialized academic vocabulary or fail to grasp specific references essential for understanding course content, thus impacting their academic performance. Moreover, US educational systems often emphasize critical thinking, active participation, and independent learning pedagogical approaches that may differ significantly from those in many Asian, African, or Middle Eastern countries, for example. In cultures where education is more passive, students may feel overwhelmed by the demand for independent thought, classroom debate, and collaborative group work (Wu, 2015). International students, particularly those from more hierarchical or traditional educational systems, may find it challenging to adapt to the less formal and more interactive US classroom environment. The resulting discomfort can hinder their academic success, contributing to feelings of inadequacy and exclusion.

Visa-related barriers, such as restrictions on work authorization and the uncertainty surrounding H-1B visas post-graduation, can create significant stress for students seeking employment (Jiang & Altinyelken, 2021). The Optional Practical Training (OPT) program allows students to gain work experience post-graduation; however, securing employment within the permitted timeframe remains a significant challenge. Many students face difficulties finding employers willing to sponsor an H-1B visa due to the complex lottery system and uncertainties attached with the lottery system (Institute of International Education, 2022). The employment search process presents additional hurdles. International students often lack the professional networks that domestic students have developed over time, making it more challenging to secure internships and job opportunities (Hofstede, 2001). Moreover, cultural differences in job-seeking strategies, such as resume writing and interview techniques, can further complicate their ability to navigate the job market effectively (Hsu et al., 2017). Networking and mentorship play an essential role in career advancement for international students. Universities can support students by fostering mentorship programs that connect them with industry professionals and alums who have successfully navigated similar challenges (Guo & Chase, 2011). Career services departments should also provide tailored resources, including workshops on job searching, interview preparation, and strategies for leveraging LinkedIn and other professional networking platforms (Gabriel, 2023). Despite these challenges, international students bring valuable skills to the global job market. Their multilingual abilities, cross-cultural competencies, and adaptability make them attractive to employers (Glass & Westmont, 2014).

Cultural dissonance presents a significant challenge for international students. As they adjust to the social norms, behaviors, and values of the US, many experience culture shock. This can lead to confusion, frustration, and a sense of lost identity. These feelings are often worsened by the struggle to stay connected to one's cultural roots while adapting to the expectations of a new society (Chennamsetti, 2020; Jibreel, 2015). For international students, especially those from collectivist cultures, the individualistic nature of US society, which focuses on personal achievement, independence, and casual social interactions, can feel strange and intimidating. Students from these backgrounds may struggle to navigate the expectations of open and informal communication, contributing to feelings of isolation and disconnection from their peers. Language barriers further complicate these cultural challenges. Students from countries where English is not the primary language may feel reluctant to participate in classroom discussions, fearing judgment or misunderstanding (Leong, 2015). These social barriers can also affect their integration into campus communities, where pre-existing social networks may make it difficult for new students to form meaningful connections. In addition, the emotional toll of being away from home, particularly for students from close-knit families or communities, can contribute to homesickness and depression (Chennamsetti, 2020). Social isolation, combined with academic pressures, may lead to significant mental health challenges for international students.

International students face various psychological stressors that can significantly affect their academic performance and overall well-being. Homesickness, discrimination, and acculturative stress are among the most common challenges (Bekteshi & Kang, 2020). Several students experience culture shock and struggle to adapt to the new academic and social environments, often resulting in isolation and anxiety (Ammigan et al., 2022). The transition to a new country can bring about stressors related to language barriers, unfamiliar educational expectations, financial burdens, and difficulty forming social connections (Bista & Foster, 2016). Homesickness is a common issue among international students, as they are often separated from their families and support networks for long periods. The absence of familiar cultural and social environments can lead to feelings of loneliness and emotional distress. Studies show that prolonged homesickness can cause depressive symptoms, low motivation, and poorer academic performance (Forbes-Mewett & Nyland, 2008).

Discrimination is another significant stressor that international students face. Experiencing microaggressions, stereotypes, and exclusionary behaviors can negatively impact students' mental health, self-esteem, and sense of belonging. Research has shown that perceived discrimination is linked to increased levels of anxiety and depression among international students (Lee & Rice, 2007). Universities must implement policies and awareness programs to combat discrimination and create inclusive campus environments. Acculturative stress results from the psychological impact of adapting to a new cultural environment.

It can include difficulties in understanding new social norms, adjusting to different teaching methodologies, and coping with changes in daily life. The pressure to assimilate while maintaining one's cultural identity can create an internal conflict that worsens stress (Glass & Westmont, 2014). Fostering cultural exchange programs and mentorship initiatives can help reduce these challenges. Despite increased awareness of mental health issues among international students, accessing mental health services remains a major obstacle. Many institutions in the US lack culturally competent counseling options, which can discourage students from seeking help (Cena et al., 2021). Language barriers, financial limitations, and concerns about confidentiality also serve as deterrents to utilizing mental health resources (Cooper & Yarbrough, 2016).

Also, the stigma surrounding mental health in certain cultures prevents students from openly discussing their struggles. In many countries, mental health concerns are often viewed as a personal weakness rather than a legitimate health issue (Bekteshi & Kang, 2020). Consequently, students may avoid seeking professional help, instead relying on informal support networks such as friends or online communities. Universities can address this issue by providing mental health resources in multiple languages, offering culturally sensitive counseling services, and conducting outreach programs to normalize discussions about mental health.

**Coping Strategies and Resilience Among International Students:** Despite these challenges, A significant number of international students develop coping strategies to enhance resilience. Building strong social networks is a key factor in maintaining mental well-being. Peer support groups provide emotional support, shared experiences, and practical advice on navigating academic and cultural challenges (Brunton & Jeffrey, 2014). Participation in cultural student organizations, mentorship programs, and international student associations can foster a sense of belonging and reduce feelings of isolation. Self-care practices, such as mindfulness, exercise, and maintaining cultural traditions, also help students manage stress. Research suggests that students who actively practice stress management techniques experience lower anxiety levels and better academic performance (Ali et al., 2020). Universities can support these efforts by offering wellness programs, meditation and mindfulness workshops, and recreational activities tailored to international students.

**The Role of Peer Support Groups and Cultural Identity in Maintaining Mental Well-being:** Peer support groups play a vital role in assisting international students in navigating the complexities of adapting to a new environment. These groups offer emotional reassurance, foster open discussions about shared experiences, and serve as valuable networks for both academic and social integration. Studies have found that students who engage in peer-led mental health initiatives report higher levels of well-being and reduced stress

(Glass & Westmont, 2014). Cultural identity also serves as a protective factor in maintaining mental well-being. When students can maintain connections with their cultural heritage while engaging in new cultural experiences, they experience higher self-esteem and lower rates of depression. Encouraging cultural expression through campus events, international festivals, and heritage celebrations helps reinforce students' sense of identity and belonging (Guo & Chase, 2011).

International students often face unique challenges in seeking help for academic, mental health, and personal concerns. Cultural background, acculturation experiences, and stigma associated with mental health issues significantly shape their help-seeking behaviors (Boafo-Arthur & Boafo-Arthur, 2016). While many institutions offer support services, international students may underutilize these resources due to a lack of awareness, perceived social consequences, language barriers, and cultural norms that discourage external help-seeking. One of the primary barriers to help-seeking among international students is stigma. Many students come from cultures where discussing mental health or seeking professional assistance is considered a sign of weakness or failure (Boafo-Arthur & Boafo-Arthur, 2016). In collectivist societies, the fear of bringing shame to one's family or community can deter students from utilizing counseling services, even when they experience significant stress, anxiety, or depression.

Furthermore, students may fear judgment from peers or negative implications for their academic or immigration status. These fears can worsen isolation, preventing students from seeking timely support. Language and communication barriers further hinder access to support services. A considerable portion of international students may struggle to articulate their concerns in English or feel that mental health professionals may not understand the cultural nuances of their experiences. This linguistic difficulty can result in misdiagnosis, ineffective communication, or reluctance to seek professional help.

Furthermore, the unfamiliarity with the North American and Western European psychological framework can make students skeptical about the effectiveness of therapy and counseling. Acculturation stress also plays a significant role in shaping help-seeking behaviors. Adjusting to a new academic and social environment can be overwhelming, particularly for students who experience discrimination, loneliness, or financial stress (LaMontagne et al., 2023). The pressure to succeed academically while navigating cultural transitions can increase psychological distress, yet many students prefer to cope independently rather than seek institutional support. Differences in communication styles, unfamiliarity with available services, and skepticism about the effectiveness of mental health interventions in North America and Western Europe contribute to this reluctance. Another primary concern is the lack of awareness and accessibility of services. A significant number of international students arrive in the US without prior knowledge of mental health support systems, and some universities fail to promote their counseling and wellness services to this demographic actively. The absence of culturally sensitive outreach efforts can result in the underutilization of mental health resources. The Theory of Planned Behavior (TPB) provides a helpful framework for understanding international students' help-seeking intentions. According to TPB, three key factors influence help-seeking behaviors: attitudes, subjective norms, and perceived behavioral control (Yee & Ryan, 2023).

**Attitudes**: Students who view seeking help as beneficial and effective are more likely to engage with available services. However, they may avoid therapy, counseling, or academic support if they hold negative perceptions about these services.

**Subjective Norms**: Social influences, including cultural expectations, peer perceptions, and family values, impact on students' willingness to seek help. If help-seeking is viewed negatively in their home culture, they may feel discouraged from accessing services.

**Perceived Behavioral Control**: This factor reflects a student's belief in their ability to seek help. They may avoid using them altogether if they feel that services are difficult to access, culturally insensitive, or ineffective.

### 1.7 Forthcoming: A Deeper Exploration of Cultural Influences on Education

This book aims to offer a comprehensive exploration of how cultural backgrounds shape the academic experiences of international students in the US to provide a robust, data-driven foundation for these insights. Chapter 2 presents original findings from the American College Health Association's National College Health Assessment (ACHA-NCHA) 2022 dataset, offering empirical evidence of the lived experiences and well-being of international students. By examining the intersections of culture, education, and identity, the book will provide a nuanced understanding of the challenges and strategies for success that international students encounter. The book will shed light on the complexities of sociocultural adaptation and identity development for international students through detailed discussions on learning styles, classroom participation, language barriers, faculty-student relationships, and peer interactions. Additionally, the book will examine the practical implications for educational institutions, providing research findings and strategies to help create more supportive and inclusive learning environments. By comparing the perspectives of international students and emphasizing the cultural factors that influence their educational experiences, this book aims to contribute to a deeper understanding of how universities can better support international students in navigating the US academic system while respecting their cultural identities. Ultimately, this book aims to offer practical recommendations to promote the academic success and well-being of international students, thereby fostering an educational environment that supports the thriving of students from diverse backgrounds.

# Chapter Two
# Lived Experiences of International College Students in the US

Although individual experiences, like my own, provide valuable qualitative insights into the significant challenges faced by international students, a single testimony, no matter how compelling, does not offer full evidence of widespread issues. Therefore, to support these personal stories and better understand the broader situation of international student experiences in the US, it is essential to analyze nationwide data. This chapter presents a quantitative foundation for understanding the lived experiences of international students in US higher education. Drawing on the American College Health Association's National College Health Assessment (ACHA-NCHA) 2022 dataset, this analysis captures self-reported data from 13,242 international students across the United States. The dataset comprised $N = 102,905$ college students nationwide. The current analysis focused on international students ($n = 13,242$) who reported their experiences. The dataset, approved for use by the Institutional Review Board (IRB #2023-0755), allows for a comprehensive secondary analysis of non-human subjects.

The American College Health Association's National College Health Assessment (ACHA-NCHA) is a nationwide survey that collects comprehensive data on students' health behaviors, activities, and perceptions. The 2022 dataset was selected for this analysis due to its thoroughness and the significant context it provides for international students in that year. Notably, the 2022 dataset marks a record number of international students in the US, with 1,362,157 F-1 and M-1 visa holders, indicating a remarkable recovery to pre-pandemic levels following a decline in 2020 (Boundless, 2023; IIE, 2022). This rebound is crucial for understanding the experiences and mental health dynamics of international students, particularly as universities adapt their support systems in response to the COVID-19 challenges. Data collection involved distributing the NCHA survey to partner academic institutions in the Spring and Fall of 2022. The survey was conducted digitally, allowing students to participate and complete it once they voluntarily provided consent. It was self-reported, ensuring confidentiality and participants' approval for data usage. Highlighting this crucial period, the 2022 dataset offers valuable insights into the psychological well-being and resilience of international students as they navigate the complexities of reentering academic life after significant disruptions. Various frequencies were calculated using the Statistical Package for the Social Sciences (SPSS) Version 26.0. Responses from the Diener Flourishing Scale – Psychological Well-Being provide nuanced insights into the internal states of international students. For example, 4,763 students (36.1%) agreed and 3,323 (25.2%) strongly agreed that they lead a purposeful and meaningful life, resulting in a combined agreement of 61.3%. Similarly, 4,955 (37.6%) agreed and 3,180 (24.1%) strongly agreed that their social relationships are supportive and rewarding. In comparison, 4,635 (35.2%) agreed and 2,714 (20.6%) strongly agreed that they are engaged and interested in their daily activities, totaling 55.8% in agreement. However, nearly 10% of students disagreed or strongly disagreed with these statements, signaling a need for enhanced well-being interventions.

### Resilience and Kessler Psychological Distress Scale

Resilience, as measured by the Connor-Davison Resilience Scale (CD-RISC), yielded generally optimistic results. When asked whether they can adapt when changes occur, 5,964 students (45.3%) responded "often true," and 3,885 (29.5%) said "true nearly all the time," for a combined 74.8%. Regarding their ability to bounce back after illness or hardship, 5,165 (39.3%) answered "often true" and 4,174 (31.8%) "true nearly all the time," totaling 71.1%. Kessler 6 offers insight into psychological distress over the past 30 days. Regarding nervousness, 5,336 students (40.5%) reported feeling nervous "some of the time," 3,303 (25.1%) felt nervous "a little of the time," and 2,392 (18.2%) felt nervous "most of the time." A smaller group, 1,058 students (8.0%), reported feeling nervous "all of the time," while only 1,074 (8.2%) indicated feeling nervous "none of the time." Feelings of hopelessness were similarly distributed: 3,480 students (26.6%) felt hopeless "some of the time," 3,671 (28.1%) "a little of the time," 1,100 (8.4%) "most of the time," and 540 (4.1%) "all of the time." Meanwhile, 4,288 (32.8%) felt none of it. Restlessness or fidgetiness was felt "some of the time" by 4,163 students (31.8%), "a little of the time" by 3,509 (26.8%), and "most of the time" by 2,019 (15.4%). Notably, 903 students (6.9%) reported feeling this way "all of the time." Regarding sadness, 2,871 (21.8%) felt "so sad nothing could cheer them up" "some of the time," 3,788 (28.8%) "a little of the time," and 437 (3.3%) felt this sadness "all of the time." Just under 40% of students reported never experiencing this feeling. A total of 3,603 students (27.7%) reported that everything felt like an effort "some of the time," and 1,785 (13.6%) experienced it "most of the time." Approximately 6.9% of students, or 902 individuals, reported feeling this way "all of the time." Finally, feelings of worthlessness were reported by 2,296 students (17.5%) "some of the time," 841 (6.4%) "most of the time," and 564 (4.3%) "all of the time," while nearly half of the respondents (49.0%) reported no such feelings.

## Academic and Social Stressors

Challenges reported in the last 12 months highlight the academic and social pressures faced by international students. Nearly half the respondents (6,433 students or 48.9%) reported experiencing academic challenges, and 6,360 (48.5%) faced financial difficulties. A majority of 8,310 students (63.4%) identified procrastination as a concern. Career-related issues affected 5,413 students (41.3%), while family problems were reported by 3,983 (30.4%). Relationship concerns were cited by 4,405 students (33.7%), and 3,161 (24.2%) experienced conflicts with roommates or housemates. Peer-related issues were faced by 2,688 students (20.6%), and 5,541 (42.4%) experienced stress related to personal appearance. Health problems of someone close affected 4,692 students (35.9%), and the death of someone close impacted 2,904 (22.2%).

## Loneliness, Isolation, and Integration Barriers

Responses to the loneliness scale further illustrate the struggles with social integration. A total of 2,491 students (18.9%) reported often lacking companionship, 2,243 (17.0%) usually felt left out, and 2,537 (19.3%) frequently felt isolated from others. Experiences of discrimination and exclusion were also reported, with 912 students (7.0%) experiencing bullying and 2,082 (15.9%) encountering microaggressions.

## Suicide Ideation and Help-Seeking Barriers

Lifetime suicidal ideation and behaviors present a serious concern. Approximately 2,583 students (19.6%) had brief passing thoughts of suicide. Additionally, 886 (6.7%) had a plan. However, it did not attempt; 475 (3.6%) had a plan and wanted to die, 232 (1.8%) attempted suicide but did not want to die, and 247 (1.9%) attempted and hoped to die. Collectively, about 33.5% of international students reported some level of suicidal ideation.

## Mental Health Impacts on Academic Performance

Mental health concerns not only affect students' well-being but also influence academic outcomes. For anxiety, 2,926 (22.6%) noted that it negatively impacted class performance, and 535 (4.1%) indicated that anxiety delayed progress toward their degree. When considering depression, 1,914 (14.7%) reported depression but had no academic effect, 1,906 (14.7%) experienced negative classroom impact, and 526 (4.0%) saw their degree progress delayed. Regarding stress, 4,249 (32.6%) remained unaffected academically, 3,603 (27.7%) experienced academic decline, and 766 (5.9%) reported delayed academic progress.

## Demographic Characteristics of International Students

The majority of respondents self-identified as female, with 57.8% ($n$ =7,633) indicating the "Female" category, compared to 42.2% ($n$ = 5,568) for "Male." Looking at self-reported gender identity, 56.0% ($n$ = 7,390) identified as "Woman," and 41.6% ($n$ = 5,489) as "Man." A smaller percentage identified with various other gender identities, including Non-binary (1.1%, $n$ =139), Genderfluid (0.3%, $n$ = 44), Genderqueer (0.3%, $n$ = 40), another identity (0.3%, $n$ = 34), Trans man (0.2%, $n$ = 23), Trans woman (0.1%, $n$ = 13), Agender (0.2%, $n$ = 32), and Intersex (0.0%, $n$ = 1). The data also indicates that 2.3% ($n$ = 306) of respondents identified as transgender. The dataset was almost equally split between undergraduate and graduate students. Specifically, 55.4% ($n$ = 7,235) were "Undergraduate Students," and 44.6% ($n$ =5,828) were "Graduate Students."

**Sexual Orientation:** A vast majority of international students, 83.4% ($n$ = 10,928), identified as "Straight." Other sexual orientations included Bisexual (7.9%, $n$ = 1,032), Questioning (2.3%, $n$ = 298), Gay (1.9%, n=247), Pansexual (1.2%, $n$=163), Lesbian (1.2%, $n$ = 153), Queer (1.0%, n=133), and Asexual (0.7%, $n$ = 96). A small percentage (0.4%, $n$ = 58) indicated, "My identity is not listed above."

**Age Distribution:** The age distribution showed the following percentages: 10.9% ($n$ = 1,442) at 18 years old, 13.2% ($n$ = 1,727) at 19, 10.5% ($n$ = 1,380) at 20, and 9.8% ($n$ = 1,283) at 21. The percentages gradually decrease with increasing age, with a notable drop after the mid-20s. For instance, 4.8% ($n$ = 628) were 26 years old, and 2.4% ($n$ = 310) were 30 years old, with the percentages tapering off to minimal levels for ages above 40.

**Racial and Ethnic Backgrounds:** Among those identifying as Hispanic or Latino/a/x, 40.5% ($n$ = 690) identified as "Mexican, Mexican American, Chicano," 5.0% ($n$ = 85) as "Puerto Rican," 3.2% ($n$ = 54) as "Cuban," and 53.2% ($n$ = 906) selected "Another Hispanic, Latino/a/x, or Spanish origin." For those identifying as Asian or Asian American, 43.9% ($n$ = 2,666) identified as "East Asian (e.g., Chinese, Japanese, or Korean)," 11.7% ($n$ = 708) as "Southeast Asian (e.g., Cambodian, Vietnamese, Hmong, or Filipino)," 43.9% ($n$ = 2,664) as "South Asian (e.g., Indian, Pakistani, Nepalese, or Sri Lankan)," and 2.0% ($n$ = 124) as "Other Asian."

## Conclusion

This chapter is intended to lay a crucial quantitative foundation for understanding the varying lived experiences of international students in US higher education, drawing comprehensively from the ACHA-NCHA 2022 dataset. Although the data indicate a general sense of purpose, supportive social relationships, and resilience among the students, it simultaneously reveals pervasive challenges across critical domains. Substantial percentages reported significant psychological distress, academic and financial difficulties, procrastination, relationship concerns, and profound feelings of loneliness and isolation. Critically, these findings strongly highlight the concerning rates of suicidal ideation and the severe academic impacts caused by anxiety, depression, and stress. The ACHA-NCHA dataset thus offers compelling empirical evidence for the complex struggles often described in qualitative reports, providing an essential quantitative context for the rest of this book. Subsequent chapters will delve deeper into the specific academic implications and cultural barriers explained by these results, exploring how universities can proactively address these complex issues to foster a more supportive and equitable educational environment for this population.

# Chapter Three
# **Cultural Backgrounds and Learning Styles**

There have been many instances throughout my educational journey where I have been misjudged or misunderstood due to my cultural background. In India, I was always told to respect elders, especially professors and teachers. However, addressing the professors at the university as "Sir" or "Madam" made them angry with me. As a young student, I did not understand the professor's anger, but eventually, one professor told me that I should not address them as sir or madam. Until twelfth grade, I learned that I should follow my teachers' and professors' instructions, not talk in class, or do anything outside the curriculum. So, when the Sociology professor asked me to write a paper in my own words, I was unsure what to write about or what topic to choose. My professor informed me that he used Turnitin to analyze my paper and found similarities; hence, he is going to report me for plagiarism. However, I believe I have done nothing wrong. For me, applying APA or MLA style citation was a foreign concept that took a massive toll on my confidence. The professors' constant reminders that English is my second language made me feel incapable of writing a paper.

Building on the quantitative insights from Chapter 2, which highlighted the prevalence of psychological distress, social isolation, and academic stressors among international students as reported in the ACHA-NCHA 2022 dataset, this chapter delves into the fundamental role of cultural background in shaping international college students' academic experiences and social integration within the US educational system. The data presented in the preceding chapter underscore that many international students struggle with feelings of loneliness, anxiety, and challenges in their daily academic lives, often linked to the complex cultural, social, and emotional adjustments they face. As the enrollment of international students in US institutions continues to rise, understanding the intricate cultural, social, and emotional challenges these students face is more important than ever. Not only do these challenges influence their academic performance, but they also impact their overall well-being and sense of belonging on campus. As Rivas et al. (2019) observe, feelings of isolation and an acute sense of disconnection from the host culture are everyday experiences for international students. These feelings often manifest as difficulties in navigating the academic environment, forming meaningful peer relationships, and understanding the social expectations of their new environment. The authors argue that cultural integration is not merely an issue of adaptation but involves a complex process of balancing and reconciling one's own cultural identity with the cultural norms of the US. The method of cultural integration is multifaceted. It goes beyond simply learning to adapt to a new environment; it involves negotiating the complexities of a foreign academic system, unfamiliar social structures, and a different set of values. International students are often expected to conform to the social practices and academic expectations of US institutions. This pressure can result in significant stress, particularly when students feel torn between maintaining their cultural traditions and meeting the demands of the American educational system. The struggle for cultural integration often leads to alienation, making it harder for international students to fully immerse themselves in the academic and social aspects of their university experience. This alienation can significantly hinder their academic success, as students who feel isolated or marginalized may lack the confidence or motivation to perform to their best abilities (Rivas et al., 2019).

As the cultural divide between international students and their American peers often seems insurmountable, it can be challenging for these students to form meaningful relationships. This challenge is a critical barrier to social integration, as the ability to create a strong social support network is a key determinant of academic and personal success. For many international students, the lack of a readily available social network and the challenge of understanding new social cues can increase feelings of loneliness and stress. These emotional challenges can significantly impair the student's academic success, as emotional and social well-being are closely tied to cognitive functioning and academic performance.

Throughout my educational journey, there have been countless instances where I was profoundly misjudged or misunderstood due to my cultural background. In India, I was raised with the deeply ingrained value of respecting elders, especially professors and teachers. However, when I first addressed my university professors in the US as "Sir" or "Madam," it consistently evoked an unexpected anger. As a young student, I initially could not comprehend their irritation until one professor patiently explained that such a formal address was not customary. Moreover, my K-12 schooling in India taught me to strictly adhere to teachers' instructions, to refrain from speaking in class unless called upon, and to follow the curriculum closely. This ingrained approach created a significant culture shock when, in my very first Sociology class, the professor asked me to write a paper "in my own words." The concept of expressing original thoughts on a topic of my choosing was entirely foreign, leaving me utterly bewildered. My confusion was compounded when my professor later informed me that Turnitin had flagged similarities in my paper, and I would be reported for plagiarism. In my mind, I had done nothing wrong; applying APA or MLA style citation was a completely foreign concept. This experience, coupled with continuous reminders from professors that English was my second language, reinforced my understanding. Therefore, I was inherently "not capable of writing a paper," which took a massive toll on my confidence.

Research on the experiences of international students in the US has consistently highlighted how cultural factors play a significant role in shaping academic journeys. These factors include language barriers, differing communication styles, and varying expectations about how students should behave in educational settings (Rivas et al., 2019). For example, students from cultures that emphasize collectivism, often seen in many Asian and Latin American societies, are accustomed to hierarchical learning environments where teachers and professors are viewed as the central authority figures. In these cultures, learning is often a passive process, with students expected to absorb information from their instructors without engaging in active debate or questioning. This contrasts sharply with the US educational system, which highly values active participation, critical thinking, and independent learning. These differing expectations can create significant barriers to integration, as international students must adjust to new academic norms and a new style of classroom interaction. International students from collectivist cultures may find engaging in the US system's emphasis on individualism and personal initiative challenging. Lin (2012) explains that this cultural shift can result in feelings of inadequacy or frustration for students who struggle to express their ideas confidently in class discussions or group projects. The unfamiliarity with US expectations for classroom behavior, such as the need to express opinions openly, engage in debates, or seek clarification from professors, can make these students feel like outsiders in their classrooms. Language barriers can often pose an additional challenge, as students who are non-native English speakers may struggle to communicate their thoughts and ideas effectively. This can affect their ability to participate in classroom discussions, complete assignments, and interact with peers and professors.

Research by Wu et al. (2015) underscores that international students' cultural and linguistic hurdles can have far-reaching consequences for their academic performance. In addition to language barriers, social isolation and cultural misunderstandings are significant challenges that hinder the academic success of international students. Many students struggle to navigate the complexities of social life on American campuses, where informal communication, peer interactions, and networking are essential to academic success. These challenges can lead to heightened stress and a diminished sense of belonging, negatively affecting their academic performance and emotional well-being. The inability to fully integrate into the academic and social life of the campus often leads to a sense of alienation and isolation, which, if not addressed, can perpetuate a cycle of academic underachievement and personal distress. In discussing the transitions international students experience, Hsu (2019) emphasizes the need to recognize that these students face not only academic challenges but also significant emotional and social adjustments. Moving to a different cultural context involves rediscovering one's sense of self as students navigate the contrast between their home culture and the culture of their new environment. These transitions can be overwhelming, especially when students struggle to reconcile their prior educational practices and cultural norms with those of the US education system. Urban and Bierlein Palmer (2014) highlight that while international students enrich the US educational landscape by bringing diverse perspectives and knowledge, their academic success and social integration highly depend on the support systems that institutions put in place. For US institutions to fully harness the potential of their international student populations, it is essential to provide tailored support services that address their unique needs. Orientation programs, cultural sensitivity training, and mentorship opportunities can help international students bridge the gap between their home cultures and the demands of US academia. By creating an environment that values diversity and fosters inclusion, universities can ensure that international students survive and thrive academically and socially.

The specific needs of international doctoral students are particularly noteworthy in this context. As Campbell (2015) illustrates, these students face unique challenges related to their academic rigor and the emotional burden of adjusting to a new cultural and educational system. They are often isolated from their domestic peers, as the demands of doctoral study limit opportunities for social interaction. Moreover, the transition into academia can be more pronounced for international graduate students, who may encounter difficulties adapting to American pedagogical styles and expectations. Lin and Scherz (2014) point out that these students may struggle with self-confidence in academic discussions, particularly when they are asked to contribute their perspectives in a field that may be culturally unfamiliar to them. The importance of social support networks for international students cannot be overstated. As Zhai (2004) emphasizes, these networks are critical in mitigating students' challenges during their cultural and academic adjustment. Support from peers, faculty, and staff is essential for fostering a sense of belonging and alleviating feelings of isolation. Moreover, the ability to navigate and adapt to different writing conventions in the US can significantly affect academic success, as Angelova and Riazantseva (1999) note. International students are often required to adjust to the academic writing standards of US institutions, which may differ from those of their home countries. Mastery of these conventions is vital for academic success. However, it is also an area where international students face considerable challenges. The cultural backgrounds of international students significantly impact their academic experiences and social integration within the US educational system. As institutions continue to welcome students from diverse cultural backgrounds, providing support and understanding is essential to help these students navigate their challenges.

The rise of online and hybrid learning has transformed the educational experiences of international students, particularly in the wake of the COVID-19 pandemic (Boundless, 2023). Although digital platforms have facilitated access to education, they have also introduced challenges, such as time zone differences, internet accessibility issues, and limited interaction with faculty and peers (Adeoye, 2021). Artificial intelligence (AI), language learning apps, and other digital tools have become valuable resources for international students. These technologies help bridge language barriers and improve academic performance by providing personalized learning experiences (Alanya-Beltran & Panduro-Ramirez, 2021). However, the transition to digital learning has also revealed disparities in technological adaptability among students from different regions, highlighting the need for more targeted digital literacy programs (Ardila & Gómez-Restrepo, 2021). Despite the advantages, adapting to online assessments and digital platforms remains a significant challenge. Several international students struggle with unfamiliar testing formats, limited access to academic resources, and decreased engagement in virtual classrooms (Bianchi & Martini, 2023).

### 3.1 Intersectionality & Identity: The Complex Layers of International Student Adaptation

Multiple intersecting factors, including race, gender, and socioeconomic background, shape the experiences of international students in US higher education. While cultural adaptation is already challenging, these identity dimensions add extra layers of complexity, affecting academic performance, social integration, and mental health (Bista & Foster, 2016). Recognizing these intersections is crucial for understanding the distinct challenges that various groups of international students encounter and for creating more comprehensive institutional policies and support systems.

Race and ethnicity play an important role in shaping the experiences of international students. While all international students face adjustment challenges, students from underrepresented racial and ethnic backgrounds often encounter additional hurdles related to discrimination, microaggressions, and systemic bias (Lee & Rice, 2007). For instance, African and South Asian international students report experiencing racial biases both in academic settings and daily social interactions (Rahman & Rollock, 2004). These students may face stereotypes influencing faculty expectations, peer interactions, and employment opportunities. In particular, African students studying in predominantly white institutions (PWIs) have reported difficulties forming peer relationships due to cultural and racial barriers (Xu, 2022). Such experiences contribute to feelings of loneliness and anxiety, affecting both academic motivation and mental health (Bekteshi & Kang, 2020). In addition, East Asian students frequently face the "model minority" stereotype, which assumes high academic competence but can also lead to undue academic pressure and social exclusion (Leong, 2015). On the other hand, Middle Eastern students have reported experiencing Islamophobia and other forms of racialized discrimination that can impact their sense of belonging in the classroom and broader campus life (Gabriel, 2023).

Gender identity further shapes how international students experience adaptation in US institutions. Female international students, particularly those from patriarchal societies, often experience gender-based barriers that limit their academic and social participation (Constantine et al., 2005). For example, South Asian and Middle Eastern female students frequently navigate cultural expectations regarding modesty, gender roles, and socialization, which may conflict with the more liberal norms of US campuses (Tochkov et al., 2010). Many female students report feeling uncomfortable during co-ed classroom discussions and social settings where direct interaction with male classmates is expected (Cooper & Yarbrough, 2016). Moreover, female African international students may face dual burdens of both racial discrimination and gender-based bias, compounding their struggles with integration (Owusu Boateng, 2022). Beyond cultural expectations, international students who identify as LGBTQ+ encounter unique challenges, including navigating different levels of acceptance in both their home and host countries. Some students come from nations where LGBTQ+ identities are stigmatized or criminalized, leading them to suppress aspects of their identity while studying abroad (Cena et al., 2021). The intersection of gender identity and cultural background thus requires targeted institutional support to ensure a safe and inclusive learning environment.

Socio-economic background is another crucial factor influencing international students' adaptation. Students from wealthier backgrounds may find it easier to navigate tuition costs, housing, and academic resources. In contrast, lower-income people often face significant financial stress (Li, 2020). Numerous international students struggle. With limited scholarship opportunities and visa restrictions that prevent them from working off-campus, students are facing increasing financial difficulties (Institute of International Education, 2022). Studies show that students from low-income backgrounds are more likely to experience challenges with food and housing, making it stressful to focus on their studies (Forbes-Mewett & Nyland, 2008). Financial stress also impacts mental health, with students from economically disadvantaged backgrounds reporting higher levels of anxiety and depression (Poyrazli &

Lopez, 2007). Moreover, students from low-income regions may lack familiarity with digital learning tools and academic writing standards, placing them at an academic disadvantage compared to peers from well-resourced educational systems (Gartman, 2016). The intersection of socio-economic background with race and gender further complicates these experiences. For instance, female students from low-income backgrounds may have fewer resources to address mental health concerns or to access career-building opportunities such as internships (Chennamsetti, 2020). African and Latin American students from economically disadvantaged regions may also struggle to secure financial aid or sponsorships, limiting their ability to complete their studies successfully (Sawesi & Tusch, 2023). International students experience adaptation in the US differently depending on their intersecting identities. By understanding how race, gender, and socioeconomic status interact to shape students' experiences, educators and administrators can develop policies that foster inclusivity and a sense of belonging. Moving beyond a one-size-fits-all approach, institutions must recognize these nuances and implement targeted interventions that support the diverse needs of international students. Addressing these challenges through an intersectional framework will help create a more equitable educational environment, ensuring that all international students, regardless of identity or background, can thrive academically and socially. Religion represents a central dimension of cultural identity that shapes the academic, emotional, and social experiences of many international students. For those navigating the transition to US higher education, religious beliefs and practices often serve as powerful coping mechanisms, sources of social support, and frameworks for understanding the unfamiliar cultural landscape. Although rarely foregrounded in institutional discourses on internationalization and student support, religion plays a critical role in how students acculturate, engage with peers, and perform academically.

Religion often informs students' acculturation orientation, the strategies they use to integrate into or distance themselves from the host culture. Elhami and Roshan (2024) found that religious international students frequently draw on their faith to preserve cultural continuity amid the demands of cultural assimilation. Students with strong religious affiliations were more likely to adopt a *separation* or *integration* strategy, choosing to maintain their cultural and religious values while selectively engaging with the dominant culture. In this way, religion may serve as both a psychosocial anchor and a cultural compass, helping students navigate the tensions between adaptation and identity maintenance. In addition to shaping acculturation strategies, religion provides an essential mechanism for coping with acculturative stress, which refers to the psychological strain associated with navigating a new sociocultural environment. As Abu-Raiya et al. (2011) suggest, students often turn to religious coping strategies, such as prayer, spiritual reflection, or faith-based interpretations of hardship, to manage distress. These coping strategies can buffer against emotional exhaustion, homesickness, and perceived discrimination, which are common among international students (Constantine et al., 2004). Religious meaning-making helps students maintain a sense of coherence and purpose, especially when facing isolation or academic pressure.

Dietary habits and campus life accompany religious beliefs in ways that may either facilitate or hinder students' integration. For example, students who follow halal, kosher, vegetarian, or fasting dietary practices may face difficulties accessing culturally appropriate food options in campus cafeterias or grocery stores (Alakaam & Willyard, 2020). In such instances, religious observance can become a source of cultural alienation, particularly when institutional resources fail to accommodate these needs. As Leong (2015) notes, social isolation is often increased by cultural misunderstandings and the inability to participate in communal eating, a practice that is frequently a central aspect of social bonding in US college culture. As an international student who practices *Hinduism (Hinduism* is a pluralistic, ancient religion originating in India that emphasizes dharma (duty), karma (action), and the pursuit of spiritual liberation (moksha) through diverse beliefs and practices (Bhaktivedanta Swami Prabhupāda, 2008), I encountered challenges finding food options that did not contain beef or pork. These dietary restrictions, rooted in my religious beliefs, often placed me in uncomfortable situations, especially during group gatherings or campus events. On multiple occasions, I found myself needing to explain that my abstention from beef and pork was religious.

In contrast, my choice not to consume alcohol was a personal decision unrelated to my faith. Despite these explanations, I often felt excluded from peer groups and social outings because I couldn't fully participate in shared meals. These experiences, though often subtle, contributed to a sense of cultural disconnection and highlighted the importance of religious literacy in fostering inclusive campus environments.

Moreover, religious identity may increase international students' vulnerability to discrimination. Students from Muslim-majority countries or those who wear visible religious attire may experience xenophobia, stereotyping, or marginalization in and outside the classroom. This is especially salient in predominantly secular or religiously pluralistic contexts, where students may feel pressure to conceal their beliefs to fit in or avoid prejudice (Sodowsky & Plake, 1992). For these students, the classroom can be both a site of learning and a site of surveillance, where their cultural-religious identities are subtly or explicitly challenged.

Nonetheless, religious affiliation or identity can serve as a source of social connection and community integration. Many students find a sense of belonging through campus faith-based organizations or local religious institutions, which offer culturally familiar spaces where they can express their identities without fear of judgment. Faith-based institutions can also offer opportunities to participate in community-based service programs, providing a sense of belonging and a sense of home. As Campbell (2015) notes in his phenomenological study, international doctoral students often rely on these networks for emotional support and a sense of cultural continuity amid the demands of academic life. Religious groups also provide students with opportunities for leadership, volunteerism, and cross-cultural dialogue, thereby enhancing their overall engagement with the campus community (Hansen et al., 2021).

## 3.2 Cultural Identities and Learning Style

### 3.2.1 Asian Students

International students from Asia, particularly those from East Asia, are often rooted in cultural and linguistic differences (Lin & Scherz, 2014). These obstacles are frequently multiplied by the stark transition from familiar educational and social contexts to the unfamiliarity of the US educational system. As they navigate their academic journeys, East Asian students commonly experience acculturative stress, a psychological response to adapting to a new culture, which can negatively impact both their academic performance and overall well-being (Tung, 2011). This stress is often tied to the deep cultural values ingrained in East Asian societies, such as Confucian principles emphasizing respect for authority, collectivism, and harmony, which can present challenges in environments where active participation, assertiveness, and individualism are encouraged (Young, 2017). In these academic settings, East Asian students may feel uncomfortable or unprepared for the level of engagement required, contributing to feelings of alienation and stress.

Such cultural differences can lead to isolation, as students struggle to meet expectations that are drastically different from those in their home countries. Consequently, many Asian international students tend to form subcultures, primarily interacting with peers from similar backgrounds and limiting their engagement with faculty or domestic students (Li, 2016). This insular behavior, while providing a source of comfort and familiarity, can hinder their academic development and limit opportunities for intercultural exchange. Moreover, Asian international students often underutilize campus counseling and support services, which are vital resources for coping with stress and facilitating the adjustment process (Young, 2017). Stigma, shame, and taboo surrounding mental health in many Asian cultures may discourage students from seeking help, as they fear being seen as vulnerable or having an inability to cope. This hesitation to access support services worsens feelings of loneliness and anxiety, making it even more difficult for these students to adapt and thrive in their new academic environments.

Similarly, Indian international students face a unique set of challenges that are shaped by both cultural and educational factors (Johnson & Kumar, 2010). Kaur (2019) highlights the difficulties these students face due to cultural and educational disparities between their home countries and the US. These challenges are often intensified by socioeconomic factors, which Kushner (2010) notes are significant influences on their experiences in American higher education. With its different pedagogical approaches and expectations, the transition to a US educational system can be particularly daunting for Indian students. Karky (2013) highlights the pivotal role of faculty in supporting Indian students, stressing that educators sensitive to cultural differences can help ease the transition and create a more supportive learning environment. Faculty understanding of cultural nuances can significantly enhance the academic experiences of Indian international students. Moreover, Chennamsetti (2020) identifies everyday struggles among Indian students, such as homesickness, challenges with self-expression, the pressure of multitasking, and the emotional toll of living away from family, all of which contribute to feelings of isolation and stress.

For female Asian Indian international students, health-related concerns are particularly pronounced. Cooper and Yarbrough (2016) examine the specific challenges these demographics face, noting that cultural expectations can create additional layers of stress that affect mental and physical health. Tochkov et al. (2010) compare the prevalence of homesickness and adjustment difficulties among Indian students to their American peers, underscoring the emotional strain that cultural dislocation can impose on these students. The acculturation process itself is further complicated by factors such as language barriers, which Leong (2015) notes can impede academic success and contribute to the psychological burden experienced by international students, particularly those from China. Similarly, Rahman and Rollock (2004) find a significant correlation between perceived prejudice and depressive symptoms among South Asian international students, indicating the profound impact of social factors on their mental health and academic performance.

Campbell (2015) examines the acculturation experiences of international doctoral students, exploring how cultural differences and academic expectations can create additional challenges for these students. In this context, Ninnes et al. (1999) critique common stereotypes of Indian students as rote learners, emphasizing that such assumptions can undermine their potential for critical thinking and academic success. This stereotype, often reinforced by faculty perceptions, can limit Indian students' educational experiences and affect the expectations placed upon them. Constantine et al. (2005) delve into the intersection of gender, culture, and academic pressures, highlighting that Asian international female students face unique challenges due to the compounded pressures of cultural adjustment and gender expectations. Meanwhile, Zhai (2004) underscores the complexity of the acculturation process as international students grapple with academic stress, cultural differences, and language barriers.

To address these challenges and improve the experiences of international students, educators must adopt culturally responsive teaching methods sensitive to diverse cultural perspectives and learning styles (Lin & Scherz, 2014). Creating inclusive learning environments that acknowledge and celebrate cultural diversity can significantly enhance the educational experiences of international students. This approach fosters stronger relationships between domestic and international faculty and students. It promotes a more inclusive academic culture that facilitates cross-cultural understanding (Li, 2016). The relational dynamics within the classroom are crucial to enhancing the overall educational experience for international students, enabling them to feel more integrated and supported in their academic and social endeavors. By embracing these practices, educators can help ease the challenges faced by international students from Asia and other regions, creating a more welcoming and supportive environment for all students.

### 3.2.2 South and Central American Students

South and Central American international students bring a rich cultural heritage into US educational settings, significantly shaping their academic experiences and learning styles (Sawesi & Tusch, 2023). The educational system in several Latin American countries is traditionally rooted in teacher-centered classrooms, with an emphasis on rote learning, memorization, and respect for authority. This contrasts sharply with the more participatory and student-centered pedagogical approaches common in US institutions, which place a greater emphasis on independent critical thinking, problem-solving, and active participation in class discussions. This foundational difference in educational practices often presents significant challenges for students from South and Central America as they transition to the US educational system.

Latin American students, particularly those from collectivist cultures like Mexico, Peru, and Guatemala, are socialized to value conformity, group cohesion, and harmony. These values directly affect their academic engagement in the US, where individualism, self-direction, and assertiveness are encouraged (Kara et al., 2020). For instance, students from countries with collectivist values may initially struggle with the US emphasis on individual responsibility for learning and active participation. The US educational system expects students to engage in classroom discussions, ask questions, and contribute to group work, which can feel uncomfortable and even inappropriate for students who have been taught to defer to authority figures and prioritize group harmony over individual expression. As a result, these students may feel overwhelmed or inadequate when faced with new educational expectations that differ dramatically from their prior experiences, leading to academic frustration and cultural dislocation.

Research on learning style preferences among Latin American students reveals that these students exhibit diverse academic behaviors influenced by their cultural background, educational experiences, and academic discipline. For example, a study of South American students enrolled in business English courses highlighted the significant role of mobile learning (M-learning) in their academic engagement. Male students, in particular, showed a stronger preference for M-learning, appreciating the utility, enjoyment, and behavioral intention of using mobile devices for their studies (Alanya-Beltran, 2021). This suggests that Latin American students may be more receptive to adopting technology as a learning mode, particularly when it offers flexibility and convenience. However, adopting M-learning was gendered, with male students more likely to embrace this learning method than their female counterparts. This highlights the need for culturally sensitive, gender-aware teaching strategies considering these differences in learning preferences.

Similarly, the learning styles of Latin American students are also shaped by their educational experiences and cultural contexts. In a dental school in Latin America, ethnic minority students preferred reflector and theorist learning styles, focusing on reflective observation and forming abstract concepts. These preferences were linked to lower academic performance, suggesting that the pedagogical approaches in the institution may not have sufficiently supported the learning needs of these students (Ardila & Gómez-Restrepo, 2021). This highlights the importance of recognizing and accommodating diverse learning styles in educational settings, as failure to do so can contribute to academic challenges and diminished success for students who may be more accustomed to passive, teacher-directed learning environments. Research into learning styles among Latin American students further underscores the complexity of their academic experiences. In engineering programs in Peru, for example, students favored sensory-intuitive, inductive-deductive, and active-reflective learning styles, reflecting their preference for practical, hands-on experiences that blend theoretical knowledge with real-world application (Navarro et al., 2022). These learning preferences are shaped by the nature of the engineering discipline, which emphasizes problem-solving, analytical thinking, and technical skills. However, transitioning to the US educational system, where active learning, self-directed research, and classroom participation are heavily emphasized, can be challenging for students from South and Central America who are more accustomed to structured, teacher-guided instruction.

The pedagogical shift from the more hierarchical, teacher-centered classrooms in Latin America to the student-centered, participatory learning environments in the US can create substantial adjustment challenges. Latin American students often struggle with the expectation to engage with learning materials independently, participate in class discussions, and take ownership of their academic progress. This can be incredibly challenging for students from countries like Peru, Mexico, and Guatemala, where the educational culture typically places greater authority and control in the hands of teachers, with limited emphasis on student autonomy (Kara et al., 2020). Students from such educational systems may initially find the US approach to teaching disorienting, as they are not accustomed to taking the initiative in their learning or speaking up in class.

The COVID-19 pandemic notably accelerated the adoption of mobile learning (M-learning) technology, which became a key tool for many students adapting to remote learning during lockdowns. South American students embraced M-learning as a flexible, accessible alternative to traditional classroom settings. Research on business English courses found that male students demonstrated higher acceptance and utility of M-learning than female students, suggesting that technology-based learning methods may resonate differently across gender and cultural contexts (Alanya-Beltran, 2021). Although M-learning has proven to be an effective tool for increasing engagement and learning accessibility, its adoption may require different approaches based on the students' cultural and gender-specific preferences. Latin American students' collectivist values also play a significant role in shaping their learning preferences. For many students from Latin American cultures, learning is seen as a shared group experience. Collaborative learning, group discussions, and peer support are integral to their academic approach. However, this emphasis on group learning can conflict with the individualistic nature of US classrooms, where students are expected to demonstrate independent thinking, self-directed learning, and critical analysis. This tension can lead to feelings of isolation or frustration among Latin American students as they adjust to an academic environment that may seem overly focused on individual achievement rather than group collaboration (Sawesi & Tusch, 2023).

Research into the learning styles of Latin American students further underscores the importance of recognizing and accommodating cultural influences in academic settings. For example, a study of undergraduate English education students in Latin America revealed a strong preference for visual learning styles, with less emphasis on auditory and kinesthetic learning (Ariastuti & Wahyudin, 2022). This preference for visual learning is not uncommon among students from collectivist cultures, who often rely on visual cues and structured, clear guidance from instructors to navigate complex academic material. Understanding these cultural differences in learning preferences can help educators design more effective, inclusive curricula that better support Latin American students' academic success.

### 3.2.3 European Students

European international students, as a group, bring a rich diversity of cultural and educational traditions that significantly shape their experiences in US higher education. Understanding their learning styles involves examining the intersection of their cultural background, educational systems, and personal learning preferences. This requires exploring how European educational traditions influence students' engagement with instructional methods, their interactions with instructors, and their approach to learning materials. Researchers have studied these dynamics to better understand how European students navigate and adapt to US academic environments, shedding light on the unique ways they engage with the learning process. The educational systems across Europe are characterized by significant diversity. However, several common themes shape students' learning styles from various regions. Higher education systems in Western European countries, such as Germany, France, and the Netherlands, traditionally prioritize student autonomy, independence, and critical thinking. These systems often expect students to take charge of their learning, with a strong emphasis on self-directed study and the development of analytical and problem-solving skills. This emphasis on autonomy is reflected in the learning styles of Western European students, who tend to favor methods that support reflective thinking, deep analysis, and theoretical inquiry.

In these countries, students are typically encouraged to engage with content at a conceptual level, processing information through observation and reflection rather than immediate, hands-on application. For example, research by Maya et al. (2021) suggests that students from Western European nations often prefer reflective and assimilative learning styles, which involve processing information analytically and in a structured manner rather than through active experimentation or application. This preference aligns with the European tradition of critical inquiry, where students focus on understanding underlying principles and constructing knowledge through a logical, often abstract, framework. On the other hand, students from Eastern European countries, such as Poland, the Czech Republic, and Hungary, often find themselves in more structured and hierarchical educational systems. These systems strongly emphasize foundational knowledge and theoretical understanding, but with a focus on practical applications. This is reflected in the learning preferences of Eastern European students, who often gravitate towards problem-based learning. For example, Berková et al. (2020) found that Czech students frequently prefer approaches that directly tie theoretical knowledge to practical, real-world problems, where learning is seen as applying abstract concepts to tangible challenges. This pragmatic approach suggests that students from Eastern Europe value a learning environment that blends theory and practice, enabling them to see the immediate relevance and applicability of their academic work. Several theoretical models can be employed to understand further European students' learning preferences, including Kolb's Experiential Learning Theory (ELT), the VARK model, and Felder and Silverman's Learning Styles Model. Each framework offers a unique perspective on how learners engage with academic content, providing a nuanced understanding of European students' learning styles.

### 3.2.3.1 Kolb's Experiential Learning Theory (ELT)

Kolb's Experiential Learning Theory (ELT; 1984) offers a cyclic learning model involving four stages: concrete experience, reflective observation, abstract conceptualization, and active experimentation. Kolb's theory categorizes learners into four distinct styles based on how they interact with these stages:

1. Diverging – Individuals who excel in generating ideas, observing situations from multiple perspectives, and reflecting on experiences.

2. Assimilating – Learners who prefer to organize information logically and process it through reflection and analysis.

3. Converging – Learners who apply theoretical concepts to solve problems in practical ways, engaging in active experimentation.

4. Accommodating – Learners who prefer hands-on experiences and responding to situations with intuition and action.

In the European context, Kolb's theory has examined regional differences in learning preferences. For example, Maya et al. (2021) found that students in Spain, particularly in psychology, often exhibit an assimilative learning style, favoring abstract conceptualization and reflective observation. These students thrive in environments that encourage critical analysis and the logical organization of knowledge, which aligns with the broader Southern European emphasis on theoretical depth and critical thinking. This preference for abstract conceptualization and reflective observation reflects a culture in which students are encouraged to engage deeply with the theoretical underpinnings of their studies. It is not uncommon for students in countries like Spain and Italy to excel in lecture-based learning, where they are given the space to absorb, analyze, and reflect on information before applying it.

## 3.2.3.2 The VARK Model

The VARK model (Fleming, 1995) categorizes learners based on their sensory preferences: Visual, Auditory, Reading/Writing, and Kinesthetic. This model provides a sensory-based approach to understanding learning preferences. Although research explicitly examining the VARK preferences of European students is still developing, the model is valuable in analyzing how European cultural and educational backgrounds influence students' sensory learning preferences. In countries such as Germany and the Netherlands, where education systems emphasize structured organization, students may prefer visual learning, which includes charts, graphs, diagrams, and other visual aids. These visual tools help students better conceptualize and retain complex academic material. Conversely, students from countries with rich oral traditions, like Italy or Greece, may prefer auditory learning, benefiting from verbal explanations and discussions that allow them to interact with the material. These distinctions highlight how European students' sensory learning preferences are shaped by their cognitive styles and the academic cultures of their home countries. Instructors can use the VARK model to design lessons, incorporating a range of sensory modalities, ensuring that European international students feel more comfortable and engaged in the learning process.

## 3.2.3.3 Felder and Silverman's Learning Styles Model

Felder and Silverman's Learning Styles Model (1988) further refines the understanding of learning preferences by identifying several key dimensions:

1. Active vs. Reflective – Active learners engage with the material through participation and interaction. In contrast, reflective learners prefer to process information internally before responding.

2. Sensing vs. Intuitive – Sensing learners focus on facts and details, while intuitive learners prefer abstract concepts and ideas.

3. Visual vs. Verbal – Visual learners benefit from seeing images and diagrams, while verbal learners prefer written or spoken explanations.

4. Sequential vs. Global – Sequential learners prefer a step-by-step approach, while global learners grasp the big picture and work backward.

Research has shown that European students from structured educational systems, such as those in Germany or Finland, tend to gravitate towards sensing and sequential learning, focusing on details and following a logical progression through academic material. Conversely, students from regions with more abstract and theoretical traditions, like Southern Europe, may lean more toward intuitive and global learning styles, where they prefer to engage with abstract concepts and understand the larger context before delving into specific details. These distinctions provide valuable insights into the learning preferences of European students, enabling educators to design more effective instructional strategies that cater to the varied needs of these learners.

The amalgamation of Information and Communication Technologies (ICT) into European education systems has profoundly impacted learning styles. In countries like Sweden and Finland, where digital literacy is highly emphasized, students are often encouraged to incorporate technology into their learning experiences. This has increased preference among European students for visual and reflective learning methods, especially those motivated by digital tools such as online platforms, videos, and virtual collaboration spaces (Navarro et al., 2022). European students accustomed to technology-enhanced learning may find it challenging to adjust to US classrooms that rely heavily on face-to-face discussions and in-person participation, which may not align with their preference for digital and reflective learning tools. However, this digital familiarity can also be an advantage, as these students may be better equipped to use modern learning technologies in US higher education.

European international students, shaped by their diverse cultural and educational backgrounds, bring a variety of learning styles to the US higher education system. Although Western European students typically favor reflective, assimilative approaches rooted in critical thinking and theoretical analysis, Eastern European students often prefer practical, problem-based learning that bridges the gap between theory and real-life application. The growing influence of ICT on European education further complicates these preferences, as students from digitally advanced countries may prefer visual and reflective learning environments. By understanding these nuances, US educators can better support European international students, helping them navigate and succeed in academic settings that may differ significantly from their home country's educational systems.

### 3.2.4 African Students

African international students' learning styles and cultural backgrounds are pivotal in shaping their academic experiences, particularly in cross-cultural and online learning environments. As international students, they bring a rich tapestry of cultural perspectives that influence their learning preferences, communication styles, and levels of engagement with academic content. These perspectives are deeply rooted in their native educational systems, societal structures, and the value placed on communal ties, which shape how African students approach learning in North American and Western European academic settings.

One significant feature of African students' learning styles is the preference for more interactive and collaborative environments. This preference starkly contrasts with the traditional lecture-based models often found in North American and Western European institutions (Adeoye, 2021). For example, African students from countries like Nigeria often thrive in educational contexts that emphasize group work, discussions, and experiential learning methods, which reflect the communal and relational nature of African societies. In many African cultures, learning is often viewed as a shared, collective experience where knowledge is transmitted through direct instruction, dialogue, collaboration, and the integration of community wisdom. This communal approach to learning can create a gap when these students are placed in environments where the dominant educational model emphasizes individualization, with limited focus on group work or peer interaction. In online learning contexts, these cultural preferences become even more apparent. African students, including those from Nigeria, tend to engage more when courses incorporate collaborative components, such as group discussions, peer reviews, and interactive assignments. These components help foster a sense of community and facilitate a richer exchange of ideas. For instance, online learning environments that focus on interactive tools, such as video conferencing, discussion boards, and real-time collaborative projects, allow African students to feel more connected to their peers and the learning process. These methods align more closely with their cultural background, where learning is about absorbing information and engaging in dynamic, social interactions that foster mutual support and shared learning experiences. Therefore, online courses designed with these interactive components can provide a more inclusive environment for African students, allowing them to participate more fully and effectively in their academic journey.

However, African students studying abroad often face multiple challenges, especially in terms of language barriers, cultural differences, and perceived discrimination. Studies have shown that these barriers significantly impact African students' academic and social integration in various global contexts (Owusu Boateng, 2022). For instance, African students may struggle to adapt to the educational demands of institutions where English, French, or other European languages dominate, especially if these students are not fully proficient. This linguistic hurdle can hinder their ability to comprehend academic content, engage in discussions, and form relationships with faculty and peers. Discrimination, whether overt or subtle, also plays a role in their educational struggles, further compounding their sense of isolation. African students often report feeling marginalized or excluded from mainstream campus activities, and this lack of belonging can lead to diminished academic motivation and lower performance.

The lack of shared cultural understanding between African students and local students or faculty members further compounds these issues. The cultural disconnect may manifest in various ways, from different approaches to communication and classroom behavior to varying expectations about academic performance and social interaction. In these situations, African students may find adapting to the new learning environment challenging, especially if faculty members and classmates are unaware of or insensitive to their cultural backgrounds. This is why faculty support is critical in the adaptation process. Culturally informed pedagogical practices are crucial for promoting inclusivity in countries where there is limited cultural overlap between African students and the local population. For instance, research by Xu (2022) highlights that in China, African students benefit from forming affective relationships with their instructors, especially in language learning settings. These relationships can be crucial support systems, helping students feel more comfortable, secure, and understood academically.

Beyond language and discrimination, the learning preferences of African students are also shaped by their educational backgrounds and cultural norms. In many African countries, education is often more practical and communal, focusing on experiential and kinesthetic learning approaches. These students may thrive in settings emphasizing hands-on activities, case studies, role-playing, and collaborative projects. African students may find these learning methods more aligned with their cultural experiences, making it essential for educational institutions to design programs that accommodate these preferences. For example, a study on South African students in Collaborative Online International Learning (COIL) environments found that South African students preferred structured and interactive course designs (Naicker et al., 2021). These courses helped ease the feelings of isolation by promoting collaboration and cultural exchange, which ultimately enhanced their adaptability and openness to learning in a diverse, international context. By incorporating interactive and community-based elements into online learning environments, educators can help African students feel more engaged and supported, leading to improved academic outcomes and cultural integration.

In addition to the challenges of academic adaptation, African international students face significant social challenges, particularly related to loneliness and isolation. According to Neto (2021), African students in North America and Western European countries often experience heightened levels of loneliness due to factors such as financial constraints, perceived discrimination, and strong emotional ties to their cultural heritage. Many African students report feeling disconnected from the local student body. This feeling can be worsened by financial difficulties that limit their ability to socialize or participate in extracurricular activities. These feelings of isolation can significantly hinder their adjustment to their new environment and negatively affect their academic performance. Loneliness is often compounded by the emotional weight of being far from family, and many African students face challenges related to maintaining cultural connections while adapting to the norms of the host country.

### 3.2.5 Middle Eastern Students

Middle Eastern international students bring distinct learning styles and cultural perspectives that can significantly influence their academic experiences, engagement, and performance in US educational settings. These learning preferences, deeply rooted in their home countries' cultural norms and educational traditions, can sometimes create challenges in adapting to North America and Western Europe's educational environments that emphasize different approaches to learning. A comparative study by Naik et al. (2012) examining business students in Egypt and the US underscores the significant role in shaping learning preferences. The study specifically explored the Felder-Silverman model of learning styles, which identifies key dimensions such as sensing-intuitive and visual-verbal learning preferences. The findings revealed that Middle Eastern students, particularly those from Egypt, strongly preferred sensory-based learning, favoring concrete, practical information over abstract theories and concepts. This inclination reflects educational systems in many Middle Eastern countries, where rote memorization, structure, and clarity are often prioritized, contrasting with North American and Western European universities' more open-ended, interpretive, and student-driven learning methods.

This cultural tendency towards structured and sensory-focused learning aligns with broader educational traditions in the region, where curricula often emphasize memorization and the mastery of factual knowledge. This focus on acquiring and retaining concrete information, rather than abstract or theoretical frameworks, can be particularly challenging for Middle Eastern students in US classrooms, where critical thinking, analysis, and interactive learning are often emphasized. Although students from the Middle East may excel in subjects that require memorization and clear-cut answers, they may struggle in environments that demand abstract thinking, group discussions, or open-ended problem-solving.

Further studies on perceptual learning preferences provide additional insight into the learning styles of Middle Eastern students. Wahyudin and Rido (2020) conducted a survey involving international students from Libya and Iran studying in Malaysia, which revealed distinct preferences for kinesthetic and visual learning, respectively. Middle Eastern students, particularly those from these countries, tend to favor learning through visual aids such as diagrams, charts, and multimedia presentations. For others, physical engagement with the material through hands-on activities or kinesthetic learning was preferred. This preference for tangible, visual, and interactive forms of learning suggests that Middle Eastern students are more likely to excel in environments where lessons are supplemented with concrete, sensory experiences rather than purely abstract or theoretical content. Such learning styles emphasize the importance of providing Middle Eastern students with opportunities for hands-on engagement and visual representation of academic concepts, such as using models, experiments, and interactive demonstrations to facilitate their learning process.

In a broader context, Gabriel's (2023) review of learning style preferences among students from Gulf countries further reinforces these findings. It identifies a strong preference for collaborative learning environments among students from countries such as Saudi Arabia and Kuwait, reflecting the profoundly ingrained collective cultural values of many Middle Eastern societies. In these cultures, group cohesion, teamwork, and social learning are highly valued, and students tend to thrive in environments that promote group work and collaborative efforts. This contrasts with the individualistic approach often seen in North America and Western Europe's educational systems, where independent study and personal achievement are emphasized. The preference for collaboration among Middle Eastern students suggests that group-based projects, peer learning, and interactive classroom environments can be particularly effective in enhancing their academic experiences. Providing opportunities for students to work together in teams and engage in discussion-based learning can help improve their academic performance and cross-cultural adaptation.

Although the preceding discussion has touched upon the broad cultural dynamics influencing international students of Arab descent, it is crucial to delve deeper into specific challenges, particularly those faced by female students whose apparel serves as a visible cultural marker. The period following 9/11 significantly intensified scrutiny and profiling within the US, creating an environment where individuals perceived as 'Other,' including those of Arab and Muslim backgrounds, often became subjects of suspicion. For female students, outwardly visible garments like the hijab or other forms of modest dress, while deeply personal and religious expressions, sometimes became unintentional barriers to full socialization and integration. These forms of apparel, unfortunately, can trigger misconceptions and stereotypes among segments of the host community who may lack familiarity or hold pre-existing biases. This can manifest in subtle, yet impactful, ways: a reluctance from peers to initiate conversations, curious or suspicious glances in public spaces, or even direct, intrusive questions about their attire or beliefs. One challenge I witnessed, and heard recounted by many, was the palpable shift in social dynamics. Students would describe attempting to join a casual campus group, only to encounter an invisible wall, a hesitance from others to engage beyond superficial pleasantries (Flannery, 2025; US Commission on Civil Rights, 2003).

Beyond classroom activities, Middle Eastern students' cultural backgrounds also influence their interactions with instructors and their expectations of the academic process. Singh et al. (2021) conducted a study on Emirati students in the UAE, highlighting the cultural misalignments that can occur between Middle Eastern students and expatriate faculty members. The study found that Middle Eastern students often view instructors as authority figures and are less likely to challenge or question academic content openly. This cultural difference, in which respect for authority and hierarchy is emphasized, can create barriers to active participation in the classroom, as students may feel uncomfortable speaking out or engaging in discussions that challenge the instructor's viewpoints. This lack of engagement can be incredibly challenging in North America and Western Europe classrooms, where active learning, critical thinking, and student-led dialogue are key components of the educational experience.

This dynamic underscores the need for culturally relevant pedagogy that bridges the gap between Middle Eastern students' cultural expectations and the more participatory, open-ended teaching methods often used in US classrooms. Educators must be aware of these cultural differences in student-instructor relationships and create an environment where Middle Eastern students feel comfortable engaging in discussions, asking questions, and challenging ideas. Faculty who recognize the importance of building trust and rapport with students can help ease the transition for Middle Eastern international students by encouraging open communication and creating a more supportive and inclusive classroom environment. By adopting a more flexible and culturally sensitive approach to teaching, instructors can help these students adapt to the academic norms of their new educational setting while respecting their cultural perspectives.

Understanding Middle Eastern students' learning preferences and cultural backgrounds is crucial in developing a supportive academic environment that fosters their academic success and overall well-being. By employing nuanced teaching strategies such as visual aids, kinesthetic learning, and collaborative group activities, educators can help Middle Eastern students thrive in US classrooms. Structured learning, hands-on activities, and collaborative learning environments that align with students' cultural expectations can promote academic performance and cross-cultural adaptation (Yousef, 2021). These approaches enhance students' academic experiences, facilitate their social integration, and help them navigate the challenges of studying abroad.

Ultimately, creating a culturally responsive and inclusive academic environment that embraces diversity will contribute to the success of all students, particularly those from Middle Eastern backgrounds, ensuring that they can adapt to their new academic settings while retaining and celebrating their cultural heritage.

### 3.3 Conclusion

This chapter offered an intricate relationship between cultural backgrounds and learning styles, shedding light on how deeply ingrained cultural norms, values, and traditions influence the academic approaches of international students. Cultural frameworks inherently shape the education system and are instrumental in determining how students approach learning, engage in classroom activities, and interact with students and faculty. These cultural dynamics affect how students learn and engage with information, as well as their participation and contributions within the academic environment. Recognizing the influence of culture on these educational experiences is essential for fostering an inclusive academic setting that accommodates the diverse learning needs of all students.

# Chapter Four
# Classroom Participation and Academic Expectations

International students in the US often face significant hurdles in navigating academic expectations and participating in classroom activities due to cultural differences, systemic barriers, and unaccommodating classroom practices. These challenges can greatly affect their academic success and well-being as they try to adapt to new academic and social settings. Despite their potential to enrich the campus experience with diverse perspectives, international students frequently encounter exclusion and marginalization within classroom settings.

My own journey vividly illustrates this struggle. Throughout my 14 years in the US academic system, from my initial arrival in 2010 to my final year of Ph.D. in 2024, surprisingly little changed regarding my classroom participation. The frequent comments from peers and professors, "You have an accent," or "English is your second language," took away my confidence, leaving me an introvert, shy, and hesitant to participate in discussions. In my home country, I was a confident speaker, someone who eagerly took part in elocution and speech competitions that occurred in the British English language. However, in the US, I transformed into a quiet, reserved individual, developing a genuine stage fright and an adrenaline rush whenever someone prompted me to speak. This profound shift was primarily driven by the paralyzing fear of being misunderstood or, worse, laughed at for my language differences. This experience highlights a critical, often underestimated aspect: the necessity of mastering American English, including its everyday conversations, academic terminology, and the informal slang integral to American social interactions. This subtle yet crucial linguistic and cultural transition took me years, proving vital not only for academic success but also for social confidence and professional networking.

## 4.1 Classroom Exclusion and Cultural Norms

International students, particularly those from Confucian Asian and other high-context cultures, often face difficulties in classroom participation due to cultural norms that differ significantly from those prevalent in US higher education. These students are accustomed to educational systems emphasizing respect for authority, indirect communication, and collective harmony. In contrast, US classrooms typically promote individualistic, direct, and assertive participation, making it challenging for international students to adapt. For instance, Confucian Heritage Cultures (CHC) students may struggle with classroom practices that emphasize open, unstructured discussions, which are common in many US universities (Rienties et al., 2013). In these educational contexts, the expectation for students to actively engage in verbal discussions and assert their opinions can be overwhelming and culturally incongruent with their background.

The struggle to align with these expectations often leads to feelings of isolation and academic disengagement. As these students are not accustomed to speaking out in class or challenging authority figures, their reluctance to participate may be misunderstood as disinterest or lack of engagement. This misinterpretation of behavior can result in faculty perceiving these students as passive or unprepared, reinforcing a cycle of marginalization. Furthermore, because the US classroom setting frequently prioritizes oral participation over written assignments or other forms of engagement, students who are more comfortable expressing themselves through written work may feel excluded. This exclusionary dynamic limits their ability to demonstrate academic competence and contributes to their social isolation within the educational environment (Valdez, 2016).

### 4.2 Language Barriers and Communication Styles

Language barriers are another significant challenge that international students face in US classrooms. While many international students are proficient in English, the pressure to communicate effectively in academic settings can be overwhelming. In addition to linguistic challenges, cultural differences in communication styles can increase feelings of exclusion. For example, students from high-context cultures, like those in Asian countries, often favor indirect communication, depending on non-verbal cues and context to express meaning. In contrast, US classrooms value low-context communication, prioritizing directness and verbal clarity. This cultural clash can lead to difficulties participating in classroom discussions and forming meaningful academic relationships (Hall, 1976). The need for frequent clarification of concepts or instructions is also a sign of disengagement by professors who are unaccustomed to these cultural differences.

The preference for oral participation in US classrooms can also create a communication barrier for international students. In many cultures, students are taught to listen attentively and absorb information rather than actively engage in discussions. Therefore, the emphasis on verbal participation in US classrooms can disadvantage students who feel more comfortable expressing their thoughts in writing or through other less vocal means of communication.

This mismatch in expectations often leads to feelings of inadequacy and frustration, further contributing to social and academic isolation (Valdez, 2016). Moreover, the cultural differences in classroom behavior can result in faculty misinterpreting international students' silence as disengagement when, in fact, these students may be processing information and reflecting before speaking, which is more typical in their home countries.

## 4.3 Acculturation and Integration Barriers

The acculturation process for international students is multifaceted and extends beyond mere academic adjustments. Cultural dislocation, homesickness, and the emotional strain of adapting to a new environment contribute to their challenges. The transition to an individualistic educational system can be disorienting for many international students, particularly those from collectivist cultures. Their academic and social experiences in their home countries have likely shaped them to value collective harmony, respect for authority, and a focus on group over individual achievement. In US higher education, where independent thinking, self-advocacy, and open classroom discussions are emphasized, international students may feel like outsiders. As Rienties et al. (2013) discovered, these students often form subgroups within the classroom, bonding primarily with students from similar cultural backgrounds rather than engaging with US students or students from other cultures. This insular behavior may limit the students' opportunities for intercultural learning and hinder their full integration into the academic community.

Additionally, the pressure to succeed academically while adapting to a new culture can affect the mental health of international students. Many report feelings of stress, anxiety, and depression related to their academic and social experiences. These mental health issues are often worsened by cultural stigmas about mental health from their home countries, making it harder for them to seek the help they need (Young, 2017). As a result, their emotional well-being may decline, leading to further disengagement from academic and social activities.

## 4.4 The Role of Faculty and Culturally Responsive Teaching

Faculty members must urgently adopt culturally responsive teaching practices that recognize and accommodate their students' diverse cultural backgrounds and learning styles. Culturally Responsive Teaching (CRT) involves adapting instructional strategies to be inclusive of all students' cultural, linguistic, and academic needs. This includes providing clear participation guidelines, acknowledging and respecting cultural differences, and offering alternative communication and assessment methods that leverage their cultural strengths.

For example, faculty members can create more structured classroom environments that ease the transition for international students who are used to more teacher-led discussions. They can also incorporate written forms of participation and assessment, which allow students to engage more comfortably and effectively with course content. Furthermore, faculty members can be trained in intercultural communication and the specific needs of international students, helping them recognize when students are struggling with cultural or linguistic barriers. This training can foster a more inclusive classroom environment and enhance international students' academic experiences by providing them with the tools they need to succeed.

Moreover, universities must provide comprehensive support services that address both academic and social needs. This includes offering tutoring, language assistance, and counseling to help students handle the challenges of living and studying abroad. Support services should also foster intercultural understanding and create opportunities for meaningful interactions between international and domestic students. By encouraging intercultural dialogue and collaboration, universities can help international students feel more part of the academic community and reduce feelings of isolation.

### 4.5 Impact of Classroom Dynamics

Classroom dynamics significantly shape international college students' academic and social experiences, influencing their participation, sense of belonging, and overall academic success. These dynamics are the product of complex interactions among students, faculty, and institutional structures. Together, they impact the ability of international students to adapt to unfamiliar educational landscapes and excel in their academic endeavors. As institutions become increasingly diverse, understanding and addressing these dynamics are essential for fostering equitable educational environments that support the success of all students, particularly those from international backgrounds.

The ability to participate in classroom discussions is a central component of academic success in many North American and Western European educational systems. This shift can be particularly challenging for international students, especially those from educational traditions that emphasize rote memorization and passive learning. According to Tatar (2005), international students often experience considerable anxiety when adapting to classroom environments that differ significantly from their home countries. In many Asian educational systems, for example, students are typically expected to listen and absorb information, with minimal emphasis on active participation or questioning. By contrast, North America and Western Europe's pedagogical practices often emphasize critical thinking, open debate, and the expression of personal opinions. This can be overwhelming for international students who may feel that their perspectives are invalid or valued in a more interactive classroom. Mustapha (2010) underscores the role of faculty in mitigating these challenges. Faculty who adopt inclusive teaching strategies such as providing clear guidelines for participation, using culturally sensitive examples, and encouraging structured discussions can ease the transition for international students. Such practices create an environment where international students feel more comfortable contributing to class conversations. For example, faculty might provide specific prompts to guide discussions or offer smaller, more intimate settings for student interaction, allowing a smoother transition into more participatory academic settings. Conversely, when faculty fail to recognize cultural differences and adopt a one-size-fits-all approach, they may inadvertently create an environment where international students feel marginalized or excluded.

The behavior of faculty members is one of the most critical factors in determining how international students navigate classroom environments. Hsu (2019) emphasizes the importance of teacher confirmation behaviors, such as offering positive feedback, providing encouragement, and acknowledging diverse perspectives. These behaviors help build a supportive classroom environment where students feel validated and encouraged to participate. For international students, positive reinforcement can help counter feelings of alienation and insecurity, enabling them to develop the confidence to engage with the material and contribute to class discussions. In contrast, the absence of supportive behavior can intensify students' feelings of anxiety and disengagement. Guo and Chase (2011) observe that faculty often misinterpret international students' silence in class as disinterest or lack of preparation rather than because of cultural differences or language barriers. This misinterpretation can lead to a cycle of disengagement, where students may feel withdrawn even further from the classroom experience due to a lack of support or understanding from their instructors. The disconnect between student and teacher expectations can leave students unprepared to navigate academic challenges, ultimately affecting their educational success. Faculty training in intercultural competence and inclusive pedagogy is vital in addressing these issues. Educators who understand the nuances of cultural diversity are better equipped to support international students and help them overcome barriers to engagement.

Classroom dynamics extend beyond the student-faculty relationship to include interactions between peers, which are equally important for fostering a sense of belonging. Peer relationships in the classroom profoundly impact international students' social integration, academic engagement, and mental well-being. Glass and Westmont (2014) highlight that supportive peer interactions contribute to a more positive academic experience by providing a network of support. These interactions are essential for students to navigate the social aspects of academic life, including group work, collaborative learning, and informal discussions outside of the classroom. However, international students often face significant challenges in forming these relationships due to cultural differences, language barriers, or perceived discrimination. Andrade (2006) suggests that these difficulties can lead to social isolation, negatively affecting academic outcomes and mental health. Students who struggle to find common ground with their peers may feel excluded from classroom discussions and group activities, further hindering their academic success. Institutions can help alleviate these challenges by implementing peer mentoring programs and facilitating group-based learning opportunities. Such programs offer a structured environment where international students can interact with their domestic peers and form cross-cultural friendships. By promoting positive peer interactions, institutions can create a more comprehensive and supportive classroom environment that benefits all students.

Beyond faculty and peer interactions, the broader institutional context shapes classroom dynamics. Guo and Chase (2011) emphasize the importance of integrating international students into the academic community by providing targeted support services, including orientation programs, workshops on academic norms, and resources for language development. These services help students understand the expectations of their host institutions and navigate the cultural and academic differences they encounter. For example, institutions can provide resources that help international students understand the participatory nature of North America and Western Europe classrooms and offer guidance on engaging with faculty and peers in an assertive yet respectful manner. Language support services are particularly critical for international students whose proficiency in English may impact their classroom experience. Providing English as a Second Language (ESL) programs, conversation clubs, or writing assistance can improve students' ability to communicate constructively in the classroom and social settings. Andrade (2006) notes that language support is helpful for academic success and social integration. When international students feel confident in their ability to communicate, they are more likely to engage with their peers and participate in classroom discussions, which enhances their overall academic experience.

The pressure to adapt to unfamiliar academic norms, combined with the fear of making mistakes in front of peers, can create heightened stress and anxiety. Tatar (2005) explains that international students often experience self-doubt about their academic abilities, which is increased by the perceived demands of the North American and Western European education system. Adapting to new teaching and learning methods can become overwhelming, which leads to feelings of inadequacy and fear of failure. In addition to these emotional stressors, many international students experience a lack of academic self-efficacy, stemming from the differences in how critical thinking, problem-solving, and independent learning are valued in their home countries. These feelings of inadequacy can affect their participation in classroom activities and hinder their academic progress. Institutions must recognize the psychological toll that classroom dynamics can take on international students and provide comprehensive mental health support. This includes offering counseling services tailored to international students' unique challenges, such as homesickness, language-related stress, and cultural dislocation. Furthermore, creating a classroom culture of empathy and understanding can alleviate some psychological burdens that international students face. When faculty and peers understand cultural adjustment difficulties, they are better equipped to offer the support needed to navigate academic challenges.

One of the most significant aspects of cultural adaptation for international students is understanding and aligning with the educational expectations and classroom culture prevalent in US institutions. Many international students arrive with academic backgrounds that emphasize rote memorization, strict hierarchical relationships between students and instructors, and passive learning modes. In contrast, the US educational environment often encourages interactive discussions, critical thinking, and participatory engagement. This pedagogical shift can pose challenges for students who are not accustomed to voicing their opinions, questioning instructors, or working collaboratively in group settings. A significant area of adjustment involves student–teacher interactions. In many cultures, educators are regarded as authoritative figures whose perspectives are not to be questioned. However, in the US, students are often encouraged to engage respectfully with faculty, ask questions, and challenge ideas constructively. Additionally, office hours represent a distinctive component of the American academic system. Several international students may be unfamiliar with this practice, yet attending office hours can deepen their understanding of course content and foster stronger academic relationships.

Classroom participation and collaboration are also integral elements of the US academic experience. Participation is frequently incorporated into course grading criteria, which may be intimidating for students from cultures where classroom silence is equated with respect. Moreover, group work and collaborative projects are common and require students to navigate diverse communication styles, leadership expectations, and teamwork dynamics. Independent learning and self-directed initiative are highly valued in US education, contrasting with the more guided and structured approaches often seen in other countries. Another critical aspect of adaptation pertains to academic integrity and writing standards. US institutions maintain stringent policies regarding plagiarism, and international students may require explicit instruction on citation practices and academic honesty. Furthermore, the emphasis on research-based writing, critical analysis, and argumentation may necessitate a shift in writing style and academic conventions for students unfamiliar with these expectations.

Beyond academics, social integration and extracurricular engagement play a vital role in cultural adaptation. Developing social connections, understanding local norms, and participating in campus life contribute meaningfully to both the personal and academic success of international students. Navigating social norms, including indirect communication styles, casual small talk, and individualistic attitudes, can help students interact more comfortably within their new environment. Forming friendships with domestic students often provides deeper cultural understanding and reduces feelings of isolation. Involvement in extracurricular activities such as student organizations, sports, and volunteer work can significantly aid cultural adaptation by fostering informal peer interactions as well. Participation in campus events that celebrate diverse cultures not only promotes cross-cultural exchange but also reinforces a sense of identity and belonging for international students. Finally, mental health and access to support services are essential for a successful transition. The process of adjusting to a new cultural and academic setting can trigger culture shock, stress, and anxiety. Many universities offer counseling services, international student offices, and peer mentoring programs to assist students during this transition. However, in some cultures, seeking mental health support may carry stigma. It is therefore crucial for institutions to actively promote the availability, confidentiality, and cultural sensitivity of mental health resources.

# Chapter Five
# Language Barriers and Academic Communication

As data revealed, academic challenges are a significant concern for nearly half of international students, often manifesting as difficulties with class performance and delayed degree progress. A primary contributor to these academic struggles is language barriers, profoundly affecting their academic performance, social integration, and psychological well-being. These barriers are not limited to basic vocabulary or grammar; they extend to more complex issues, such as understanding academic discourse, cultural nuances, and social expectations crucial for academic success. For international students, particularly those from non-English-speaking countries, language proficiency is intrinsically tied to their overall adaptation to new cultural environments and their educational experiences. A mainly overlooked aspect is the necessity of mastering American English. As an international student, I can attest to the profound challenges posed by transitioning from British English, which I learned in India, to American English. Becoming comfortable with everyday conversations, academic terminology, and the informal slang integral to American social interactions took years. This transition is often underestimated but is crucial to academic success, social confidence, and professional networking.

Towards the culmination of my dual undergraduate degree, an internship with an outside organization was a mandatory requirement. I successfully secured an internship, but I did not clearly understand the instructions provided by the dean regarding its nature. Any internship within my field would suffice, as I am unaware of the dean's specific emphasis on lab-based work over fieldwork. When he subsequently rejected my chosen organization, I felt utterly frazzled and bewildered. In a state of intense stress, I sent an urgent email to the dean, pleading for his understanding, explaining my international student status, and highlighting the strict time constraints I faced to complete my degree. His denial of my request was a crushing blow. I apologized multiple times, desperate for a solution, but ultimately had to forgo that invaluable internship opportunity. I instead completed an independent study with a faculty member to fulfill the graduation requirement. Exactly a year later, when I sought admission to the Master's program, the same dean denied my request. I firmly believe this denial was a direct consequence of the miscommunication that had occurred. It was a harsh, yet indelible, lesson: I learned then the critical importance of clear academic communication in the US context, and how crucial it is to ask probing questions; otherwise, vital opportunities can be missed, misunderstandings can jeopardize one's academic standing, and for an international student, the stakes for entire career are too high to afford such errors.

## 5.1 Academic Challenges and Performance

Language barriers pose a significant and multifaceted challenge for international students in US academic settings, fundamentally hindering their ability to comprehend complex material, participate effectively in discussions, and meet course expectations. Although students with advanced English proficiency might navigate everyday conversations with ease, their challenges often lie in mastering academic language, a level of communication that extends far beyond general English. For those with lower proficiency, the hurdles are even greater, encompassing difficulties in understanding lectures, assignments, and the specialized terminology required in their fields of study.

Beyond the speed and dialect of spoken English, international students often face a more hidden linguistic challenge: the widespread use of idiomatic expressions and highly specialized academic language jargon. These elements, while natural parts of native English communication and disciplinary discourse, can make conversations and lectures almost impossible to understand for those still learning their fluency. Idiomatic expressions, by their very nature, resist literal translation and can cause significant confusion. Imagine a student hearing a professor casually say, "That's a piece of cake" when referring to a simple assignment, or a peer exclaim, "Let's hit the books" before an exam. Without the underlying cultural context, these phrases are nonsensical. I recall a student recounting how she missed the punchline of a joke because the speaker "spilled the beans" – a phrase that left her completely bewildered, leading to an awkward silence and a feeling of being outside the social circle. These moments, seemingly minor, accumulate and contribute to a pervasive sense of social exclusion, making it difficult for students to engage in informal interactions fully.

Similarly, academic jargon presents its own unique set of hurdles. Every discipline in US higher education operates with its distinct lexicon, often assuming a baseline understanding that international students may not possess from their home countries. Terms like "synergy," "paradigm shift," "heuristic," "discourse community," or "scaffolding" might be commonplace in a US classroom yet be entirely novel or used with different connotations elsewhere. For instance, a professor might casually refer to "doing a lit review" or "conducting due diligence" in a research methodology class. Native English speakers readily understand these as "literature review" and "thorough investigation." An international student, having mastered general English, might still struggle to grasp the immediate, specific meaning, let alone the implicit academic expectations tied to such terms. This often forces students to constantly mentally translate or look up terms, slowing down comprehension and inhibiting real-time participation in lectures and discussions. These subtle yet pervasive linguistic differences significantly contribute to the challenges of academic and social integration. This can trigger anxiety, diminish confidence in participating, and reinforce feelings of alienation, as students grapple with a language that is both familiar in its grammar but elusive in its nuances. Overcoming these specific hurdles requires not just English language proficiency, but a nuanced understanding of American cultural communication patterns and the specific "language" of US academic discourse.

Ennin and Manariyo (2023) corroborate this by stating that even proficient English speakers often struggle with idiomatic expressions, academic jargon, and subject-specific content. International students in disciplines such as the social sciences and humanities may find it especially challenging to comprehend culturally embedded references, metaphors, and rhetorical devices, which frequently rely on assumptions of understanding that do not translate seamlessly across cultures. Classroom participation, a vital component of academic success in many US universities, presents another significant challenge directly impacted by language proficiency. As Hussein and Schiffelbein (2020) point out, students with lower language proficiency often hesitate to speak in class due to fears of miscommunication or judgment. This reluctance can lead professors to perceive them as disengaged or uninterested, further intensifying feelings of isolation and disconnection. Without opportunities to actively engage in discussions, these students miss critical educational experiences essential to their academic growth and social integration.

Moreover, language proficiency critically affects students' ability to seek clarification and request help when needed. Many international students are reluctant to approach professors, not only because they fear their linguistic skills may be inadequate but also due to a lack of familiarity with the academic help-seeking culture prevalent in different educational contexts. As Wang and colleagues (2025) observe, Chinese international students, for instance, often struggle to communicate with professors, which limits their ability to receive constructive feedback and build essential academic relationships. This communication gap can result in missed opportunities for mentorship, hindering both their educational development and motivation.

## 5.2 Social and Psychological Impacts

The effects of language barriers go beyond academic challenges; they profoundly impact social and psychological adjustment. Language is the primary vehicle through which people connect. When international students face language difficulties, their ability to form social bonds and experience a sense of belonging is severely limited. Research by Ali Yoenanto and Nurdibyanandaru (2020) indicates that many international students report stress due to language barriers. For example, 68% of participants in a study at Universitas Airlangga acknowledged that language difficulties contributed to their psychological strain. The constant challenge of navigating a foreign language environment generates anxiety and frustration, further hindering their ability to adapt socially. Zhang and Mi (2010) found that many international students tend to avoid social interactions due to fear of making mistakes or feeling embarrassed about their language skills. This self-imposed isolation can add to students' challenges, preventing them from accessing social networks and support systems crucial to their overall well-being. Interestingly, the social isolation triggered by language barriers is not limited to interactions with native speakers. Peer groups within the international student community are often linguistically segregated, as students tend to group with others who speak the same language. While this clustering can serve as a natural coping mechanism, it inadvertently hinders meaningful intercultural exchanges. It impedes the broader learning experience that international education aims to provide. This segmentation can reinforce feelings of exclusion, as students miss opportunities to practice their language skills and engage with the diverse perspectives that make a multicultural academic environment unique.

### 5.3 Cultural and Communication Style Differences

The cultural differences in communication styles further complicate language barriers. International students often struggle with the language and understanding of how communication is expected to unfold in the US academic context. In many countries, academic discussions are more formal, with students showing deference to instructors and adopting a more passive role in learning. In contrast, US classrooms encourage active participation, open debate, and disagreement (Chauhan, 2023). This cultural shift in expectations can create confusion, as students may feel uncertain about expressing their opinions or engaging with professors and peers in a more participatory environment. Moreover, American conversational norms, including the use of humor, sarcasm, and informal phrases, can be challenging for international students to interpret accurately. The ability to grasp these nuances is essential for engaging in academic discussions, as well as for social and professional interactions. International students may feel excluded or hesitant to contribute in academic and informal settings without clear guidance or opportunities for immersion. Universities must provide targeted communication training that familiarizes students with formal and informal language, bridging the cultural gap and fostering greater confidence in diverse communicative contexts. Non-verbal communication adds another layer of complexity. Gestures, body language, and facial expressions carry different meanings across cultures, and international students often struggle to interpret or use these cues effectively (Battye & Mak, 2008). Misunderstandings of non-verbal cues, such as eye contact or posture, may lead to incorrect assumptions about the student's level of engagement or comprehension. These misinterpretations impede effective classroom participation and hinder international students' ability to connect with their peers and instructors on a personal level.

### 5.4 Faculty Perceptions and Academic Engagement

Faculty members play a crucial role in international students' academic success and social integration. However, language barriers often shape how faculty perceive and engage with these students. As Hussein and Schiffelbein (2020) note, professors may interpret students' language difficulties as a sign of a lack of motivation or interest, particularly when students struggle to communicate in ways that align with classroom expectations. Instructors not trained to recognize and address international students' linguistic and cultural challenges may unintentionally reinforce feelings of inadequacy and exclusion. This is especially problematic in disciplines like the humanities and social sciences, where communication skills are essential for academic success. The lack of faculty training in managing linguistic diversity can result in missed academic support and mentorship opportunities. Lutfiana et al. (2020) highlight that misunderstandings stemming from language barriers were a significant obstacle for Thai students studying in Indonesia, further underscoring the importance of addressing these challenges to improve international student success. Faculty awareness and sensitivity are crucial for creating an inclusive academic environment that fosters the engagement and growth of international students.

### 5.5 Strategies for Addressing Language Barriers

Language barriers pose significant challenges to international students, impacting their academic performance, social integration, and overall well-being. As higher education institutions increasingly enroll students from diverse linguistic backgrounds, addressing these barriers has become critical to supporting international students. To lighten the challenges associated with language differences, universities have implemented various strategies and support systems to enhance language proficiency, foster social connections, and create an inclusive academic environment. These strategies are designed to enhance language skills, alleviate anxiety, and foster a sense of belonging among international students.

One of the most fundamental strategies for addressing language barriers is providing dedicated language support programs. These programs typically include English language courses tailored to international students, focusing on general language skills and academic English proficiency. For example, Intensive English Programs (IEPs) are structured courses designed to help students improve their reading, writing, speaking, and listening skills. These programs equip students with the essential language tools for academic success and prepare them for the linguistic demands of university life. According to Lee (2018), IEPs provide a bridge between the students' current language abilities and the advanced language requirements of higher education, ensuring that they can participate fully in academic discussions, engage with course materials, and complete assignments successfully. In addition to formal language programs, universities often offer tutoring services to help students refine their language skills. These services typically provide one-on-one or small group sessions where students can receive personalized instruction, ask questions, and practice specific aspects of language use that may pose challenges. Tutoring programs help students improve their academic language and foster a sense of connection to the university community, as students can seek assistance in a supportive, non-judgmental environment. Tutoring services provide targeted assistance by focusing on individual needs, ensuring that students can progress at their own pace.

Peer mentoring programs have emerged as one of the most effective and socially rewarding strategies for addressing language barriers. These programs pair international students with domestic students or other international students who have achieved a higher level of language proficiency. Peer mentors assist their mentees by providing guidance, helping them navigate academic tasks, and offering practical advice on improving their language skills. More importantly, peer mentoring programs provide a platform for informal language practice, allowing international students to engage in meaningful conversations and receive feedback on their language use in a supportive, low-pressure environment. As Zhang and Mi (2010) point out, peer networks offer a space for language practice free from the fear of judgment. This environment is particularly valuable for students who may feel self-conscious about their language abilities and are hesitant to participate in formal classroom settings. Through regular interactions with their mentors and peers, international students improve their language proficiency and help develop social bonds that can reduce feelings of isolation. Peer mentoring also serves as a bridge for building intercultural competence, as mentors and mentees share their cultural experiences and perspectives, enriching their social interactions.

The role of faculty in supporting international students is crucial and cannot be overstated. Professors trained in intercultural communication and aware of the linguistic challenges that international students face can make a significant difference in the academic experiences of these students. Intercultural training for faculty involves educating professors on the cultural norms, communication styles, and educational expectations that may vary between international and domestic students. By understanding these differences, faculty members can adjust their teaching strategies to create more inclusive and supportive learning environments. Domínguez and Cheng (2022) highlight the importance of faculty awareness in improving student engagement and participation. Culturally sensitive faculty members can modify their teaching methods to accommodate diverse language backgrounds, for example, by offering alternative forms of assessment, providing more explicit instructions, and encouraging student participation in ways that consider language barriers. By adopting inclusive teaching practices, professors can help international students feel more comfortable and confident in their academic abilities.

## 5.6 Conclusion

Language barriers are among the most significant obstacles international students face, impacting their academic success, social integration, and overall sense of belonging. Universities must recognize the profound influence of language proficiency on students' experiences and take proactive steps to support their linguistic development. Comprehensive language support programs, peer mentoring, faculty training, and collaborative learning opportunities are essential components of a multifaceted strategy for addressing these challenges. By creating an inclusive, supportive academic and social environment, universities can empower international students to succeed academically, integrate socially, and build meaningful connections with their peers, ultimately enhancing their overall well-being and enriching their educational experience.

# Chapter Six
# Faculty-Student Relationships and Cultural Perceptions

Given the ACHA-NCHA data in Chapter 2, which underscored the prevalence of social isolation, loneliness, and academic challenges among international students, the quality of faculty-student relationships becomes particularly critical. Faculty-student relationships are foundational to the experiences of international students in the US, often shaping their academic success, emotional well-being, and cultural adjustment (Ma, 2022). These relationships bridge the unique challenges faced by international students, such as cultural and linguistic barriers, and their ability to integrate into US academic and social environments. Positive faculty-student interactions foster academic confidence, social belonging, and cultural adaptation. At the same time, challenges in these relationships can intensify feelings of isolation and hinder academic engagement.

Throughout my 14 years in academia, it has been a profound rarity for only a handful of faculty members who truly saw beyond my color, my accent, my origin, or my "different" English. Since childhood, I have been an inherently bright student, driven to excel academically and determined to succeed, regardless of the obstacles. However, after coming to the US, my entire perception of academia shifted. My ambition narrowed; I no longer yearned to excel but to *make it through*. My daily prayer before each new semester became a silent plea: "Please, let this year bring a professor who sees me as a human, who recognizes my potential, and who looks past my 'otherness.'"

I clearly remember one academic semester. On the very first day, the professor started the lecture by saying that all international students would need to attend the writing lab every week, emphatically stating, "*because I am not here to teach them English.*" She then warned that failing to show proof of attendance would result in a failing grade for the course, and she would personally see to it that these students would not be allowed to graduate. I was terrified. This was the first and only time in my academic career that I dropped a class purely out of fear of a professor. This professor, who began her course with such biased comments, would never have known my true potential, nor would she have ever looked beyond my perceived "otherness." I have many similar experiences where I was belittled in class or made fun of for reasons entirely unrelated to academics or my ability to perform. For those who might question my academic abilities, I hold two Master's degrees, one with Honors due to a 4.0 GPA, and a Ph.D. with a perfect 4.0 GPA. This contrast between my documented academic success and the biases I encountered highlights how faculty perceptions can deeply affect the experiences of international students.

### 6.1 Cross-Cultural Challenges in Faculty-Student Relationships

Cultural differences significantly shape faculty-student relationships, while creating opportunities but also creating challenges, as international students and faculty navigate complex intercultural dynamics. For students, the challenges of transitioning to US academic norms often require adaptation to new expectations surrounding participation, interaction, and learning styles. Language barriers frequently complicate these transitions, making it difficult for international students to express their thoughts, ask questions, or seek clarification that aligns with US academic and cultural expectations (Stojanović & Robinson, 2021). Moreover, the egalitarian and participatory teaching methods commonly promoted in US classrooms can feel unfamiliar or disorienting to students from cultures that value hierarchical or teacher-centered approaches (Hussein & Schiffelbein, 2020). The impact of these cultural differences is further highlighted in the work of Mok (2013), who underscores the importance of faculty interactions in shaping the academic outcomes of international students. Cultural differences, like reluctance to participate in class or seek help during office hours, can be misunderstood as disinterest or lack of effort. This misinterpretation may hinder students' academic performance and reduce their ability to build rapport with faculty, creating a cycle of disengagement that is difficult to overcome. For international faculty, similar challenges arise in adapting to the expectations of the US academic culture. Faculty accustomed to teaching styles that emphasize lectures, rote memorization, or strict authority in their home countries may face difficulties engaging students who are encouraged to think critically, challenge ideas, and collaborate with peers. Language proficiency and culturally nuanced communication styles further complicate these interactions. For instance, even minor linguistic nuances, such as idiomatic expressions or tone, can result in miscommunication, confusion, or perceived distance between faculty and students (Stojanović & Robinson, 2021).

The challenges extend beyond individual interactions, as faculty also play a critical role in creating inclusive classroom environments that support diverse learning styles. Wang and BrckaLorenz (2018) stress that fostering trust and overcoming cultural divides requires intentional and sustained intercultural communication from both students and faculty. This involves recognizing and addressing implicit biases, cultivating cultural humility, and employing teaching practices that are flexible and adaptable to diverse student needs. Faculty who try to learn about their students' cultural backgrounds and experiences are better equipped to create environments that promote inclusivity, respect, and mutual understanding. Moreover, the dynamics of cultural adjustment are not one-sided; they necessitate collaboration and empathy from students and faculty. For international students, engaging with faculty attuned to their cultural and linguistic challenges can foster a sense of belonging and empowerment, encouraging active participation and deeper learning. Conversely, faculty who develop cultural competence enhance their effectiveness in teaching international students and enrich the overall classroom experience by fostering a multicultural perspective that benefits all students. In essence, the interplay of cultural and linguistic factors in both faculty and students encourages practices that bridge cultural divides. These institutions can strengthen connections between international students and faculty, laying a foundation for academic success and mutual enrichment.

## 6.2 Hierarchy and Authority in Academic Relationships

Just like any other student traveling to a different state or city for education, international students often bring deeply ingrained cultural norms and expectations shaped by educational systems where authority and hierarchy play central roles in faculty-student interactions. In such contexts, formalities, deference, and a passive learning style are accepted and often seen as markers of respect and proper academic conduct (Ma, 2022). These norms can lead to significant challenges when transitioning to US classrooms, where informal, collaborative, and egalitarian relationships between students and faculty are encouraged and often expected.

Faculty in the US typically value active participation, critical questioning, and open dialogue as essential components of the learning process. However, for international students, these expectations can feel culturally dissonant. For instance, asking questions or challenging ideas in class might be perceived as disrespectful or confrontational in their home cultures. This can create discomfort and hesitation, further inhibiting participation and engagement (Hussein & Schiffelbein, 2020). The disconnect between cultural norms becomes even more pronounced when faculty misinterpret the culture of these students as their disregard. For example, a student's reluctance to contribute to discussions or reliance on faculty guidance might be seen as a lack of motivation or interest rather than an adherence to cultural norms that value respect for authority and structured learning. These misinterpretations can strain faculty-student relationships, limiting mentorship, support, and academic success opportunities.

Encouraging faculty to develop cultural competence and an awareness of these nuances is critical for bridging these gaps. Faculty attuned to their students' cultural and educational backgrounds are better equipped to interpret behaviors accurately and respond sensitively. Adapting teaching methods to include a mix of participation styles, such as small group discussions or written reflections, can help create an inclusive environment where international students feel comfortable engaging without fear of violating cultural norms. Brunton and Jeffrey (2014) emphasize that understanding these dynamics is essential for fostering learner empowerment among international students. When faculty acknowledge and accommodate cultural differences, students are more likely to feel confident, respected, and motivated to engage actively in their education. Kwon (2009) highlights how cultural expectations influence the adjustment of international students to US academic settings, particularly in their interactions with faculty. For many students, these interactions are critical in determining their academic success and overall sense of belonging in a new cultural and educational environment. Classroom participation may provide the much-needed confidence to these international students.

Institutional efforts to support faculty and students in navigating these cultural divides can have far-reaching benefits. Training programs on cross-cultural communication, mentorship strategies, and inclusive teaching practices can equip faculty with the tools to foster positive relationships with students from diverse backgrounds. At the same time, orientation programs for international students can help set realistic expectations about US academic norms, providing them with strategies to adapt while maintaining their cultural identity. By fostering mutual understanding and creating spaces where cultural differences are respected and valued, educational institutions can strengthen faculty-student relationships, enhance academic outcomes, and promote a more inclusive and supportive learning environment for all students.

### 6.3 The Role of Cultural Sensitivity in Mentoring Relationships

Cultural dynamics significantly shape mentoring relationships, particularly when international faculty mentor students from diverse or marginalized backgrounds. In these relationships, the intersection of cultural differences, academic expectations, and personal experiences can create unique challenges and opportunities for both mentors and mentees. One critical area of concern is how international faculty approach mentorship, often prioritizing technical expertise and academic achievement, which may inadvertently overlook the broader social and cultural challenges faced by marginalized students.

Merriweather and colleagues (2022) highlight these complexities in their study of mentoring relationships between international faculty and Black and

Brown STEM doctoral students. They note that these students, often navigating multiple layers of identity, may experience a lack of empathy and understanding from their mentors, who may focus primarily on technical expertise and scientific rigor rather than acknowledging the social and cultural obstacles these students encounter. These obstacles include experiences of racism, discrimination, and microaggressions, which can significantly impact students' academic performance and well-being. By not addressing or even recognizing these challenges, mentors can unintentionally contribute to feelings of isolation, alienation, and underperformance among marginalized students.

The importance of recognizing the broader cultural and social contexts of mentoring relationships is also reflected in the work of Jin and Schneider (2019), who examine faculty perspectives on international students. They find that many faculty members, especially those without significant experience in cross-cultural teaching, may lack awareness of the cultural nuances that influence international students' behavior and expectations. For instance, students from collectivist cultures might hesitate to initiate personal conversations with faculty or openly express concerns, interpreting such behaviors as a sign of respect or deference to authority. Faculty, in turn, may misinterpret these actions as a lack of engagement, leading to missed opportunities for mentorship and support. These gaps in understanding can create barriers to effective mentoring and limit the potential for international students, particularly those from marginalized backgrounds, to thrive academically and personally. When successful, mentoring relationships go beyond academic guidance to offer emotional support, validation, and a sense of belonging. However, suppose faculty are unaware of or dismissive of the cultural dynamics at play. In that case, they may fail to provide the holistic support these students need to succeed academically and personally.

Mentoring practices must be more culturally responsive and attuned to the unique needs of international and marginalized students. International faculty mentoring students from diverse backgrounds means engaging in self-reflection to recognize their cultural biases and assumptions. Furthermore, faculty can benefit from professional development opportunities emphasizing cultural competence, emotional intelligence, and awareness of the social and cultural factors influencing student experiences. Creating mentoring relationships that embrace cultural sensitivity involves more than just technical guidance; it requires empathy, active listening, and understanding how a student's background shapes their academic journey. Faculty mentors must be willing to engage in open conversations about race, identity, and the personal challenges students face, particularly concerning issues of systemic inequality and discrimination.

Moreover, faculty can foster a more inclusive and supportive mentoring environment by providing opportunities for students to connect with other students and faculty members who share similar backgrounds or experiences, promoting a sense of community and belonging. Ultimately, the goal of mentoring should be to empower students, helping them navigate the complexities of academic life while addressing the personal and cultural challenges they may encounter. By cultivating culturally responsive mentorship practices, institutions can better support the success of international students and ensure that they feel valued, understood, and prepared to succeed in both academic and professional settings.

### 6.4 Encouraging Mutual Understanding and Collaboration Between Faculty and Students

Building bridges between faculty and international students requires a dual approach: fostering an environment where faculty can navigate cultural complexities and ensuring that international students feel empowered and supported as they engage with US academic culture. This collaboration can be cultivated through mutual understanding and respect, where faculty approach their students with empathy and openness to the diverse backgrounds they bring into the classroom. For international students, it means recognizing the value of their cultural perspectives and academic approaches when embracing opportunities for learning and adaptation to US educational norms. Institutions can play a key role in facilitating this mutual understanding by organizing workshops, orientation programs, and discussion forums for students and faculty. These initiatives can provide students with practical tips on adjusting to US academic expectations, such as approaching professors with questions, participating in class discussions, and engaging in critical thinking. Similarly, workshops on cultural competency can guide faculty in creating welcoming environments, understanding the cultural contexts behind students' actions, and developing inclusive teaching practices that accommodate a wide range of learning preferences and communication styles. Moreover, students benefit from learning about the institutional culture and the expectations of their professors. Orientation programs or modules that outline the US educational system's focus on collaboration, active participation, and self-directed learning can be beneficial. These efforts help set clear expectations and offer students the tools to engage with faculty effectively. For example, assisting students to recognize that asking questions or seeking clarification during lectures is seen as a sign of engagement rather than disrespect can reduce hesitation and increase classroom participation. Additionally, equipping students with effective communication strategies, such as emailing professors respectfully, asking for office hours, or initiating academic conversations, can create a more seamless interaction between students and faculty.

### 6.5 Support Networks and Resources for International Students

The importance of building a supportive network cannot be overstated. International students often feel isolated due to their distance from family and unfamiliarity with the US social and academic systems. Faculty can be key in providing this support through academic mentorship and connecting students to broader institutional resources. These resources may include peer support groups, international student associations, counseling services, and workshops to promote mental health and emotional well-being. By actively referring students to these resources, faculty can play a vital role in ensuring that international students are academically and personally supported. In addition, institutions should consider creating specific programs to foster strong faculty-student relationships. Programs that connect international students with faculty outside the classroom, such as informal lunch discussions or faculty-led interest groups, can break down barriers and foster community. These interactions allow students to discuss personal experiences, academic goals, and cultural adjustments in a more relaxed setting, allowing them to feel seen and heard as individuals. Furthermore, mentoring programs that pair international students with faculty mentors with backgrounds or expertise in cross-cultural issues can offer valuable support. These programs can help international students navigate the academic system while providing a safe space to discuss their challenges. The mentorship can extend beyond academic guidance, offering emotional support, practical advice for living in the US, and assistance with adjusting to the cultural shifts that come with studying abroad.

### 6.6 Continuous Feedback and Reflection in Faculty-Student Interactions

An essential part of improving faculty-student relationships is the ongoing process of feedback and reflection. Faculty must be receptive to feedback from their international students, as it can provide valuable insights into the effectiveness of teaching methods and classroom interactions. This feedback loop should encourage students to express their thoughts and feelings about the course structure, teaching methods, and their level of comfort in communicating with faculty. Creating an anonymous channel for students to provide feedback can help alleviate concerns about reprisal, especially for those who may not feel comfortable voicing their concerns directly. Faculty should also reflect on their teaching practices and the inclusiveness of their classroom environment. Regular self-reflection enables faculty to evaluate their teaching and mentoring approaches, making necessary adjustments to support their students better. For example, faculty might reflect on how they communicate with students, the language in their instructions, and whether they create opportunities for students from diverse backgrounds to contribute to discussions. By continuously striving for improvement, faculty can create a more inclusive and effective learning environment that benefits all students, not just international ones.

## 6.7 Institutional Commitment to Cultural Competence and Inclusivity

The commitment to fostering positive faculty-student relationships for international students must extend beyond individual faculty efforts and be deeply institutionalized. The ACHA-NCHA data indicate significant academic challenges, psychological distress, and feelings of isolation among international students, highlighting that a piecemeal approach to support is insufficient. Therefore, universities must take deliberate, systemic steps to embed cultural competence and inclusiveness into the very fabric of academic life, ensuring a comprehensive and consistent approach. This can be achieved through the development and implementation of institutional policies that prioritize diversity, equity, and inclusion across all facets of academic experience, from curriculum design to student support services.

To cultivate a faculty body capable of effectively engaging with diverse student populations, institutions should ensure that hiring practices reflect a profound commitment to diversity. Beyond initial recruitment, robust faculty development programs are essential, providing ongoing training in cultural competence and inclusive teaching strategies. Such training should specifically address the findings from Chapter 2, for example, by equipping faculty to recognize and respond to the signs of psychological distress or academic disengagement that might stem from acculturative stress or cultural misunderstandings. This proactive approach can help reduce the loneliness and anxiety reported by many international students.

Furthermore, universities must regularly and systematically assess the institutional climate for international students. This rigorous assessment should move beyond anecdotal evidence, incorporating data collection methods such as the ACHA-NCHA, including comprehensive surveys, structured focus groups, and qualitative interviews with international students regarding their experiences with faculty and academic staff. By gathering and analyzing such data, institutions can precisely identify areas where cultural misunderstandings or barriers to engagement persist, thereby pinpointing specific gaps in support. For instance, if survey data reveals that a significant percentage of international students feel uncomfortable approaching professors during office hours (as suggested by the cultural differences discussed in Chapter 5), this pinpointed issue can lead to targeted interventions. With this granular information, universities can develop refined support systems, such as enhanced orientation sessions for new international students that explicitly cover US classroom expectations and the purpose of office hours. They can also implement training for faculty to encourage more approachable and culturally sensitive interaction styles, ultimately fostering a more inclusive academic culture where international students feel seen, understood, and supported in their educational journey and overall well-being.

## 6.8 Conclusion

In conclusion, this relationship between faculty and international students is an essential aspect of academic and personal success. As the ACHA-NCHA data consistently highlight, international students face significant challenges related to academic stress, social isolation, and overall well-being. These struggles often become heightened by the subtle yet profound friction caused by cross-cultural differences in communication, hierarchical expectations, and persistent language barriers. However, these challenges are not insurmountable. They present a vital opportunity for both faculty and students to approach their interactions with a spirit of collaboration, mutual respect, and a genuine openness to learn from each other's diverse perspectives. For this to happen on a meaningful scale, responsibility cannot rest solely on the efforts made by an individual. Institutions must actively support this process by embedding cultural competence into the very fabric of academic experience. This requires a systemic commitment to providing comprehensive training for faculty on inclusive teaching strategies and cross-cultural communication. It also requires establishing a structured mentorship program and readily available resources that facilitate communication, foster cultural understanding, and promote student well-being. By proactively investing in cultural competence, universities can create a more inclusive and dynamic academic environment where both faculty and students can thrive. Ultimately, strengthening faculty-student relationships is an ongoing process that requires continuous effort, reflection, and adaptation from all parties, ensuring that every international student feels valued, supported, and empowered to succeed in their academic journey.

# Chapter Seven
# Peer Interactions and Social Integration

The data presented in Chapter 2 indicate that loneliness, feelings of being left out, and isolation are prevalent challenges among international students. This empirical evidence underscores the critical importance of effective peer interaction. Indeed, the academic and personal experiences of international students in the United States are intricately linked to their ability to navigate peer interactions and achieve social integration. These two elements significantly shape their experiences, profoundly influencing their emotional well-being, academic performance, and overall success in their new environment. As international student populations continue to grow in US universities, understanding the challenges they face in establishing peer relationships becomes essential for creating inclusive, supportive, and thriving academic environments that directly address the isolation many students report.

Now that you have learned a little about my academic determination and the biases I faced with faculty, you might assume that over 14 years of education, I must have cultivated a vast network of friends and a vast social support system. However, let me assure you that it was not as easy as it seems, and often, it felt nearly impossible. Although some students might have initially expressed a desire for friendship, deep-seated differences in religious beliefs, cultural norms, and ideologies frequently created insurmountable barriers to meaningful interaction. Over the past 14 years, I have never been invited to a birthday party or a wedding. On one occasion, I directly confronted peers who had distributed invitations to the entire class, only to be told that I would be "the only brown person there, and they did not want that." Another student once bluntly stated that I "looked like I was from the Middle East" and that their family "would not approve." Still another rationalized the exclusion by citing my abstinence from alcohol and my dietary restrictions against beef and pork. Initially, these rejections were devastating; I felt a profound, aching loneliness. Even now, the lack of proper social integration leaves me feeling isolated at times. As a spiritual person, I find solace in believing that some individuals are not meant to be in one's life, but in my case, it often felt as though *no one* was meant for me.

Adding to this social alienation, during my Ph.D. program, I found myself "othered" by my peers, who perceived me as an "overachiever" and the "teacher's favorite," labels that further isolated me. For international students like me, the journey to forming genuine friendships is fraught with unique difficulties. Even attempts to connect with fellow Indian students proved futile, as most hailed from regions of India that held biases against the part of India I was from, preventing any genuine camaraderie. This intense personal experience highlights the complex and often heartbreaking reality of social integration for international students, where cultural, racial, and even regional differences within one's heritage can create persistent barriers to belonging.

## 7.1 The Role of Peer Interactions in Academic Success and Emotional Well-Being

Peer interactions frequently serve as a cornerstone of both academic success and emotional well-being for international students. These interactions extend beyond classroom collaboration, as they also serve as a primary social outlet and an essential component in establishing a support system in an unfamiliar academic environment. Research consistently demonstrates that cultivating positive peer relationships can lead to enhanced academic engagement and improved mental health outcomes (Bianchi & Martini, 2023). However, peer relationships in the US educational context also take on additional importance for international students, given the unique cultural and social dynamics they navigate. For example, studies have shown that international students who engage in academic collaborations, whether through group assignments, study sessions, or discussions, perform better academically (Jiang & Altinyelken, 2021). These collaborations improve subject comprehension and help students develop critical thinking and problem-solving skills in an interactive, peer-supported environment. Furthermore, peer groups, particularly in collaborative contexts, foster a learning atmosphere that encourages creativity, innovation, and the shared exchange of knowledge, a vital aspect for students who might otherwise feel intellectually isolated.

From an emotional standpoint, peer relationships can act as a crucial buffer against the stress of adjusting to a new academic system and culture. Research by Bianchi & Martini (2023) and other scholars suggests that emotional support from peers significantly reduces the likelihood of international students experiencing depression, anxiety, or other stress-related disorders. For example, peer mentoring programs, where more experienced students guide newcomers, have proven effective in bridging both emotional and academic gaps, thereby fostering a stronger sense of community and belonging (Patel et al., 2024). These mentoring relationships provide practical assistance with adapting to coursework and concurrently establish a robust support network for coping with culture shock, homesickness, and feelings of isolation. To further leverage these benefits, universities must prioritize creating structured opportunities for peer interaction, which can be achieved through initiatives such as peer mentoring programs, academic clubs, and cultural exchange events that enable international students to forge meaningful connections. Recognizing the importance of cultural nuances in peer interactions is also paramount; institutions should offer training for domestic students in intercultural communication to facilitate smoother social integration.

## 7.2 Social Isolation: Its Impact on Academic and Emotional Well-Being

Social isolation remains one of the most profound and pervasive challenges encountered by international students in the United States. This isolation is frequently a result of both external and internal barriers that prevent students from establishing meaningful, deep connections with their peers, professors, and the wider community. These multifaceted barriers encompass everything from cultural and language differences to a dearth of support networks and feelings of inadequacy. Consequently, the emotional toll of this isolation is substantial, with a notable proportion of students reporting elevated levels of loneliness, anxiety, and depression (Cena et al., 2021). The psychological repercussions of isolation can be severe, contributing to emotional distress that negatively impacts students' overall well-being and, crucially, their academic performance.

When international students experience emotional isolation, particularly in the absence of familial support, they can feel profoundly disconnected and vulnerable. The emotional weight of such isolation often leads to a spectrum of psychological difficulties, ranging from pervasive sadness and homesickness to more severe issues such as depression or anxiety. The absence of familiar support structures, including family or community networks, further compounds these feelings of loneliness. Moreover, the demanding task of managing life in a foreign country while simultaneously striving for academic excellence can be overwhelming. This strain can significantly detract from students' academic capabilities, especially if they lack effective coping mechanisms for stress or struggle to find emotional stability. Studies indicate that students who feel socially isolated from their peers are less inclined to engage in crucial academic and social activities, such as study groups, extracurricular events, and class discussions. These activities are vital for academic success and simultaneously provide essential opportunities for social interaction that can lessen the emotional toll of being far from home (Lin, 2012). Without these essential connections, international students frequently withdraw from both academic and social experiences, thereby deepening their isolation. This withdrawal can culminate in a profound sense of not belonging within the university community, often leading to diminished academic performance and increased emotional distress. The inability to forge relationships with peers and professors can erode a student's sense of belonging, which is critical for their emotional well-being. The absence of this foundational sense of belonging can result in feelings of alienation and hopelessness, which, in some instances, may lead students to decide to return home or discontinue their studies.

Language barriers are among the most significant obstacles to social integration for many international students. Although a considerable number of international students arrive in the US with proficient English skills, communication challenges often persist. These challenges extend beyond basic grammar and vocabulary to include colloquialisms, slang, and culturally specific references that may not be immediately understandable. Even students who excel in formal English communication may struggle with the informal speech frequently used by domestic peers in social situations. As a consequence, students may feel excluded from social interactions or conversations, further perpetuating their sense of isolation. This issue is particularly pronounced for students from non-English-speaking countries, who may feel overwhelmed by the rapid pace of conversations or the nuanced use of culturally specific humor and idioms that are unfamiliar to them. These difficulties with communication can deter students from participating in social activities or speaking up in class, creating a vicious cycle of isolation and exclusion.

Cultural differences also play a significant role in shaping social interactions. For instance, students from more hierarchical cultures may find it challenging to adapt to the relatively informal, egalitarian norms of US academic and social environments. In many cultures, deference to authority figures, such as professors, is expected, and interactions with them may be formal and highly respectful. However, in the US, a more relaxed approach is often adopted, with students encouraged to engage in casual conversations with professors or peers. This cultural dissonance can lead to hesitation in initiating conversations, sharing opinions, or participating in class discussions. In addition to these cultural differences, stereotypes and biases held by domestic students can further reinforce the social divide between international students and their peers. Domestic students may inadvertently perceive international students as "outsiders," even when the latter are actively striving to integrate into social circles. These negative perceptions can further isolate international students and make it more difficult for them to form meaningful friendships or connections.

The experience of social isolation among international students is further compounded by the lack of established support networks within their host country. Unlike domestic students, who often have family or local community connections to rely on, international students frequently find themselves without these crucial safety nets. This absence of support not only heightens feelings of loneliness and homesickness but also amplifies anxiety and stress, both of which can significantly impair students' academic performance and mental health. Research consistently highlights the crucial role of social support in alleviating these challenges. Students with a robust network of friends, family, or other sources of support are generally better equipped to manage the complexities of living and studying abroad (Rivas et al., 2019). Without such support, students are left to navigate a multitude of academic, emotional, and social challenges independently.

Furthermore, the lack of social support can lead to increased academic stress and burnout. International students often face the added burden of adjusting to unfamiliar teaching styles, grading systems, and educational expectations, which can differ substantially from what they were accustomed to in their home countries. The pressure to meet these new expectations, combined with the challenges of cultural adaptation and isolation, can result in overwhelming stress. Wu et al. (2015) found that this isolation can create a feedback loop, where feelings of emotional distress lead to further isolation, thereby multiplying the distress. The inability to engage with peers or professors in meaningful ways can leave students feeling alienated, contributing to higher levels of anxiety, stress, and, ultimately, academic burnout.

The mental health implications of this social isolation are severe. Studies consistently demonstrate that international students who experience social isolation are at a higher risk of developing mental health problems such as depression and anxiety, and are also more likely to experience suicidal ideation (Wu et al., 2015). These mental health challenges are further compounded by the stigma associated with seeking mental health support, especially in cultures where mental health issues are often viewed negatively. International students may feel reluctant to reach out for help, fearing that they will be misunderstood or judged. This reluctance, coupled with the absence of social support, can significantly impact students' overall well-being. Given the profound impact of social isolation on international students, universities must implement programs and policies that specifically address these challenges. Providing spaces where international students can interact with domestic students and peers from other countries is essential in combating isolation. Universities can create cultural clubs, networking events, support groups, and other social spaces that foster inclusivity and allow students to form meaningful connections. Additionally, targeted outreach efforts aimed at international students, particularly those from regions with lower representation on campus, can help ensure that these students feel seen, supported, and valued within the academic community. By addressing isolation through these supportive programs and initiatives, universities can cultivate a more inclusive environment that promotes both international students' academic success and emotional well-being.

### 7.3 Barriers to Peer Interactions

Language barriers remain among the most formidable challenges international students face in navigating social interactions and academic engagement during their time in the United States. Although many international students possess advanced proficiency in English, they often encounter significant challenges in everyday communication. These challenges go beyond basic grammar and vocabulary, as language use in informal and social contexts usually involves idiomatic expressions, slang, and culturally specific references unfamiliar to those from different linguistic and cultural backgrounds (Jiang & Altinyelken, 2021). These aspects of the English language, which are essential for full participation in social and academic settings, can be challenging to grasp, even for technically fluent students. This discrepancy between formal and colloquial language can create a barrier to integration, leaving students feeling excluded, isolated, and frustrated in their attempts to engage with peers. For instance, everyday conversations among domestic students frequently include slang terms, colloquialisms, or references to pop culture, sports, or local events that international students may not fully understand. Even with a strong command of English, international students may find themselves lost in these exchanges, unable to comprehend the subtleties of humor, jokes, or casual references prevalent in these interactions. The resulting feelings of exclusion can be compounded by the rapid pace of conversation, which may leave international students feeling overwhelmed and reluctant to participate. The speed at which domestic students speak, combined with informal language and slang, may create a sense of disconnection for international students who are still adjusting to the language and the cultural context in which it is used.

The fear of making mistakes or being misunderstood in academic settings also contributes to the reluctance of international students to engage in peer interactions. In particular, students from cultures where humility and restraint are highly valued may feel uncomfortable voicing their opinions or contributing to group discussions. In many cases, these students may hesitate to speak up in class, express their thoughts during group work, or participate in collaborative learning environments because they are self-conscious about their language proficiency (Cena et al., 2021). This sense of insecurity can be especially pronounced in academic settings, where there is often an implicit expectation that students will actively participate in discussions and contribute to group projects. The apprehension of being judged for making grammatical errors, using improper language, or speaking with an accent can discourage students from participating in discussions, ultimately leading to missed academic collaboration and socialization opportunities. Moreover, linguistic differences can result in significant miscommunications between international students and their peers. These miscommunications, which may stem from differences in accents, speech patterns, or pronunciation, can worsen feelings of alienation and contribute to being misunderstood or overlooked. For example, international students with strong accents may find that their ideas or contributions are dismissed not because of their substance but because their peers struggle to understand their speech. The inability to communicate clearly and effectively can make students feel isolated, invisible, or marginalized in academic or social settings. This cycle of miscommunication and misunderstanding can ultimately result in social withdrawal, reinforcing the isolation many international students experience and further hindering their ability to form meaningful relationships with their peers.

In addition to verbal communication challenges, differences in non-verbal communication practices between cultures can further complicate peer interactions. Non-verbal communication, such as body language, facial expressions, and gestures, is critical in interpreting social interactions. However, these practices can vary significantly from one culture to another, leading to misunderstandings and misinterpretations. For example, maintaining direct eye contact is seen as impolite or confrontational in some cultures. In contrast, in US culture, it is often considered a sign of attentiveness, respect, and engagement. International students not accustomed to these cultural norms may inadvertently give the impression of being disengaged or disinterested in conversations, even though they may be fully engaged in the discussion. Such differences in non-verbal cues can contribute to the perception that international students are distant, aloof, or uninterested in socializing when, in fact, the root cause may be a simple misunderstanding or cultural mismatch. These misinterpretations can create additional barriers to forming relationships and isolate international students from their peers.

Furthermore, cultural norms surrounding communication styles, such as the level of formality in interactions and indirect versus direct communication, can influence how international students perceive their interactions with domestic students and vice versa. For example, students from more hierarchical cultures may feel uncomfortable engaging in casual conversations with professors or peers, as they may be accustomed to more formal, deferential interactions. This cultural difference in communication expectations can lead to reluctance on the part of international students to approach professors or classmates informally, which can hinder academic and social integration. The perceived "informality" of US academic and social norms may create confusion or hesitation for international students, who may feel uncertain about navigating these more casual communication styles.

Given the different challenges international students face regarding language barriers and cultural differences, universities need to implement comprehensive strategies that support language development or awareness and intercultural communication. Language support programs that provide students with the tools and resources to improve their speaking and listening skills in informal, everyday contexts can help ease the transition to a more comfortable social and academic environment. These programs could include conversational English practice, peer mentoring, and language exchange partnerships, allowing international students to practice communication in real-world settings without any judgment or bias. In addition to language support, universities should offer cultural exchange initiatives that promote cross-cultural dialogue and foster understanding between international and domestic students. These programs could include international student clubs, cultural events, or social gatherings to encourage interaction and exchange between students of various backgrounds. Additionally, these programs should not restrict domestic students or focus only on international students from certain backgrounds. Students can build greater cultural awareness and develop the communication skills necessary for navigating intercultural interactions by participating in these activities. Promoting awareness of cultural differences in communication styles, such as body language, tone, and directness, can help domestic students better understand and engage with international students. Training faculty and staff to recognize and address these communication challenges can also ensure international students feel supported inside and outside the classroom. This may also help international students gain more confidence to go off campus and explore the surroundings without the fear of people not being able to understand them or being misunderstood. By creating an environment where cultural differences are recognized and valued, universities can support international students in overcoming challenges in building meaningful connections and engaging fully in academic and social activities. These efforts may help international students adapt to life in the US and foster a richer, more diverse educational experience for everyone, promoting mutual understanding and respect among individuals from different cultural backgrounds (Cena et al., 2021).

## 7.4 Cultural Differences and Peer Relationships

Cultural differences are central to shaping peer interactions among international and domestic students, as these differences may guide the communication styles, values, and expectations surrounding relationships and socialization. The cultural divides, stemming from varying worldviews, attitudes, and social norms, can create opportunities for growth and challenges in forming connections. Among the most significant cultural differences that affect peer relationships are the contrasting orientations of individualism and collectivism, which profoundly shape how students approach interactions with others (Hofstede, 2001).

In collectivist cultures, such as Asian, Latin American, and Middle Eastern, relationships are typically characterized by long-term trust, mutual dependence, and a focus on group harmony. In these cultures, social interactions are often viewed through the lens of family and community, and loyalty to one's group is considered paramount. The value placed on interdependence and respect for the needs of others over individual desires is reflected in how students from collectivist cultures interact with their peers. For international students from these backgrounds, forming meaningful relationships requires time, patience, and shared experiences. They tend to prioritize deep, personal bonds built over an extended period, emphasizing loyalty, respect, and understanding. The concept of personal space and boundaries in collectivist cultures may be more fluid, and a greater emphasis is placed on group activities and shared responsibilities. For instance, students from collectivist cultures may place higher importance on group cohesion and expect their interactions with peers to be more involved and less transactional. As such, social engagements may involve more significant, close-knit groups, where connections develop gradually through experiences and activities that foster trust. Additionally, communication may be more indirect, with students expressing themselves subtly to maintain harmony and avoid confrontation or disagreement (Markus & Kitayama, 1991). The collectivist student's expectation of loyalty, trust, and interdependence in relationships might make socializing in a US context feel initially unappealing or isolating, especially when relationships appear more superficial or transactional.

In contrast, with its individualistic orientation, US culture tends to prioritize personal autonomy, self-reliance, and direct communication (Markus & Kitayama, 1991). In this environment, students are encouraged to assert their opinions, engage in self-promotion, and pursue immediate relationship reciprocity. The US educational system and social norms emphasize independence and personal achievement, often placing value on "getting to the point" in interactions and valuing directness in communication. Students from the US may expect their relationships to develop quickly and on a more transactional basis, where mutual benefits are sought almost immediately. For example, in group projects, US students may expect each member to actively contribute and take ownership of their roles in the team. They may also be more inclined to discuss personal opinions openly. They may see it as usual to debate or assert themselves in class and social settings. This directness, although seen as a virtue in the US, can be perceived as abrasive or rude by students from more reserved, collectivist cultures.

For international students accustomed to indirect forms of communication or more reserved socialization styles, the US approach can feel overwhelming, abrupt, or even alienating. The rapid pace of interactions, the emphasis on self-promotion, and the expectation of assertiveness may create stress or anxiety for students unaccustomed to these norms. International students from collectivist cultures may interpret the openness and directness of US students as confrontational or impolite. For example, making eye contact or speaking out in class may be uncomfortable for international students from cultures where these actions are not typical or may even be considered disrespectful.

The differences in communication styles due to cultural nuances can lead to misunderstandings. Domestic students, for instance, may interpret the more reserved or passive behavior of international students as disinterest, disengagement, or a lack of initiative, which may hinder the formation of friendships or collaboration. On the other hand, international students may view the assertiveness and directness of their US peers as off-putting. They may feel that their cultural approach to communication, which emphasizes respect and humility, is undervalued or misunderstood. This expectation gap can create tension and feelings of alienation, making it harder for international students to form authentic relationships.

Compounding these difficulties is the issue of perceived prejudice or stereotyping, which can significantly impact peer interactions. International students may encounter stereotypes based on accents, academic abilities, or cultural practices. For example, they may be subject to assumptions about their English proficiency or educational performance, reinforcing negative stereotypes and contributing to social exclusion (Jiang & Altinyelken, 2021). These stereotypes can manifest subtly, such as peers speaking more slowly or louder when interacting with international students, assuming they cannot understand or participate in discussions, or even making dismissive comments about their accents. Over time, these experiences of discrimination or bias can discourage international students from seeking out social connections, making them feel as though they do not belong or are unwelcome in social circles.

For international students, these experiences of stereotyping and exclusion can profoundly impact their sense of belonging and their willingness to engage with domestic students. They may begin to withdraw from social situations, feeling self-conscious or worried about being judged based on their cultural background. This social isolation can lead to mental health challenges such as stress, anxiety, and depression as students struggle to navigate an environment in which they feel they are constantly judged or misunderstood.

In conclusion, cultural differences, particularly in individualism versus collectivism, significantly shape peer relationships among international and domestic students. These differences can create barriers to social integration and academic collaboration, often leading to feelings of isolation and exclusion for international students. However, by promoting cross-cultural understanding, offering support through peer mentoring, and creating inclusive spaces for cultural exchange, universities can help bridge these divides, fostering a more welcoming and supportive environment for all students. These efforts benefit international students and enrich the educational experience for domestic students, cultivating a more global perspective that prepares all students for success in an increasingly interconnected world.

### 7.5 Unfamiliarity with US Academic Systems

Social integration and peer interactions are profoundly influenced by the academic systems and expectations that international students encounter when they arrive in the US. In addition to facing language and cultural barriers, international students often struggle with adapting to the unfamiliarity of the US academic system, particularly the emphasis on group-based projects, participatory learning, and active class discussions (Tinto, 1993). These challenges are rooted in significant differences between the educational systems they are accustomed to and those they experience in US institutions, which can profoundly affect their academic performance and social integration within peer groups. Many international students come from educational environments where teaching is predominantly lecture-based, with a strong emphasis on listening, absorbing information, and memorizing content. In these systems, students typically have limited opportunities for active participation in class discussions or collaborative work with peers. The teacher is often seen as the authoritative figure, and students are expected to focus on content absorption rather than engaging critically with the material or with other students (Hounsell, 1984). This contrasts sharply with the US educational model, which emphasizes critical thinking, assertiveness, and independent contributions from students. Active participation is often a key indicator of academic engagement and success in US classrooms. Students are expected to question ideas, debate concepts, and collaborate with their peers in group projects, which can be unfamiliar and intimidating for international students from more passive educational systems.

For these students, the expectation to engage in group projects and class discussions can feel daunting. The US model encourages students to express their opinions freely, challenge prevailing ideas, critique arguments, and participate in collaborative learning. This active engagement is central to academic success in the US, and students are often graded based on their contributions to group work and class discussions. However, for international students who come from more hierarchical or authority-respecting academic environments, this expectation may cause anxiety. In some cultures, students are taught to defer to the teacher's authority and avoid questioning or confronting ideas presented by professors. Challenging authority or participating in debates may not be appropriate or respectful in these cultures. As a result, the transition to US classrooms, which encourages such behaviors, can lead to discomfort, confusion, and frustration for international students, particularly if they struggle with language barriers or unfamiliar cultural norms in communication (Bozdogan & Comeaux, 2007).

For international students unfamiliar with participatory learning, the prospect of group work or classroom debates can be overwhelming. The fear of making mistakes, being judged for language limitations, or misunderstanding social cues in classroom interactions can lead to avoidance or withdrawal from group activities or class discussions. In some cases, this anxiety can be multiplied by the pressure to perform at the same level as domestic students, who are more accustomed to the US interactive and critical learning model. As a result, international students may avoid speaking in class, hesitate to engage in group work, or refrain from offering alternative viewpoints, which can hinder their academic success and ability to form social bonds with peers. The reluctance to participate actively in discussions or group work can significantly affect peer interactions and social integration. Much of the social bonding and collaboration among US classrooms occurs through group projects and class discussions. These activities facilitate academic learning and provide opportunities for students to interact, share ideas, and build relationships with their peers. International students who struggle with participation may miss these opportunities, resulting in social isolation and difficulty forming meaningful connections with domestic students. This lack of interaction can add to the alienation and marginalization that many international students experience in a foreign academic and social environment. They may find it harder to make friends, join study groups, or engage in extracurricular activities, which are often key avenues for social integration. Moreover, international students may also face challenges adjusting to the US academic work pace and structure. The emphasis on deadlines, self-directed learning, and active engagement in coursework may be unfamiliar to students from educational systems where instruction is passive, and the teacher is the primary source of knowledge. The transition to a system where students are expected to take greater responsibility for their learning can be overwhelming, especially if they are unfamiliar with time-management strategies or the expectations around independent research and critical writing.

International students face significant challenges related to unfamiliarity with the US academic system, which can hinder their academic success and their social integration. Differences in teaching styles, expectations around class participation, and group work can lead to anxiety, frustration, and isolation. By providing clear guidance, fostering inclusive learning environments, and promoting opportunities for peer interaction and support, universities can help international students better navigate these challenges and develop the skills necessary to succeed academically and socially. With proper support, international students can adjust to the US academic system and become active, engaged members of the university community, building meaningful connections with domestic students and contributing to the richness of the educational environment.

### 7.6 The Importance of Peer Support Networks

Peer support networks play an indispensable role in international students' social integration and overall well-being, providing a critical framework through which they can navigate the complexities of academic life and the emotional challenges of living in a new country. These networks offer educational assistance and foster personal connections, which can significantly lessen the feelings of loneliness, isolation, and cultural dislocation that often accompany international students' transitions (Bekteshi & Kang, 2020). The research underscores that establishing robust peer relationships is central to international students' academic and emotional success, and the benefits extend far beyond immediate academic support.

International students often face academic challenges when transitioning to new educational systems, particularly when adapting to unfamiliar pedagogical approaches. The social environment within peer networks is pivotal in helping students navigate these challenges. Positive peer interactions serve as a bridge to understanding academic expectations, developing collaborative skills, and becoming familiar with learning styles that may differ from those in their home countries (Lorenzetti et al., 2023). For example, students from countries with more hierarchical education systems may struggle to adjust to the American emphasis on critical thinking, independent learning, and active participation in class discussions. In this context, peer networks provide essential support. Domestic students, who are more familiar with US academic norms, can guide international students through various academic processes, such as understanding the importance of questioning, making arguments, and presenting one's viewpoint. Group projects and study groups, common in US universities, become informal spaces for international students to acclimate to new academic standards. These collaborations also offer a space to practice and refine English language skills in a low-stakes environment, allowing international students to engage with complex ideas and academic discourse while being supported by peers. Moreover, peer networks can serve as informal mentorship platforms where domestic students share insights into navigating the broader university experience, such as understanding grading systems, using university resources, and balancing academic and personal lives. This type of mentorship is crucial, as it fosters academic integration and helps students feel connected to the academic community. These peer relationships can reduce stress and foster a greater sense of competence and belonging for international students who may struggle with unfamiliar processes and expectations.

Beyond academics, peer networks are essential for the emotional well-being of international students. The transition to studying in a foreign country can be overwhelming, often accompanied by homesickness, culture shock, and social isolation. Peer support plays a key role in alleviating these challenges by offering emotional and practical assistance. Engaging with peers who may share similar struggles or experiences can provide a sense of solidarity, reminding international students that they are not alone in their difficulties. For many international students, sharing experiences and feelings with peers, whether through informal chats or more structured support groups, becomes a meaningful way to manage stress and combat isolation. Research indicates that peers' emotional support can help students navigate homesickness, cultural anxiety, and the academic pressures inherent in university life (Holmes et al., 2015). These peer relationships provide comfort, validation, and a sense of community that can make international students feel more rooted in their new environment, enabling them to persevere through the challenges of adjusting to a new country and culture. Moreover, peer networks offer an informal yet vital source of resilience-building. As international students experience difficulties acclimating to new environments, peers act as emotional anchors, providing encouragement and empathy. This emotional support can significantly increase students' resilience, empowering them to tackle academic and personal challenges more confidently. For international students, especially those from collectivist cultures where emotional well-being is often centered around community, peer support provides a form of social cohesion that promotes mental health and emotional stability.

The interactions that occur within peer networks also contribute significantly to the development of intercultural competencies. Since international students often come from different cultural backgrounds than their domestic peers, these interactions provide a unique opportunity for mutual learning and personal growth. Daily exchanges expose students to diverse perspectives on social norms, values, traditions, and beliefs. These intercultural engagements help broaden students' attitudes, challenge preconceived notions, and promote a deeper understanding of cultural diversity (Gudykunst & Ting-Toomey, 1988). Engaging in conversations about cultural differences through casual chats, collaborative projects, or cultural events helps foster mutual respect and understanding. These interactions help domestic and international students gain a more nuanced appreciation of the complexities of other cultures and provide a platform for them to develop skills such as empathy, flexibility, and intercultural communication. These competencies are increasingly valuable in today's globalized world, where cross-cultural interactions are commonplace in academic and professional settings. Cultural exchange within peer support networks can also lead to long-lasting friendships and meaningful connections (Tang & Zhang, 2023). International students who engage with domestic peers not only enrich their own lives but also contribute to the campus's cultural diversity. In turn, domestic students who participate in these exchanges gain global awareness and learn to navigate multicultural environments, skills essential in both personal and professional realms. As international students become more integrated into the social fabric of the university through peer interactions, they develop a more holistic understanding of the academic and social expectations of their new environment, contributing to a more prosperous and fulfilling educational experience.

### 7.7 The Role of Peer Interactions in Academic and Personal Growth

Collaborative learning environments are among the most powerful tools for enhancing academic performance and personal growth. For international students, academic success is intricately tied to their ability to engage effectively with peers and contribute to group activities. These environments provide opportunities for students to work alongside individuals with different backgrounds and perspectives, enhancing individual learning outcomes and developing critical social and cognitive skills. Research by Barkley et al. (2005) underscores the significance of collaborative learning in academic settings, arguing that students learn best when actively engaged in solving problems with others. This engagement encourages students to ask questions, exchange ideas, and critique each other's perspectives in a way that deepens understanding of the course material. For international students, working in such settings can bridge their previous educational experiences and the expectations of their new academic environment. Often, these students may come from educational systems emphasizing rote learning or teacher-centered instruction. This contrasts sharply with the more interactive, student-centered learning approaches common in US universities. Through collaborative learning, international students can refine their problem-solving abilities, develop communication skills, and gain confidence in their academic contributions, regardless of their cultural background or prior educational training.

Moreover, peer interactions within collaborative settings allow international students to navigate cultural and educational differences that might otherwise pose challenges in their academic journey. For example, while US students might be more accustomed to engaging in debates and presenting arguments, international students may have come from educational systems where such behaviors are not typically encouraged. In a collaborative learning environment, international students can learn to embrace these approaches and develop a stronger sense of ownership over their ideas and opinions. By participating in group projects or study sessions, they also become more adept at negotiating differences in academic approaches and expectations, honing their ability to adapt to various problem-solving strategies. Over time, these experiences build their academic resilience, preparing them for the demands of a globalized workforce where cross-cultural collaboration is the norm.

In addition to enhancing academic skills, peer interactions are integral to personal growth, influencing academic success. Positive interactions with diverse peers create an environment where international students are exposed to multiple worldviews, helping them challenge their assumptions and broaden their understanding of the world. Such experiences foster the development of intercultural competence, the ability to communicate effectively and respectfully with individuals from various cultural backgrounds. This skill is invaluable not only in academic settings but also in professional and personal spheres as international students prepare to engage in increasingly multicultural societies. As Bennett and Bennett (2004) suggest, intercultural competence is a key attribute for students who will later navigate complex, international work environments. For international students, understanding and respecting cultural differences enables them to engage more deeply with academic material that addresses global issues, while also helping them form stronger social connections with their peers.

Engaging with peers from diverse backgrounds also provides international students with a richer and more nuanced understanding of cultural dynamics. It helps them develop essential social skills, such as empathy, adaptability, and negotiation, critical skills for navigating academic challenges and thriving as global citizens. By participating in diverse group discussions, international students learn to appreciate the complexities of different perspectives while honing their ability to negotiate and communicate with others constructively. These experiences play a vital role in the development of emotional intelligence, which enables students to manage their own emotions while understanding and responding to the emotions of others in a culturally sensitive manner. Through peer interactions, international students also gain exposure to the differing values and priorities that shape their peers' academic and personal lives. For example, students from collectivist cultures might gain a deeper understanding of the individualistic values that shape the behavior of their US peers while also offering their insights into collectivist practices. These exchanges can lead to moments of reflection as students begin to question their cultural assumptions and learn to see the world through others' eyes. In this way, academic growth is intimately tied to personal growth as students develop the intellectual flexibility and emotional maturity required to work with diverse groups in educational, professional, and personal settings.

Additionally, positive peer relationships create a supportive academic community where international students can seek guidance, share resources, and receive peer encouragement. This peer support network reduces isolation and fosters a sense of belonging. As international students face academic challenges that stem from language barriers, cultural differences, and the pressures of adjusting to a new educational system, having a supportive peer group can make all the difference. Peer interactions, whether academic or social, help create a safety net for students, providing reassurance and camaraderie during times of stress or uncertainty.

The role of peer relationships in academic and personal growth extends beyond immediate interactions in the classroom. Peer mentorship programs, where senior students guide newcomers, are particularly effective in fostering a culture of inclusivity and academic success. These programs not only provide academic support but also offer a platform for cultural exchange. Mentors can help international students navigate the practical aspects of life in the US, such as understanding classroom dynamics, accessing academic resources, or improving language skills. Through these relationships, mentees can gain confidence and a sense of belonging, positively impacting their academic performance and emotional well-being.

Peer interactions are foundational to international students' academic and personal development. These interactions enable students to navigate the complex landscape of a new educational system, refine critical skills like communication and problem-solving, and develop intercultural competence. More importantly, they foster personal growth by helping students broaden their perspectives, challenge their assumptions, and learn to adapt to diverse cultural contexts. As international students build meaningful relationships with their peers, they gain academic success and the skills needed to thrive in a multicultural world. Institutions that prioritize fostering positive peer interactions and social integration not only support their students' academic success but also prepare them to become globally aware and socially responsible leaders in an interconnected world.

## 7.8 Institutional Strategies to Enhance Peer Interactions

To foster social integration and enhance peer interactions among international students, institutions must implement strategic initiatives that address the unique challenges faced by this diverse population. Social integration is crucial not only for the well-being of international students but also for their academic success and overall campus experience. Given the cultural differences, language barriers, and possible feelings of alienation, institutions need to create spaces and opportunities where international and domestic students can interact meaningfully, develop friendships, and engage in the academic and social life of the university.

Language proficiency is one of the most significant barriers for international students in terms of social integration. Effective communication is key to building connections with peers, participating in classroom discussions, and engaging in social activities. Institutions can provide language workshops beyond basic language instruction to include conversation clubs, where students can practice speaking English in an informal, non-judgmental setting. These clubs allow international students to engage in dialogue with native speakers and practice language skills while gaining insights into cultural nuances. Conversation clubs also offer domestic students the chance to interact with international students, breaking down language barriers and encouraging mutual learning (Bianchi & Martini, 2023). Peer tutoring programs are another way to improve language skills and academic confidence. These programs pair international students with domestic or advanced international students who can offer educational support, help clarify course material, and provide guidance on writing, presentation skills, or research. By providing tailored academic support, peer tutoring fosters a sense of belonging, helps students build self-efficacy, and strengthens peer networks crucial for integration.

Intercultural competence training is a powerful tool for bridging the cultural gap between international and domestic students. Many misunderstandings and tensions arise from cultural differences that influence communication styles, social expectations, and ways of engaging with others. By offering workshops promoting awareness of these differences, institutions can foster student empathy and respect (Cena et al., 2021). This training type helps international and domestic students understand each other's perspectives, which is crucial for positive peer interactions and social integration.

Faculty and staff members also benefit from intercultural competence training as they shape the campus climate. Educating faculty about the diverse cultural backgrounds of their students and the challenges international students face can help them adopt inclusive teaching practices. Faculty trained to recognize and respond to their students' cultural and linguistic needs are more likely to create an inclusive classroom environment where all students feel valued and able to contribute to discussions. Furthermore, faculty members can serve as cultural mentors, facilitating peer interactions and encouraging students to form cross-cultural relationships.

Social events, such as cultural festivals, international student orientations, and campus-wide celebrations of diversity, are critical in helping international students feel included and welcomed. These events allow international students to showcase their cultures, traditions, and customs. In contrast, domestic students can gain exposure to new experiences and perspectives. By creating spaces for students to share their cultural heritage, institutions can facilitate cross-cultural understanding and foster connections between students who may otherwise have limited opportunities to interact.

International student orientations are fundamental, providing students with essential information about navigating campus life, adjusting to academic expectations, and accessing support services. These orientations also serve as a social bridge where international students meet peers undergoing similar adjustment processes. As a result, they can form lasting friendships and networks of support from the very beginning of their academic journey (Tang & Zhang, 2023). Group-based learning activities encourage collaboration among students from diverse cultural backgrounds and effectively promote peer interaction and cross-cultural understanding. Collaborative projects, whether in the classroom or outside, encourage students to collaborate, exchange ideas, and draw on their unique cultural perspectives. For instance, when international students collaborate with domestic students on research projects, group assignments, or presentations, they gain exposure to diverse perspectives, problem-solving approaches, and communication styles. These projects foster academic success and facilitate social bonding as students learn about each other's strengths, personalities, and cultural viewpoints. Faculty need to design group activities that are equitable and inclusive, ensuring that all students have the opportunity to contribute to the project and that no student is marginalized. Faculty can also encourage students to reflect on their experiences working in diverse teams, which can deepen their understanding of intercultural communication and collaboration.

Faculty play a critical role in enhancing peer interactions and promoting social integration by adopting inclusive teaching practices that reflect the diverse cultural backgrounds of their students. Inclusive teaching involves creating a classroom environment where all students feel valued, respected, and encouraged to participate. Faculty members can integrate diverse examples and case studies into their lectures, which can help students from various cultural backgrounds feel that their experiences and perspectives are represented and validated. Faculty use diverse teaching materials to signal to students that cultural differences are valued and recognized.

Additionally, faculty should offer multiple modes of participation to accommodate students with diverse communication styles, enabling them to engage with the course content. For example, some students may be more comfortable expressing their ideas in writing or smaller group discussions than speaking in large class settings. By encouraging a variety of participation formats, faculty can ensure that students from different cultural backgrounds are given equitable opportunities to contribute to the class and connect with their peers. Clear expectations for group work are also essential for ensuring all students can collaborate effectively. Faculty should clearly define the roles and responsibilities of each group member, ensuring that international students are aware of the expectations surrounding teamwork and communication. Additionally, faculty should actively facilitate group dynamics to ensure that all students have a voice and that cultural differences are respected during collaboration.

Tailored support services are essential for ensuring international students' academic, social, and emotional well-being. In addition to language support and academic mentoring, institutions must provide mental health resources sensitive to international students' unique experiences. Many international students may face stress, anxiety, and depression related to acculturation, academic pressures, and isolation. Culturally sensitive counseling services can help students address these challenges while respecting their cultural values and norms. Another critical strategy is creating safe spaces for international students to share their experiences and challenges. Support groups, counseling sessions, or student organizations focused on the needs of international students can help them connect with others who share similar experiences. These spaces allow students to discuss their emotional well-being, share coping strategies, and find support in their journey toward integration.

## 7.9 Conclusion

In conclusion, peer interactions and social integration are foundational to the well-being and success of international students in the US. Forming meaningful relationships with peers, navigating cultural differences, and finding a sense of belonging are essential for their academic success and personal growth. Universities can create environments where students thrive by addressing international students' challenges and investing in initiatives that foster inclusivity and cross-cultural understanding. These efforts benefit international students and enrich the academic experience for domestic students, faculty, and staff, ultimately creating a more vibrant, innovative, and globally aware campus culture. In doing so, institutions invest in a future where diversity is celebrated, collaboration knows no boundaries, and global citizenship is at the heart of academic experience.

# Chapter Eight
## Adapting to US Academic Culture

Adapting to US academic culture presents a complex and multifaceted challenge for international students, requiring a substantial shift in their approach to learning, social interactions, and self-perception. This process of adaptation is shaped by several factors, including language barriers, unfamiliarity with the US educational system, and differences in learning and communication styles (Krsmanovic, 2022; Wang, 2022). For international students, the academic expectations in the US may differ significantly from those they experienced in their home countries, leading to frustration and isolation, particularly during the early stages of their academic journey. However, over time, most international students find ways to adjust and succeed, although this journey can be long and often requires significant emotional and psychological resilience.

Let me tell you, no one can truly prepare you for the profound shock you experience upon entering the US classrooms and academic system. In India, my educational trajectory was meticulously charted; teachers and authorities predetermined schedules, and students were not required to select their preferred classes, times, or even instructors. This stark contrast utterly disoriented me during my very first semester when I attempted to enroll in courses. I vividly recall my academic advisor essentially "hand-holding" me through the registration process, guiding me on which classes to take because I was utterly incapable of making those decisions on my own.

The first day of classes was nothing short of frightening. My schedule, filled with unfamiliar abbreviations for building names, left me struggling to locate my classrooms. I navigated the campus to the best of my ability, only to have an eye-opening, and frankly humiliating, revelation a week later: I had been mistakenly attending all the wrong classes, including graduate-level courses, as a first-year undergraduate student. One professor, noticing my consistent attendance despite my name not appearing on the roster, called the registrar, only to be informed that I was never meant to be in her class. The next day, I retraced my steps, first to the academic advisor and then to my actual, assigned classes. I had missed a whole week of coursework, and some professors were visibly upset by my unexplained absence. Upon trying to explain my situation, they simply refused to believe my bewildered account.

Once the semester truly began, I developed a strong aversion to MLA and APA citation styles; they made no sense to someone accustomed to a different writing convention. Even today, I find multiple-choice questions frustratingly deceptive, feeling as though they are designed to trick you into second-guessing your knowledge rather than honestly assessing it. These early experiences profoundly shaped my academic journey, underscoring the deep cultural and systemic gaps international students often face upon arrival.

### 8.1 Understanding Academic Expectations

One of the most prominent challenges international students face when adapting to the US academic culture is understanding the academic expectations that govern student learning and performance. These expectations often vary dramatically from many other educational systems' more rigid, teacher-directed learning models. In countries where education is highly structured and teachers take on an authoritative role in delivering content, international students may be unprepared for the independence required in US classrooms. The US system emphasizes skills such as critical thinking, independent research, and active participation in class discussions, values that may not be noted in the same way in other educational systems (Ammigan et al., 2022; Moussa, 2021).

For example, in many US classrooms, students are expected to engage with the course material critically, analyze different perspectives, and express their ideas openly during discussions. This level of intellectual engagement can be unfamiliar and even intimidating for students from more passive learning environments, where rote memorization and lecture-based learning are the norm. Additionally, in countries with more hierarchical teacher-student relationships, questioning or challenging a professor's ideas may seem disrespectful. In contrast, in the US, students are often encouraged to evaluate content and ask questions to deepen their understanding critically. In many educational systems, assessments focus heavily on exams, and one or two high-stakes tests typically determine grades. In contrast, the US system emphasizes continuous assessment, including participation, homework assignments, and group projects, which may be new to international students (Ammigan et al., 2022). International students may find it challenging to adapt to this more holistic approach to grading, particularly when the grading criteria and evaluation methods are unfamiliar.

### 8.2 Adapting to Classroom Dynamics

The US classroom environment can starkly differ from what international students are used to. In many cases, US classrooms are more informal, interactive, and student-centered than traditional, lecture-based classrooms in other parts of the world. Professors in the US are generally seen as facilitators of learning rather than authoritative figures who impart knowledge. This shift in role can be disorienting for students in highly structured learning environments. In addition to emphasizing discussion, US classrooms often encourage collaborative learning through group work, peer reviews, and presentations, which may require international students to adjust their learning styles to be more participatory and communicative. The informal nature of US classrooms also manifests in the expectations around communication. Many US professors encourage students to engage in casual, open communication, where it is acceptable to address instructors by their first names or ask for clarification on assignments without fear of judgment. This shift can be challenging and intimidating for international students accustomed to a more formal, hierarchical relationship with professors. Some individuals may struggle with approaching instructors or engaging in classroom interactions, particularly when they are uncertain about cultural norms related to authority, communication, and respect.

### 8.3 Navigating Grading Systems and Academic Calendars

Another significant adjustment for international students involves navigating the distinct US grading system, which typically employs letter grades (A, B, C, etc.) alongside a Grade Point Average (GPA). This system often presents a stark contrast to grading practices in students' home countries, where marks might be presented as varied numerical percentages (e.g., on 5-point, 10-point, or 20-point scales), descriptive results like "Pass/Fail" or "Distinction," or entirely different numerical interpretations where lower numbers signify better performance. In some countries, the grading scale may be less granular, or top marks might be awarded to a much smaller percentage of students, making the US system's nuances of A, B, and C grades, and its emphasis on GPA, particularly perplexing. Consequently, international students may initially struggle to fully grasp how their performance is being evaluated or may feel confused by the US system's continuous assessment approach, which differs from more exam-focused traditions abroad.

Similarly, adapting to the US academic calendar can be a considerable challenge. Many countries adhere to academic schedules that feature longer breaks between terms, or markedly different semester start and end dates. International students may find adjusting to the fast-paced, cyclical nature of the US calendar particularly demanding, especially if they are unfamiliar with the concept of a protracted summer break, the intensive period of midterms, or the concentrated timing of significant final exams. These differences necessitate a rapid adaptation to new rhythms of study, assignment submission, and assessment.

## 8.4 Social and Cultural Integration Challenges

Beyond the academic challenges, international students must navigate significant social and cultural integration challenges. Adapting to a new educational environment is intertwined with learning how to integrate into campus life and connect with domestic students. One significant hurdle in this process is language proficiency, particularly in an academic setting requiring advanced reading, writing, and verbal communication skills. While international students may be proficient in conversational English, academic English poses a distinct challenge, especially in writing research papers or delivering presentations. Misunderstandings or language barriers can lead to feelings of embarrassment or self-doubt, further increasing the sense of alienation that many international students experience. Language difficulties are not limited to the basics of speaking and writing; they also extend to understanding the nuances of language, such as idiomatic expressions, humor, or slang. What may be considered humorous or acceptable in a US classroom may be confusing or even offensive to international students, creating potential social and emotional barriers. Body language, gestures, and nonverbal cues can also be misinterpreted, further complicating communication. These challenges can make it more difficult for international students to form connections with domestic peers, leading to feelings of isolation and loneliness.

## 8.5 Academic Level and Time in the US

The academic level, undergraduate or graduate, plays a crucial role in how international students adapt to the US educational system. This section highlights the differences in experiences between these two groups and the role of time spent in the US in facilitating adaptation. Graduate students generally have a clearer sense of purpose and more relevant academic experience, which aids their transition to the US educational system. Their motivations are often more research-driven, and they typically possess stronger academic skills, such as critical thinking and scholarly writing, which ease their adaptation. In contrast, international undergraduate students may struggle with the shift from high school to university, as they are often required to shift from passive learning to more active, participatory learning methods. Moreover, the classroom culture in the US frequently emphasizes independent learning, critical analysis, and debate skills that may not have been stressed in their home countries (Tu, 2021). The challenges are particularly pronounced for first-year international undergraduates, who face difficulties understanding the academic system, building relationships with domestic peers, and managing the independence required for self-directed study. These students often come from educational systems where rote memorization is emphasized, making the transition to US academic systems, which value critical thinking and active participation, particularly challenging.

First-year international undergraduate students often experience a steep learning curve. As they face academic culture shock, they must navigate differences in classroom dynamics, assessment methods, and social expectations. Additionally, the transition to self-directed learning, where students are expected to manage their academic workload independently, can be overwhelming. This can be magnified by a lack of familiarity with US teaching styles, including the emphasis on active class participation and group discussions, which may be new to students from more teacher-centered cultures. In addition to academic challenges, many first-year international undergraduates face social isolation and homesickness. Due to differences in communication styles and cultural norms, the difficulties in forming connections with domestic peers often lead to feelings of exclusion. This emotional barrier can impact academic performance, as students may struggle to engage with their studies without the social support they require (Zhang, 2022). Time spent in the US significantly influences how international students adapt academically and socially. In the initial months, students primarily focus on overcoming language barriers, adjusting to unfamiliar grading systems, and managing academic workload, which can be particularly difficult for those who are not proficient in English. Social isolation is also common during the early stages, as students often face challenges connecting with their peers.

By the second year, many international students have become more familiar with the US academic system. Their language skills have likely improved, and they may have established stronger social networks. By this time, they are often more comfortable with classroom expectations, such as contributing to discussions and engaging in collaborative work. Over time, as they gain more exposure to group projects, faculty mentorship, and peer study groups, their confidence in their academic abilities grows, contributing to improved academic performance (Bethel et al., 2020). Adaptation becomes a more integrated process for those who have spent more than three years in the US. Students who stay longer typically experience better academic outcomes, develop stronger relationships with faculty, and participate in extracurricular activities that enhance their educational and social integration. However, challenges related to identity negotiation and cultural dissonance may persist, even for long-term residents, as they may feel caught between the expectations of their home and host cultures (Wu et al., 2015).

### 8.6 Acculturation Strategies and Adaptation Outcomes

International students' strategies for acculturating to the host country significantly influence their academic success and emotional well-being.

Building on John W. Berry's (1997) foundational framework of acculturation, these strategies describe how individuals engage with both their heritage culture and the new host culture. Berry identified four primary acculturation strategies: assimilation, separation, integration, and marginalization. Each strategy carries different implications for students' experiences and educational outcomes.

**Assimilation:** This strategy involves individuals prioritizing the adoption of the host culture while essentially relinquishing their heritage culture (Berry, 1997). For international students, complete immersion into the US culture can accelerate language proficiency and expand networking opportunities. However, for some students, this may result in a profound loss of cultural identity, potentially leading to feelings of isolation or internal identity conflict. While this strategy can be effective for some in terms of rapid social and linguistic adjustment, it may have long-term emotional consequences for others (Erturk & Nguyen Luu, 2022).

**Separation:** In contrast to assimilation, separation occurs when individuals maintain strong ties with their heritage culture while engaging minimally with the host culture (Berry, 1997). Students adopting this strategy may initially feel more comfortable due to the familiarity of their cultural traditions. However, this approach can significantly limit academic and professional growth opportunities in the host country. They may find building relationships with domestic peers and professors challenging, thereby restricting their exposure to academic collaboration and vital networking opportunities (Lai et al., 2023).

**Integration:** Often considered the most adaptive strategy, integration involves individuals maintaining their heritage culture while also actively participating in and adapting to the host culture (Berry, 1997). Students who successfully balance their home culture with the US academic environment typically experience the most favorable academic and social outcomes. These students effectively integrate their cultural knowledge and skills into the educational setting while simultaneously embracing aspects of US culture. This dual engagement allows them to succeed academically while preserving a strong sense of cultural identity, contributing to higher levels of academic achievement, social integration, and overall well-being (Lai et al., 2023).

**Marginalization:** This strategy is characterized by a lack of engagement with both the heritage culture and the host culture (Berry, 1997). Students experiencing marginalization may feel disconnected from both their home and host cultures, leading to higher stress levels and significant difficulty adapting both academically and socially. This challenging position can result from being unable to identify with the cultural norms or values of either the host country or their heritage culture, frequently leading to profound feelings of dislocation and alienation (Lai et al., 2023).

It is crucial to note that while sociocultural adaptation, ease in social interactions, and understanding cultural norms are essential, they do not necessarily guarantee psychological adaptation. Some students, despite being socially integrated, may continue to struggle with internal conflicts, identity challenges, and mental health issues, which can negatively impact their academic performance and well-being (Lai et al., 2023). The data from Chapter 2, showing a notable percentage of international students reporting psychological distress despite potential social engagement, provides empirical support for this distinction, underscoring the complexity of faithful adaptation.

## 8.7 The Influence of Host Country Context

The sociopolitical climate of the host country plays an essential role in shaping international students' adaptation experiences. For example, US immigration policies, political stability, and public attitudes toward foreigners significantly affect how international students perceive their ability to adapt academically and socially. Students in countries with a more welcoming attitude toward immigrants tend to have better academic and social outcomes. Supportive university policies, inclusive campus climates, and proactive social integration programs contribute to a smoother adaptation. In contrast, students in countries or regions with anti-immigrant sentiment or restrictive immigration policies may face additional barriers. These students may experience heightened stress and anxiety, which can hinder their ability to succeed academically (Erturk & Nguyen Luu, 2022).

## 8.8 Biological Sex Differences

International students face a multifaceted process when adjusting to the US education system, which often presents challenges that differ according to biological sex. The intersection of cultural differences, academic expectations, language barriers, and gender norms plays a significant role in how male and female international students navigate their educational journeys in the US. Understanding these differences can provide insights into developing gender-responsive strategies and interventions that promote equitable adaptation for all international students. By examining biological sex through neurobiological, behavioral, and sociocultural factors, we can better understand how gender shapes their responses to stress, academic pressures, and social integration challenges.

The stress adaptation process is fundamentally shaped by biological sex differences, particularly in the neurobiological and behavioral responses to challenges. Both male and female international students experience stress in varying degrees and employ different coping strategies, significantly impacting their academic success, mental health, and social integration. Understanding these differences is essential for tailoring interventions that effectively address the distinct needs of each gender in the context of higher education.

*Emotional Sensitivity and Coping Strategies:* One of the primary areas where sex-based differences emerge is emotional sensitivity. As Vuong et al. (2021) highlight, female international students tend to be more emotionally sensitive and inclined to rely on social connections to cope with stress. This relational coping style can manifest in both positive and negative ways. On the positive side, women may build strong interpersonal bonds that provide emotional support, buffering them against the adverse effects of stress. However, the emotional vulnerability that comes with relying on social connections can also intensify feelings of anxiety, homesickness, and loneliness if meaningful connections are difficult to establish. Cultural differences compound the challenge, as the difficulty in forming relationships with domestic peers who may not be attuned to these emotional cues can leave female international students feeling socially isolated, further intensifying emotional distress.

Homesickness is particularly pronounced among female international students, as they often feel a more profound sense of disconnection from their home culture, which includes not only missing family and friends but also feeling alienated from familiar routines, food, and language. This emotional disconnection is especially acute for women because they are typically more attuned to their internal emotional states and may experience these disconnections with greater intensity than their male counterparts (Vuong et al., 2021). On the other hand, male international students tend to use independent coping mechanisms that are shaped by societal gender norms. Traditional masculine norms often emphasize self-reliance and emotional stoicism, which leads many male students to avoid expressing vulnerability. While this can sometimes foster resilience, it also means that male students are more likely to suppress their emotions, making it harder for them to reach out for help when needed. Consequently, male students may avoid seeking support from campus counseling or mentorship programs due to a cultural stigma surrounding vulnerability, which may lead to unaddressed mental health concerns such as depression, anxiety, or substance abuse (Cheng et al., 2013).

*Coping Mechanisms and Mental Health Implications:* The reluctance of male international students to seek social or professional support, coupled with their tendency to tackle challenges independently, can hinder their social integration into the US academic environment. These students may not engage with the support services available on campus, such as mental health counseling, peer mentoring programs, or study groups, due to concerns about appearing weak or unable to "cope" independently. This refusal to engage with social or institutional support can result in heightened stress and reduced academic performance as male students struggle to find effective ways to manage their emotional and academic pressures. Conversely, female international students, more likely to engage with social support networks, may be more proactive in seeking help through peer mentoring or counseling services. However, if these support structures are not culturally sensitive or inclusive, female students may still face challenges obtaining the help they need. The struggle to connect with supportive individuals or groups can leave female students feeling isolated and emotionally vulnerable, undermining their academic performance and overall mental health.

American academic culture is often characterized by individualism, self-reliance, and direct communication. These expectations can be particularly challenging for international students from collectivist cultures, who are accustomed to more collaborative, hierarchical, and indirect forms of communication. The pressure to adapt to US expectations of independent problem-solving, self-advocacy, and assertive self-promotion can be particularly daunting for female international students. Female students may need to balance maintaining their cultural values of interdependence and conforming to US norms of individual achievement. This balancing act can create additional emotional strain, particularly for female students who may feel that their collectivist values conflict with the individualistic demands of the academic environment. For male international students, the pressure to demonstrate competence and self-sufficiency may align more closely with their cultural expectations. However, the emphasis on assertiveness and self-promotion in the US academic system may create anxiety for male students not accustomed to these direct modes of communication. In collectivist cultures, male students are often socialized to be more reserved and avoid self-promotion, making the US emphasis on assertiveness and self-advocacy a challenging hurdle. Male international students may feel uncomfortable advocating for themselves in classroom discussions, seeking help from professors, or participating in group projects where open communication and visibility are key.

Given the differing challenges male and female international students face when adjusting to US academic culture, universities must implement targeted interventions for biological sex differences. These interventions should enhance academic success, mental health, and social integration by recognizing and addressing the unique coping styles, emotional needs, and socialization patterns of both genders. For female international students, support programs should focus on building emotional resilience and promoting social connectedness. Universities can offer group counseling sessions that provide a safe space for female students to discuss their emotional challenges, explore coping strategies, and build supportive relationships with peers. Additionally, cultural exchange programs and peer mentoring initiatives can help female students feel more integrated into the campus community, providing opportunities to connect with domestic and international peers. Promoting belonging through social events, networking opportunities, and cultural activities can also help reduce feelings of homesickness and isolation. For male international students, universities should work to reduce the stigma surrounding emotional vulnerability and help-seeking behavior. Providing male students with tailored mental health resources, such as programs that emphasize the importance of emotional expression and seeking help, can encourage them to engage with support services. Peer mentoring programs that connect male students with mentors who understand the pressures they face can help normalize the experience of seeking guidance and support. Additionally, universities can offer training for faculty and staff on recognizing the signs of emotional distress among male students and how to initiate conversations about mental health and well-being.

Biological sex differences significantly affect how international students adapt to the US academic culture. These differences impact their coping strategies, emotional regulation, social integration, and academic performance. Female students may rely more heavily on social connections for coping. Still, they may also experience heightened emotional sensitivity and homesickness, while male students may struggle with self-reliance and underreport emotional distress due to cultural stigma. Understanding these gendered responses to the adaptation process is essential for creating inclusive, supportive academic environments. By implementing gender-sensitive interventions, universities can help male and female international students navigate the complexities of the US education system, fostering an environment where all students can thrive. Adapting to the US academic culture requires international students to navigate complex cultural and social dynamics. These students often face challenges such as unfamiliar academic expectations, social integration, and balancing their cultural identity with their educational and social experiences.

Social support is critical in successfully adapting international students to US academic and social life. A robust support network is essential in their ability to manage the pressures of academic rigor, culture shock, and homesickness. Research highlights the gender differences in how international students seek and benefit from social support (Shu et al., 2020). Females tend to be more open to building social networks, often participating in student organizations, community events, and peer support groups, which can help them better adjust to the social and cultural climate. This connection with others creates a support system that helps ease emotional stress, cultural dissonance, and academic challenges. In contrast, students assigned male at birth may be less inclined to seek social support, potentially due to cultural expectations around masculinity and emotional expression. In some cultures, emotional openness is discouraged among males, making it more challenging to reach out when they need assistance. Males often prioritize academic success and career advancement over social integration, potentially leading to isolation and a more limited support network. This gendered difference in social integration has important implications for how universities should approach support systems for international students. To promote a more inclusive environment, institutions should offer support services and programs that motivate all students, regardless of gender or background, to connect with peers, ask for help, and build meaningful relationships to enhance their academic and emotional well-being.

Adaptation to new food and lifestyle environments is a significant challenge for international students. Moving to a new country with a different food culture can lead to digestive issues, food aversions, and a sense of disconnection from one's cultural identity. For students assigned female at birth, these challenges can be more pronounced. Studies suggest they are more likely to struggle with unfamiliar food options and nutritional changes, which can intensify feelings of isolation and homesickness (Vuong et al., 2021). Additionally, students who follow religious or cultural dietary restrictions may find it even more challenging to adjust, as their options for food may be further limited, leading to feelings of alienation and discomfort. Social connectedness plays a pivotal role in addressing these challenges. For example, forming friendships with peers from similar cultural backgrounds can provide a sense of solidarity and practical support, such as sharing traditional meals or finding local grocery stores that stock familiar ingredients. Moreover, universities can create spaces for students to share their food traditions through cultural events, food fairs, or international student groups. These initiatives help international students maintain a connection to their cultural heritage and provide opportunities for cross-cultural exchange, enriching the university's social fabric. In addition to social support, universities should consider offering diverse dining options in on-campus facilities, ensuring that students with specific dietary needs can access food that aligns with their cultural or religious practices. This could include halal, kosher, vegetarian, or vegan options. Ensuring international students feel supported in their dietary needs helps them maintain their physical health and cultural identity, facilitating a smoother transition to their new environment.

Adapting to the US classroom culture is one of the most significant challenges that international students face. The US educational system is often characterized by active participation, debate, and critical thinking, values that are not always emphasized in the educational systems of other countries. For example, in many Asian and Middle Eastern cultures, students assigned female at birth may not be encouraged to speak up or assert their opinions in mixed-gender academic settings. This can cause significant challenges in the US, where participation is crucial to academic success (Ali & Sharma, 2017). For these students, the US classroom culture can seem intimidating, leading to hesitancy in expressing their thoughts and ideas, which may affect their academic performance and overall experience. Conversely, students assigned male at birth, who may come from educational systems that emphasize individual achievement and personal success, might struggle with the standards of collaborative learning methods in US classrooms. The emphasis on teamwork, group projects, and peer interactions can be particularly challenging for these students, especially if their previous educational experiences did not prioritize such collaboration. This difficulty adapting to the collaborative nature of US classrooms can impact students' ability to engage in group work, discussions, and other participatory learning activities essential to academic success. The differences in classroom participation styles highlight the importance of cultural sensitivity and support within US classrooms. Faculty members should be aware of the diverse backgrounds of their students and be mindful of the potential barriers to participation that some international students may face. Structured interventions, such as mentorship programs, workshops on academic communication, and peer-led study groups, can help students build the confidence and skills necessary to succeed in the US academic environment. For example, encouraging students to engage in smaller, informal discussions before more significant class debates can help build confidence in voicing their opinions. Additionally, faculty can create more inclusive learning environments by actively encouraging diverse perspectives, fostering a culture of respect for different communication styles, and ensuring that all students feel heard and valued.

The cultural and social adaptation process for international students is multifaceted and influenced by gendered norms, dietary challenges, and differing classroom expectations. The role of social support and connectedness cannot be overstated; strong networks of friends, mentors, and cultural communities can help students navigate the complexities of cultural transition. Universities should create an inclusive and supportive environment that encourages active participation in both social and academic spheres. To facilitate this adaptation process, universities should provide programs that foster social integration, such as peer mentoring, cultural events, and educational workshops. Furthermore, faculty and staff should receive training in cultural competence to ensure they are aware of the challenges faced by international students and are equipped to support them in overcoming these obstacles. By addressing these issues holistically, universities can create an environment where international students can thrive academically, socially, and emotionally.

Adapting to the US academic culture is a significant challenge for many international students, particularly those from educational systems and cultural backgrounds that differ markedly from those in the United States. One of the key aspects of this adaptation involves academic performance and time management, which are influenced by a range of factors, including the structure of the educational system, expectations around independent study, and cultural values regarding learning and academic engagement. Arab students, for instance, often face a dual challenge of excelling in coursework while also navigating the complexities of adapting to a new academic culture that requires different skills and approaches to learning.

Arab students, like many international students, often demonstrate strong academic performance once they have adjusted to the academic environment in the US. They are typically motivated, diligent, and committed to achieving high grades. However, their initial academic success can be delayed as they navigate the demands of a new educational system. In many Arab countries, education is often more structured and teacher-directed, with a greater emphasis on rote memorization and passive learning (Moussa, 2021). This system contrasts with the US education system, which emphasizes active learning, critical thinking, and the ability to engage in independent research and inquiry. The US system encourages students to be more self-directed, where they are expected to take ownership of their learning through activities such as group discussions, problem-solving exercises, independent research, and participation in lectures and seminars. This shift in expectations can be overwhelming for students from Arab backgrounds, particularly for those who are not accustomed to such autonomy in their academic work. The need to develop critical thinking skills, participate actively in classroom discussions, and analyze complex topics without heavy reliance on textbooks or memorized content can create an initial academic struggle for Arab students. They may find themselves spending more time than their peers on completing assignments, adjusting to different learning approaches, and ensuring they meet their professors' expectations. Furthermore, the faster pace of US courses, where assignments, exams, and projects come up quickly and frequently, may be difficult for Arab students to manage at first. In some Arab countries, the academic calendar may be more relaxed, and deadlines may not be as tight. Therefore, tight deadlines and constant assessments in the US can initially be a source of stress for students who are not used to the demands of this accelerated academic schedule. Developing effective time management strategies is critical to their success, and this is an area where many Arab students, particularly in their first year, may require additional support.

Adaptation to US academic culture often necessitates learning how to balance multiple responsibilities, including attending lectures, completing assignments, studying for exams, and participating in extracurricular activities. For students from cultures where the academic approach is more rigid and prescriptive, time management may not be a skill they have had to develop to the extent required in the US education system. The expectation in the US that students manage their own time and prioritize tasks efficiently is a skill that many Arab students, especially those transitioning from teacher-directed environments, may struggle to master initially. These students may spend a disproportionate amount of time on specific assignments as they try to grasp the new academic expectations, sometimes at the expense of other coursework or responsibilities. Moreover, the emphasis on self-reliance and independent study can be difficult for students who are accustomed to more structured learning environments. In the US, it is not uncommon for professors to give students a broad overview of the subject matter, expecting them to delve deeper into the content on their own. This shift from passive to active learning can be a daunting challenge for students who are unfamiliar with this approach. Arab students may find themselves spending considerable time trying to understand the deeper concepts and material, which may take longer than their peers who have experience with such independent learning.

For female students from more conservative Arab backgrounds, these academic challenges can be compounded by cultural and familial restrictions that limit their exposure to diverse learning environments and independent decision-making. In many conservative cultures, women are socialized to prioritize family responsibilities, respect traditional gender roles, and often face more restrictions on their social activities and academic engagement than their male counterparts. This can result in limited opportunities for these students to engage in the kinds of academic practices that are foundational to success in North America and Western Europe educational settings. For example, traditional values in some Arab cultures may discourage female students from participating in coeducational activities, engaging in academic debates, or taking the lead in group work, all of which are common in US classrooms. As a result, female students from conservative backgrounds may have limited experience with the independent learning styles and collaborative environments that characterize US education. They may struggle to adapt to the participatory nature of US classrooms, where students are expected to ask questions, express opinions, and engage in debates with peers and professors. These academic expectations can lead to feelings of insecurity or inadequacy for female students who have not had the same level of exposure to these practices in their home countries. The lack of experience with critical thinking, collaborative problem-solving, and classroom participation can hinder their ability to fully engage in academic discussions, which may, in turn, affect their academic performance. In addition, many of these students may find themselves facing the pressure of balancing academic responsibilities with traditional familial expectations. For example, in some conservative families, there may be higher expectations placed on women to maintain a specific image or behavior, which can create an emotional burden as these students try to navigate the challenges of living in a new, unfamiliar academic culture while also adhering to family and cultural norms.

Effective mentorship programs and robust faculty support systems are essential for facilitating academic success. Mentors, especially those attuned to the unique challenges these students face, can provide invaluable personalized guidance on time management, academic writing, and build confidence in classroom discussions. Culturally aware and sensitive faculty members are pivotal in fostering inclusive educational environments. By understanding the cultural barriers that influence participation or learning approaches, faculty can create supportive atmospheres where international students feel comfortable engaging in academic activities and transitioning to more independent learning. Providing structured opportunities for independent learning, such as workshops on study skills and critical thinking, and assignments encouraging research, further aids development. Faculty can also facilitate group discussions and active participation, helping students develop assertive communication skills essential for US classrooms. Cultivating inclusive classroom practices is essential to ensure international students, particularly females, feel supported. Female students from cultures emphasizing traditional gender roles, where assertiveness and open participation may be discouraged, can struggle to express themselves in US classrooms that prioritize engagement. Professors must be trained to recognize and effectively respond to the diverse communication styles of their students. Inclusive teaching strategies, such as small-group discussions, case studies that reflect varied cultural experiences, and diverse interaction modes like online forums, can enhance inclusivity. Acknowledging gender differences in participation ensures no student is inadvertently marginalized, fostering an environment that celebrates diversity and provides equal opportunity to contribute and excel.

International students face unique mental health challenges, often influenced by cultural understandings of mental health, gendered expectations, and the pressure to succeed abroad. For female students from conservative or patriarchal backgrounds, societal expectations of emotional restraint can compound these issues, leading to a reluctance to seek help. Mental health services must therefore be culturally relevant and gender-sensitive, incorporating diverse cultural approaches to support women. Creating non-judgmental spaces, making services visible through workshops and outreach, and offering multilingual counseling can ease the feelings of alienation for all international students, including males who may face societal pressure to suppress vulnerability regarding academic stress, social isolation, and homesickness. Fostering a genuinely inclusive environment hinges on equipping faculty and staff with the cultural competency necessary to create a welcoming and supportive environment. Professional development training should cover cultural differences in communication, learning styles, and participation, as well as how gendered expectations influence classroom behavior. Such training enables faculty to identify signs of academic distress or isolation related to cultural adaptation challenges, providing targeted support, particularly for female students from traditional cultures who might hesitate to seek help due to cultural norms.

Recognizing that international female students may encounter specific barriers in adjusting to the US educational system, from participating in classroom discussions to navigating social life, universities should implement gender-specific support services. These programs can provide safe spaces for discussing challenges, offering workshops on navigating academic settings, leadership training, and social networking opportunities specifically tailored to women. Support groups or mentorship programs pairing female students with culturally aware faculty and staff can build confidence, encourage open engagement, and facilitate full participation in academic and social spheres. Adapting to the US academic culture is a crucial, multidimensional process for international students, demanding time, resilience, and robust institutional support. This transition involves understanding and embracing distinct social, academic, and personal dynamics that are profoundly different from those in their home countries. Key adjustments include understanding classroom functionality, professor-student interactions, and expectations for participation. Socially, students must adapt to new communication styles and casual interactions that are essential for forming friendships and integrating into campus life. Language proficiency, often a significant hurdle, directly impacts academic engagement and social confidence. Furthermore, international students may encounter subtle or overt discrimination based on race, accent, or nationality, which creates additional emotional and psychological barriers to adaptation. Striking a balance between maintaining one's cultural identity and conforming to host culture demands, such as US ideals of independence and direct expression, can create internal conflict. However, through comprehensive support services like orientation programs, academic advising, counseling, and peer support groups, universities can significantly ease this process. Fostering an inclusive campus culture that promotes diversity, active cultural exchange, and provides opportunities for students from diverse backgrounds to connect is crucial. By providing these resources, universities not only help international students thrive academically and socially but also enrich the entire academic community by cultivating a vibrant and globally aware campus culture.

# Chapter Nine
# Implications for Educational Institutions

Cultural adaptation is a complex and dynamic process that affects multiple levels of society, ranging from students to educational institutions, policymakers, and broader societal constructs. This book examined these various dimensions, providing valuable insights to enhance the experiences of international students and promote a more inclusive academic environment. By examining the cultural adaptation process through individual, institutional, policy, and societal perspectives, this work highlighted the critical roles each element plays in facilitating the successful integration of international students into academic, social, and professional arenas.

## 9.1 Individual-Level Implications

International students often experience significant psychological and emotional stress due to a variety of factors, such as cultural differences, homesickness, new academic structure, and social isolation. Acculturative stress, a form of psychological strain that occurs during cultural adaptation, has been shown to have a profound impact on mental health, leading to conditions like anxiety and depression (Bekteshi & Kang, 2020). These emotional challenges can create academic challenges, which may hinder degree completion or graduation. Although mental health challenges are prominent, research has shown that fostering resilience, establishing peer support networks, and providing access to culturally competent mental health resources can help reduce these adverse effects and support students in their adjustment process (Gudykunst & Ting-Toomey, 1988). A supportive environment that recognizes or even accepts the unique emotional challenges faced by international students can enhance their overall well-being and academic success.

Firstly, institutions should offer culturally competent counseling services, including training multilingual therapists and trained peer support groups who can empathize with international students and understand their perspectives. These services should emphasize the understanding of the diverse cultural contexts and stressors these students face, ensuring that counseling approaches are sensitive to cultural differences. Secondly, universities should establish peer mentorship programs that pair experienced outgoing international students and/or alumni with incoming students, guiding them through their transition. Having experienced similar struggles, peer mentors can provide empathy, practical advice, and a sense of solidarity, easing the adjustment process and helping incoming students locate necessary resources for their overall health. Thirdly, awareness campaigns that are focused on mental health, stress management, and self-care should be integrated into international student orientations and continuously promoted throughout their education journey. Campaigns could include information on recognizing early signs of stress, accessing mental health resources on campus and within the community, and building resilience. Additionally, faculty members should receive training on identifying signs of emotional distress and mental health challenges in international students. This training should also focus on understanding the cultural barriers preventing students from seeking help and provide clear steps or protocols to follow in order to help international students find appropriate resources. Moreover, universities should collaborate with local community organizations to provide off-campus cultural and mental health support. This can help expand the support and social network for international students, especially those who feel uncomfortable accessing campus-based resources. This may also take away the burden on the campus-based counseling clinic, which is often overbooked and has long waiting times. Lastly, develop wellness retreats or stress-relief programs tailored specifically for international students. These could include activities such as mindfulness workshops, yoga sessions, and outdoor recreational programs designed to help students decompress and build social connections.

International students often struggle with adjusting to different learning styles and academic expectations, especially when transitioning from educational systems that emphasize passive learning to those that require active participation, critical thinking, and self-directed study (Galperin & Punnett, 2021). For students from cultures where rote memorization and authority-based teaching are prevalent, the shift to a more participatory and collaborative learning environment can be particularly challenging. These difficulties can impact students' academic success and hinder their ability to engage with the curriculum entirely. Providing structured support and understanding the varying academic backgrounds of international students is essential in fostering their educational success.

Institutions should implement structured academic transition programs that introduce international students to the expectations and learning styles of the host country's education system. These programs should include workshops on study skills, academic writing, and participation in classroom discussions, helping students adjust before taking full-degree courses. Faculty and staff members should adopt flexible assessment methods that accommodate the diverse educational backgrounds of international students. This could include offering alternative participation methods (such as written reflections instead of verbal class discussions) to ensure that students are evaluated in ways that align with their learning preferences and capabilities. Universities should offer workshops specifically designed to help international students enhance their academic writing and research skills. These workshops could focus on areas such as essay structure, thesis development, citation practices, and academic integrity, addressing the linguistic and educational challenges that international students often face. Institutions should provide technology-based tools such as AI-assisted tutoring platforms, online discussion forums, and recorded lectures to support international students who struggle with language barriers. These resources can help students review content at their own pace and deepen their understanding of course materials. Universities should develop curricula that are culturally responsive and inclusive, integrating global perspectives into course materials. This ensures that international students feel represented and that they can connect their cultural backgrounds to the subject matter being taught.

Navigating the shift from their home culture to that of the host country often leads to identity transformation for international students. Blending elements from both cultures can enrich students' perspectives but may also create internal conflict, particularly for those from collectivist cultures adjusting to individualistic academic environments (Hofstede, 2001). This tension can affect their sense of self, social integration, and academic performance. Recognizing and supporting this process of identity hybridization is key to helping international students successfully adapt while preserving their cultural identity. Institutions should create spaces for intercultural dialogue where students can share and reflect on their evolving identities. These forums could include regular meetings or online platforms where students from diverse backgrounds discuss their cultural adaptation and share personal experiences. Faculty should actively encourage diverse perspectives in coursework by integrating materials and discussions that validate students' cultural backgrounds. This approach helps international students feel recognized and enriches the learning environment for all students. Universities should organize cultural celebrations and storytelling initiatives that allow international students to express and explore their evolving identities. These events could showcase traditional music, food, art, and stories from students' home countries, fostering mutual understanding and respect. Institutions should establish identity-based affinity groups that offer safe spaces for international students to discuss their adaptation experiences and share strategies for navigating cultural differences. These groups could focus on specific regions or cultural identities and serve as support networks for students with shared experiences. Universities should provide workshops on intercultural competence to help students navigate cultural differences in academic and professional settings. These workshops help students develop strategies for communicating effectively across cultures and managing potential conflicts that may arise from cultural misunderstandings.

## 9.2 Institutional-Level Implications

Culturally responsive teaching ensures that international students engage meaningfully with course content. Faculty should be trained to implement inclusive pedagogy that considers students' diverse learning preferences (Gay, 2010). The institution can benefit by developing comprehensive faculty training modules focused on inclusive teaching strategies. These modules should incorporate a strong emphasis on intercultural communication skills, equipping faculty to effectively understand and respond to the diverse learning needs and cultural backgrounds of international students. The training should empower faculty to create a more welcoming and supportive learning environment, fostering academic success and a sense of belonging for all students. Another action that can benefit institutions is integrating global perspectives into curricula by using case studies, real-world examples, and diverse cultural backgrounds to ensure that students' own cultural experiences are represented. Offering bridge courses can help international students adapt to academic norms before they enroll in full-degree programs. These courses can focus on enhancing vocabulary skills, writing skills, critical thinking, and collaborative learning. Encouraging faculty to incorporate multilingual instructional materials and glossaries for technical terms which will help students better comprehend complex concepts. Establishing cross-cultural teaching partnerships, in which faculty collaborate with educators from students' home countries to co-develop supportive curricula that better address the students' needs in both cultural and academic contexts.

Active engagement in campus organizations and leadership roles fosters international students' sense of belonging. Cultural competency training for domestic students and faculty can also help reduce biases, stereotypes, and misjudgments and promote inclusion (Naicker et al., 2021). Some actionable implications include but are not limited to universities establishing international student ambassadors who can facilitate cross-cultural interactions on campus, serve as mentors, and create an accessible point of contact for new international students. Promoting intercultural leadership programs that prepare international students for leadership roles within student government and organizations, fostering a sense of ownership and belonging within campus life and beyond. Encouraging faculty-student engagement through informal networking events, peer mentoring programs, and faculty-led roundtables that foster deeper academic and social connections. Implementing buddy programs that pair international students with domestic students to facilitate cultural exchange, reduce feelings of isolation, and foster mutual learning, thereby making the adaptation process easier for international students. Providing cross-cultural training workshops for all students to promote intercultural understanding and collaboration. Addressing unconscious biases and encouraging empathy and cooperation among diverse student bodies.

Navigating academic systems, financial aid, and administrative processes can be particularly challenging for international students (Hussein & Schiffelbein, 2020). Universities should offer personalized advising services to address these barriers and support international students in achieving academic success. Some strategies include establishing centralized international student support offices with multilingual advisors, offering a consistent and accessible resource for academic, cultural, and administrative guidance. Developing an interactive online guide detailing academic and administrative processes for international students, including enrollment steps, visa requirements, and campus resources, to ensure students feel well-prepared for their educational journey. Offering one-on-one mentorship sessions with academic advisors trained in cultural adaptation issues to guide international students through challenges such as adjusting to US grading systems and expectations for academic integrity. Implementing real-time chat or virtual advising services for students needing immediate assistance with academic concerns, ensuring that students can access help outside regular office hours, particularly for time-sensitive issues. Providing financial literacy workshops tailored to international students to help them understand tuition payment deadlines, scholarship applications, and budgeting, taking into account the unique financial pressures they may face.

### 9.3 Policy-Level Implications

International students often face significant financial challenges due to restrictions on their ability to work while pursuing their studies. These constraints impact their financial stability and limit their ability to gain professional experience, which is crucial for career advancement. A survey by Filomeno and Brown (2022) highlights that financial stress is one of the most pressing concerns for international students, with many relying on limited part-time employment opportunities subject to strict regulations. Expanding work opportunities, such as extending post-graduation work permits and increasing allowable work hours during academic breaks, can alleviate some of these financial burdens, allowing students to focus more on their educational goals. Furthermore, such policy adjustments can lead to a more enriched academic experience, as students gain valuable work experience that enhances their learning and prepares them for their future careers.

First, policymakers should advocate for a more flexible approach to the number of hours international students are permitted to work during academic breaks. Allowing students to work more hours during these periods could help alleviate financial stress and enable them to gain additional skills and experience without violating visa regulations. Second, universities should actively collaborate with local businesses to develop internship and job placement programs that cater to international students. These opportunities could bridge the gap between academic learning and real-world work experience, enhancing students' employability. Partnerships could also benefit local businesses by bringing in a diverse, skilled workforce with international perspectives. Third, universities should take a proactive role in helping international students navigate complex visa restrictions and employment authorization processes. Providing detailed workshops, one-on-one counseling, and online resources would empower students to better understand the limitations and opportunities available under their current visa status. Third, institutions and advocacy groups should establish scholarships for international students facing financial hardship. These programs could cover tuition fees, living expenses, or other costs that may be affected by the inability to work full-time. Such initiatives would take away the financial burden on students, allowing them to focus more on their academic and professional development. Last, policymakers and higher education institutions should engage with international student representatives to discuss visa policies, work opportunities, and financial support. This involvement ensures that the needs and concerns of international students are directly addressed in policy decisions. Creating channels for these students to voice their perspectives helps ensure that policies are fair and effectively meet the diverse needs of this student population.

By taking these actions, policymakers and educational institutions can enhance the financial and academic experiences of international students, ultimately fostering a more culturally supportive environment that benefits both students and the broader scholarly community.

### 9.4 Societal and Economic Implications

International students are a critical economic force, contributing billions of dollars annually to host countries through tuition payments, fees, and local expenditures. According to the Institute of International Education (2022), the economic impact of international students is far-reaching, supporting local businesses, creating jobs, and boosting the economy. This financial infusion extends beyond the education sector to local housing, transportation, and retail industries. Additionally, international students often bring diverse perspectives and expertise to academic programs, which enriches the educational environment and enhances institutions' innovation and research capacity. Retaining these talented graduates in the workforce post-graduation is equally essential. By providing a pathway for international graduates to stay and contribute to the labor market, nations can enhance their global competitiveness and address skill shortages in key sectors (Boundless, 2023). For instance, industries such as technology, engineering, healthcare, and finance often face talent gaps, and international graduates can play a pivotal role in filling these voids, particularly in specialized and high-demand fields. Moreover, governments and institutions should develop policies and programs that promote the retention of skilled international graduates within their respective workforces. This could include offering more flexible and extended work visas, building pathways to permanent residency for graduates in high-demand sectors, and recognizing the value of international education in addressing workforce needs. Universities should enhance their career services by providing specialized support tailored to the needs of international students. This can include organizing networking events that connect international students with potential employers, offering job search resources tailored to navigating work visas, and hosting employer engagement programs that highlight the benefits of hiring international graduates. Additionally, career centers could provide workshops that help international students build resumes and practice interview skills suited to the unique expectations of the local job market. Additionally, policymakers should consider easing work visa restrictions for international graduates, especially those in fields with significant labor shortages. Offering simplified processes or even automatic work authorization for graduates with degrees in science, technology, engineering, mathematics (STEM), healthcare, and other critical sectors would make it easier for both students and employers to capitalize on the skills of international graduates, benefiting both parties and contributing to national economic growth. Governments and institutions should also promote incentives for employers to hire international students. By streamlining visa sponsorship processes, reducing bureaucratic delays, and offering tax incentives or subsidies for businesses that hire international graduates, policymakers can create a more attractive environment for employers to tap into this valuable talent pool. International students bring diverse perspectives, cultural understanding, and global experience to the workforce. Governments and institutions should further emphasize the economic and societal value of diversity, encouraging companies to leverage the unique qualities that international graduates bring to the table. Highlighting the benefits of a diverse workforce and creating policies that foster an inclusive work environment can help international graduates integrate successfully, benefiting the broader economy of the host country.

By implementing these actions, governments and universities can foster a thriving ecosystem that enables international students to continue contributing to their host countries' economic and social fabric. Ensuring that international graduates are allowed to remain in the workforce and flourish strengthens the economy and enhances the country's global standing in innovation, competitiveness, and talent retention.

## 9.5 Conclusion

Cultural adaptation is a complex and dynamic process that requires coordinated efforts at individual, institutional, policy, and societal levels. Educational institutions must actively address the unique challenges international students face while fostering an environment that promotes inclusion, academic success, and well-being. Moving forward, continued collaboration between universities, policymakers, and communities is essential in ensuring that international students succeed academically and contribute meaningfully to their host societies.

# Chapter Ten
# **Conclusion and Future Directions**

The academic journey of international students in the US is mainly shaped by the intersection of their cultural backgrounds, the educational expectations of the host country, and the institutional support. As demonstrated throughout this book, international students encounter unique challenges and opportunities that profoundly influence their overall academic experience. Their ability to succeed and thrive depends not only on their inherent efforts but also, crucially, on the institutional support systems and the broader cultural climate in which they are expected to succeed in academics. By examining different factors that influence their experiences, such as new cultural learning styles and social integration challenges in identity formation and the adaptation to new academic environments, this book has provided a clearer understanding of the dynamic and frequently vigorous nature of the educational journeys of international students.

My own 14-year journey through the American educational system, from the naive undergraduate in 2010 to the Ph.D. graduate in 2024, has been a testament to both the profound resilience of international students and the systemic gaps that persist within US higher education. I arrived in the US, a young Indian student steeped in a culture that revered elders, including teachers, and where academic paths were mainly pre-determined. The immediate shock of navigating a system where I chose my classes, times, and even professors was immense, leaving me utterly reliant on an academic advisor to guide my initial enrollment. The sheer terror of discovering I had spent a week in entirely the wrong graduate-level courses as a first-year undergraduate, followed by professors' disbelief and anger, crystallized early on that the American academic landscape would demand a level of self-advocacy and understanding of implied norms for which I was entirely unprepared. My initial struggles with APA and MLA citation, seen as mere "writing" in my home country, became sources of public humiliation, increased by constant reminders that my status as a "second-language English speaker" inherently limited my writing capabilities. These early experiences, far from unique to me, are the unspoken curriculum for countless international students.

The classroom, once a space where I, a confident speaker, excelled in elocution competitions in India, morphed into an arena of paralyzing fear in the US. The constant comments about my accent, the dismissive tone when my "different" English was noted, instilled a stage fright so profound that an adrenaline rush became my involuntary response to any prompt to speak. I became the shy, quiet student, not out of a lack of knowledge or ability, but from the petrifying fear of being misunderstood or, worse, ridiculed. I discovered that this fear extended beyond the classroom. The academic miscommunication with a dean over an internship requirement, which I believed fulfilled my degree, led to its rejection and, I strongly suspect, contributed to the denial of my master's application a year later. This was a brutal lesson in the high stakes of clear communication: as an international student, misunderstandings could put my entire career at risk.

Perhaps the most searing aspect of this journey has been the profound social isolation. Despite 14 years in academic settings, genuine friendship often felt like an unattainable mirage. Differences in religious beliefs, cultural norms, and ideologies created visible chasms. I was never invited to birthday parties or weddings. When I confronted my peers, I was told I would be "the only brown person there" or that my appearance suggested a Middle Eastern origin, which "their family may not approve of." Others pointed to my dietary restrictions or abstinence from alcohol. The loneliness was crushing, and even now, the lack of proper social integration leaves an unattended scar. As a spiritual person, I often reflect that some people are not meant for one, yet in my case, it often felt like no one was meant for me. Even within my own cohort and educational group during my Ph.D. program, I was "othered" and perceived as an "overachiever" and the "teacher's favorite," which further isolated me from the very peers with whom I shared a common heritage. This book, therefore, is not merely an academic treatise; it is a testament to these lived realities, providing both data and narrative to highlight the profound human experience behind the statistics of international student mobility.

## 10.1 Cultural Adaptation and Integration: A Two-Way Process

One of the key insights emphasized in this book is that cultural adaptation is not a one-way process. While international students must navigate the complexities of adjusting to the US academic culture, there is an equally important need for institutions, faculty, and peers to engage in this process as well. The mutual exchange between international students and their host institutions is fundamental to creating an inclusive and supportive environment. This interaction shapes the success of international students, as they are not only adjusting to the academic system but also contributing their unique perspectives, experiences, and knowledge. The process of cultural integration involves the efforts of both the students and the institution to understanding, valuing, and incorporating diversity into every aspect of educational experience. Though the academic demands of the US system are often rigorous, the social and cultural adaptation required to navigate new norms, communication styles, and expectations can be just as challenging. Students from collectivist cultures, for instance, may find it difficult to adjust to the individualistic, self-assertive nature of US academic environments. They may also struggle to find their place within peer networks, emphasizing immediate reciprocity and transactional relationships. In contrast, US students may face challenges in understanding the subtleties of different communication styles of international students, often leading to misunderstandings that can hinder social integration. However, when institutions recognize these dynamics and actively work to foster intercultural competence, students and educators can benefit from the rich diversity.

## 10.2 Institutional Support: The Role of Faculty, Staff, and Policies

Institutions play a critical role in the lives of international students and international scholars worldwide. Institutions must continue to evolve and refine their policies, teaching practices, and support structures to accommodate the diverse needs of an increasingly global student body. Academic support services, including language assistance, tutoring, and writing workshops, are crucial in helping international students succeed academically. However, beyond these services, institutions must create culturally responsive environments where students feel supported and valued for their cultural contributions. Faculty members, in particular, play a pivotal role in shaping the academic experience of international students. Teaching practices that are mindful of cultural differences in learning styles, communication, and classroom dynamics can enhance the success of international students. For instance, recognizing the importance of collaborative learning in collectivist cultures or offering alternative ways for students to express their understanding (such as oral presentations or group discussions) can help international students feel more engaged and less isolated in academic settings. By fostering inclusive pedagogical practices, faculty can ensure that international students are academically successful and feel comfortable and confident in contributing to classroom discussions. Moreover, international student support services must go beyond academic needs and address students' social and emotional well-being. Social integration challenges, including feelings of isolation and cultural alienation, are common among international students. Support structures such as peer mentoring programs, cultural exchange initiatives, and community-building activities can significantly reduce these feelings and encourage social connections. When properly integrated into university life, these initiatives may offer international students the opportunity to build meaningful relationships with both domestic peers and other international students, promoting a sense of belonging and improving overall mental health and well-being.

## 10.3 Future Directions: Shaping the Future of International Student Support

The future of international student support lies in a comprehensive, holistic approach that integrates academic, social, and emotional support into every facet of the university experience. As institutions continue to recognize the importance of cultural diversity, there is a growing need for tailored support mechanisms that account for international students' specific needs and challenges. Future research and institutional policies should focus on expanding the scope of support services to address the academic, social, cultural, and emotional needs of international students.

One of the primary ways that institutions can prepare for the future is by expanding their culturally responsive curricula. As universities continue to attract students from diverse cultural backgrounds, academic programs must evolve to reflect global perspectives and integrate cultural awareness into the academic curriculum. Universities can help promote intercultural competence among domestic and international students, to help prepare students for work and collaborate around the globe. Faculty development programs that offer training on effectively engaging with international students from diverse backgrounds should become a standard feature in teacher preparation, ensuring that educators are equipped to teach in culturally diverse classrooms. Moreover, pedagogical approaches must include various learning styles. As this book has discussed, international students from collectivist cultures may find it difficult to adjust to the US education system's emphasis on individual performance. As a result, instructors may need to create learning environments that foster collaboration, mutual respect, and group-based learning. This can be achieved by adopting a more flexible approach to assignments and grading, offering opportunities for group work, and considering the diverse communication styles of international students.

Cross-cultural exchange programs, international student organizations, and intercultural dialogue sessions can be invaluable in encouraging mutual understanding among domestic and international students. These programs provide platforms for students to share their cultural experiences, learn from one another, and break down the stereotypes and misconceptions that often create divisions socially. Universities may integrate global perspectives into campus events, social gatherings, and workshops, creating spaces for students to engage in meaningful intercultural interactions. The increasing focus on diversity and inclusion in higher education suggests that the future of international students may be hopeful. Still, it requires continued commitment from all stakeholders, administrators, faculty, staff, and students.

## 10.4 The Need for Advocacy in Supporting International Students

Cultural adaptation is a complex and nuanced process that involves more than just the individual experience of an international student. Cultural adaptation can also be considered an ever-evolving adaptation due to the changing geopolitical dynamics. It requires active participation from stakeholders at all levels, such as institutional, local, and national, to foster an environment where international students can succeed. It is essential to recognize that successful integration into US academic settings does not solely depend on personal resilience or the ability to adjust to new cultural environments. The cultural transition process also depends on systemic changes brought about through advocacy efforts. In this context, advocacy catalyzes the creation of policies, practices, and regulations that directly address the unique needs of international students, ensuring that their academic, social, and psychological well-being is prioritized. The need for advocacy can be understood on several fronts. First, higher education institutions' policies must adapt to international students' diverse backgrounds and experiences. This can include providing culturally responsive support services, offering academic mentorship programs, and creating curricula that reflect global perspectives. Second, legal protections for international students are essential to ensure they are not subjected to unfair treatment, discrimination, or marginalization. Third, societal perceptions, stereotypes, and misjudgments of international students must be reshaped, moving away from biases and fostering an inclusive atmosphere where international students are celebrated as contributors to the university and broader community. Student associations play a pivotal role in the advocacy landscape, serving as the collective voice of international students. These organizations can initiate campaigns, collaborate with university administrators, and engage with policymakers at local and national levels to address pressing concerns. Through advocacy, student associations help bring about policy changes that directly impact the well-being and success of international students. Ultimately, advocacy efforts should focus on creating a supportive ecosystem where international students can succeed academically and socially without the hindrances of systemic barriers beyond their control.

## 10.5 Institutional Advocacy: Influencing Policies Within Universities

Universities and colleges must acknowledge their responsibility to create inclusive, supportive, and equitable environments for all students, including international students. Advocacy within these institutions is crucial for addressing the unique challenges that international students face and ensuring they have access to resources and an academic environment that supports their success. Advocacy within universities can significantly impact policy changes, which in turn influence the international student experience. Institutional advocacy efforts can lead to a more inclusive academic environment by highlighting the need for policies and services that specifically cater to the needs of international students. Many international students may feel alienated or underserved within the broader campus community without this advocacy.

International students often encounter institutional policies that do not fully consider or address their specific needs. These policies, which usually reflect a one-size-fits-all approach, can overlook important factors such as cultural background, language barriers, and the pressures of adjusting to a new academic system. Advocacy efforts can help identify these gaps and promote policy changes that foster inclusivity. For example, universities may be encouraged to implement mentorship programs, academic tutoring services tailored to the needs of international students, and counseling services that are culturally competent. Another significant area of advocacy is academic policies. Many international students come from educational systems different from the US model, and their learning styles may not align with the expectations in US classrooms. Advocacy efforts can push for curricula that incorporate global perspectives and recognize the diversity of students' learning preferences. By making these adjustments, universities can create a more inclusive and equitable academic environment for international students.

Student associations, particularly those focused on international students, are key advocates for positive change. These organizations represent international students' interests and serve as an essential bridge between students and the university administration. Through advocacy campaigns, forums, surveys, and direct dialogues with university administrators, student associations can bring attention to the challenges faced by international students. One of the primary roles of student associations is to ensure that international students have access to a comprehensive range of services designed to meet their needs. These include language support programs, career counseling, mental health services, and culturally sensitive housing accommodations. By actively engaging with the administration, student associations can create an environment where international students feel academically and socially supported. Additionally, student associations can push for better representation of international students in leadership positions within student government and other decision-making bodies. This ensures that the voices of international students are heard and their concerns are addressed at the highest levels of university governance. Through these collective efforts, student associations contribute to a culture of inclusivity, ensuring that international students feel a sense of belonging on campus.

## 10.6 National Advocacy: Changing Policies at the Government Level

Although institutional advocacy focuses on policies within individual universities, national advocacy addresses broader issues, such as visa and immigration policies, that impact international students across the United States. These national-level issues have far-reaching consequences for the academic, personal, and professional lives of international students. Visa and immigration policies are among the most pressing concerns for international students. Many students face significant challenges due to restrictive visa regulations, which limit their ability to work, stay in the US after graduation, or transition to permanent residency. National advocacy efforts are aimed at reforming these policies to create more flexibility, such as expanding work opportunities for international students both during and after their studies. Advocacy groups can work to make the visa process more transparent and equitable, advocating for removing bureaucratic barriers that hinder international students' ability to integrate fully into academic and professional environments. These changes are essential to allowing international students to make the most of their educational experiences in the US. US national advocacy also plays a crucial role in ensuring that international students have access to legal protections that safeguard them from discrimination, harassment, and exploitation. Advocating for stronger protections against xenophobia, bias, and discrimination is essential for fostering a safe environment for international students. In addition to advocating for anti-discrimination laws, national advocacy efforts aim to influence policies related to healthcare, work permits, and financial aid, ensuring that international students have access to resources that enable them to succeed academically and professionally.

## 10.7 The Role of International Student Advocacy Organizations

National and international organizations dedicated to advocating for the rights of international students play an essential role in this overall system. These organizations are at the forefront of efforts to help change policies, improve student visa processes, and enhance services dedicated to international students. Such organizations include the National Association for International Educators (NAFSA) and the Alliance of International Students (AIS). These organizations partner with students, policymakers, and educational institutions to push for legislative changes that support international students' rights and improve their experiences in the US. Their advocacy efforts address immediate concerns and create long-term changes that positively impact international students nationwide. Effective advocacy requires international students to be equipped with knowledge and tools to navigate the systems affecting their lives.

Some of the strategies include building coalitions with other student groups, faculty, and community organizations. These partnerships can help demonstrate solidarity and create a unified voice that is difficult to ignore. International student organizations can work together to align their efforts with broader student advocacy groups, strengthening their collective impact. Furthermore, engaging with policymakers is essential for national advocacy. International students and their organizations should seek opportunities to meet with lawmakers and discuss issues like visa reform, work opportunities, and anti-discrimination policies. Public campaigns, petitions, and lobbying effectively bring attention to these concerns and drive legislative changes. International students should be aware of the legal resources available to them in case of discrimination, exploitation, or other legal challenges. Campus-based legal aid clinics, advocacy organizations, and legal advisors can provide support to ensure that international students are not deprived of their rights due to their non-citizen status. Advocacy is critical in ensuring international students receive the support and protection they need to succeed in US higher education. By addressing the challenges faced at the institutional, national, and legal levels, advocacy efforts can create lasting changes that benefit future generations of students. Through collective action, advocacy can help international students navigate the challenges of cultural adaptation, increase their engagement with their host society, and enhance their contributions to their host country and the global community.

## 10.8 Digital Platforms for Social Integration

Digital platforms may offer a promising solution for social isolation and integration by providing a space for connection, support, and community-building that goes beyond physical and cultural boundaries. The digital age has transformed how people communicate, form relationships, and participate in collaborative learning. International students, especially those in the early stages of their academic journey, can benefit from digital tools that support socialization and integration. Virtual spaces, including social media platforms, online communities, and educational collaboration tools, provide a low-pressure way for students to connect with peers, access mental health resources, and develop support networks outside the classroom.

For many international students, online spaces may feel less intimidating than face-to-face interactions, especially when seeking help or resources that may require cultural competence or a lack of cultural differences. These platforms provide opportunities for students to connect with others who understand their unique challenges and can be especially helpful for those hesitant to join in-person social events due to social anxiety or vivid cultural norms. Digital platforms also allow students to participate in academic discussions and collaborative projects outside the classroom, fostering a sense of scholarly community and reducing feelings of loneliness. Additionally, because of the stigma surrounding mental health issues in some cultures, digital platforms can offer a more comfortable environment for students to seek help, whether through virtual counseling or peer support groups. Moreover, international students can also seek overall health and well-being support through telehealth or other digital platforms due to the differences in medical terms or health services.

The implications of research into digital platforms for supporting international students in US higher education are significant and could transform how universities engage with these students. The growing reliance on digital tools in higher education provides innovative solutions to address international students' unique challenges, especially in regard to social integration, academic achievement, and mental health support. One of the most important areas for universities to focus on is expanding their use of digital tools to promote social integration. Social integration is a well-known challenge for international students, as they often face feelings of isolation and difficulty connecting with peers due to cultural differences, language barriers, and unfamiliar social norms. Digital platforms offer a convenient and accessible way to close this gap. Universities could develop tailored online platforms specifically designed for international students, where they can connect with other students, participate in cultural exchange activities, and share experiences. These platforms could include discussion forums, virtual meetups, and peer-led social events, helping international students build a sense of community and belonging both before and after arriving on campus.

Additionally, universities could develop platforms that provide easy access to mental health resources. Mental health issues, including stress, anxiety, and depression, are disproportionately high among international students, worsened by the stress of adjusting to a new country, culture, and academic system. Online mental health services could equip students with the tools and resources to manage their well-being. Digital platforms could offer access to counseling services, stress-management resources, mindfulness exercises, and peer support networks, all tailored to the specific needs of international students. Furthermore, partnering with existing mental health apps or platforms that specialize in student well-being could further improve support for international students, especially those who may feel uncomfortable seeking in-person help due to cultural stigmas surrounding mental health.

Another area where digital platforms could have a transformative impact is academic collaboration. For international students, academic integration is often a major challenge. They may encounter difficulties related to language proficiency, unfamiliarity with the US educational system, and a lack of peer support in coursework and study groups. Digital platforms could assist international students in connecting with domestic and other global peers to form virtual study groups, participate in academic workshops, and access tutoring services. These platforms could also host academic resources such as webinars on academic writing, research techniques, or navigating U.S. grading systems, giving students the tools they need to succeed academically.

One especially effective digital approach could be creating virtual peer mentorship programs. Senior international students, like outgoing students and alumni who have already faced the challenges of adapting to life in the US, could offer guidance and support to incoming international students. Peer mentorship could be organized through existing digital platforms or apps, providing a unique chance for social interaction, skill development, and emotional support. Mentees could ask questions, share concerns, and receive advice in a more informal, accessible setting that is free of judgment. Virtual mentorship programs not only make the transition easier for new students but also create a space to learn from peers, building important connections that could last throughout their time in the US. Additionally, digital platforms open up exciting possibilities for universities to connect with international students in ways that were not possible before. Virtual orientations, which give a thorough introduction to the university's academic programs, cultural norms, and available support services, could be vital for international students, especially those who might struggle to attend in-person sessions due to time zone differences or travel restrictions. Online career fairs, networking events, and professional development workshops specifically designed for international students could also be offered, helping students explore future career options, learn about internships, and build skills needed to succeed in the global job market. These virtual initiatives could greatly improve the overall student experience by making international students feel more connected, informed, and supported.

As the number of international students in US higher education continues to grow, understanding their unique challenges and developing targeted interventions is more crucial than ever. International students contribute significantly to US universities' academic and cultural diversity, and educational institutions should prioritize their success. However, despite the many resources available to international students, challenges such as cultural adjustment, social isolation, mental health concerns, and academic struggles remain prevalent. Longitudinal studies are essential to understanding international students' long-term experiences and trajectories. Researchers can gather critical data on their educational, social, and psychological well-being by following international students from their first year through graduation. These studies would provide insights into the factors that contribute to student success or failure, helping universities identify at-risk populations and implement early interventions. Understanding how international students' needs change over time will also guide the development of more tailored programs and support services, enabling universities to better meet the evolving needs of their international student populations. At the same time, incorporating digital tools into the university experience offers promising opportunities for improving international students' social, academic, and emotional well-being. Digital platforms offer innovative solutions to address the challenges faced by these students, especially in areas like social integration and mental health support. Virtual social spaces, peer mentorship programs, academic collaboration tools, and mental health apps can help international students feel more connected to their peers, reduce feelings of isolation, and access resources to manage stress and anxiety. Additionally, these platforms can complement traditional in-person services, creating a hybrid support system that is more accessible and comprehensive for international students.

Future research should focus on exploring the effectiveness of digital platforms in supporting international students' success. What types of digital interventions are most beneficial for students from different cultural backgrounds? How can universities ensure that these platforms are accessible, user-friendly, and responsive to the diverse needs of international students? Researchers should also investigate how digital tools can complement existing campus-based resources and their role in bridging gaps in support services, especially in situations where face-to-face interactions are limited or unavailable. Moreover, as universities continue to embrace digital tools, they must consider issues of equity and access. Digital platforms should be designed to be accessible to all students, regardless of their technological resources or familiarity with digital platforms. Institutions must ensure that international students, particularly those from lower-income backgrounds or regions with limited access to technology, are not left behind. Additionally, universities should actively work to combat digital divides by providing adequate training and support for students who may not be as familiar with online platforms. In conclusion, while digital platforms present a powerful tool for enhancing the international student experience, their effectiveness will depend on thoughtful implementation and ongoing research to refine and improve these interventions. By continuing to investigate how digital tools can foster social integration, academic success, and emotional well-being, universities can ensure that they provide the most effective support for their international student populations. Moving forward, it will be crucial to develop a comprehensive, evidence-based approach to integrating digital platforms that combine the strengths of technology with the human touch needed to truly support and empower international students. By doing so, higher education institutions can create a more inclusive, supportive, and enriching environment for students worldwide.

## 10.9 Future Directions for International Students

Researching cross-cultural dynamics in higher education is crucial as global student populations continue to grow. Future studies should explore the intersectionality of international students' identities, examining how their cultural, racial, and socioeconomic backgrounds influence their experiences and integration processes. Understanding the nuances of these experiences can help institutions create more targeted and effective support systems for international students, ensuring that they receive the necessary assistance to succeed.

The role of universities in supporting international students cannot be overstated. Beyond providing academic resources, institutions must create inclusive environments that foster social integration and mental well-being. Future research could examine how institutional policies and practices, such as orientations, peer mentoring, and extracurricular activities, impact international students' sense of belonging and overall success. Furthermore, universities should explore opportunities to incorporate international student perspectives into curriculum design and faculty training to foster a more inclusive academic environment.

In addition to institutional efforts, collaboration between domestic and international students plays a key role in fostering intercultural understanding. Future studies could focus on how to facilitate meaningful interactions between these groups through collaborative learning experiences, service-learning projects, and cultural exchange initiatives. By encouraging interaction between domestic and international students, universities can create more opportunities for peer learning and mutual understanding. As discussed earlier, longitudinal research is essential for understanding the long-term outcomes of international students' experiences in the US. Future studies should track students' academic, personal, and professional development over extended periods to assess the lasting impact of their international education. Furthermore, regular evaluation of existing programs and policies can help ensure that institutions adapt to the evolving needs of international students.

Finally, with the increasing use of technology in education, there is an opportunity to further integrate digital tools into student services. Online platforms for academic support, peer mentoring, mental health services, and social networking can all contribute to a more inclusive and supportive environment for international students. Future research should explore innovative ways to utilize technology to enhance the experiences of international students, particularly in remote learning contexts and during periods of social distancing.

## 10.10 A Story of Resilience and a Call to Action

The journey of an international student is often one walked between worlds—a dance between the heritage left behind and the new rhythms of a foreign land. My own 14 years in the US academia have been a microcosm of this experience, marked by initial bewilderment, moments of profound alienation, and a constant, often exhausting, negotiation of self. I came with a thirst for knowledge, instilled with a deep reverence for educators, only to find myself battling misconceptions about my accent and my "different" English, constantly reminded of a perceived inadequacy in academic writing, despite my inherent abilities. The fear of being misunderstood, of being made fun of, silenced the confident speaker I once was, transforming me into a shy observer in classrooms where participation was paramount. I learned the hard way about the implicit rules of academic communication, realizing that a simple misunderstanding could derail an internship or even a future degree. My loneliness was a tangible presence, a void where friendships might have blossomed, often amplified by cultural and racial biases that deemed me "too different" to include. Even within my own community, the nuances of regional identity created further divides.

Yet, this story is not one of despair, but of profound resilience. It is the story of navigating a system that wasn't always built for "me," but one in which I stubbornly carved out my own path to success. Despite the belittling, the rejections, and the profound isolation, I emerged with two Master's degrees, one with Honors and a perfect 4.0 GPA, and a Ph.D. with an equally flawless 4.0 GPA. This isn't a boast; it's a testament. A testament to the unwavering spirit of international students who, like me, refuse to let external biases define their potential. It's a testament to the belief that every international student brings a unique tapestry of knowledge, culture, and life experience that enriches the very fabric of American higher education.

My journey, and the extensive research presented in these pages, reveals a clear truth: cultural adaptation is indeed a two-way street, but it has often lacked reciprocal movement from institutions and domestic peers. This book, therefore, is not merely a narrative of challenges; it is a fervent call to action. It is a plea for universities to look beyond the surface, beyond accents, origins, or perceived "otherness" and truly *see* the individual potential, the rich cultural background, and the unwavering determination that each international student embodies. There is a demand for faculty to be trained in cultural competence, for support systems to be truly holistic and accessible, and for campus communities to dismantle the barriers that lead to loneliness and miscommunication. It is a reminder that fostering genuine social integration and celebrating diverse identities are not just "nice-to-haves," but essential components of a truly equitable and globally aware academic environment.

In the quiet moments, when the echoes of past rejections or misunderstandings surface, I find strength in my spirituality and in the profound belief that my experiences, however challenging, serve a greater purpose. My story, woven into the fabric of this book, is intended to be a beacon for future international students, a roadmap for institutions, and a catalyst for change. It is a hope that no student, regardless of their origin, will ever feel that "no one is meant for me" in a place dedicated to learning and growth. The "beautiful story" we must now collaboratively write is one where every international student is not just welcomed, but truly belongs, where their diverse voices are not just heard, but celebrated, and where their unique contributions are not just acknowledged, but fundamentally transform the academic landscape for the better.

## 10.11 Conclusion

The current exploration of cultural influences on the academic experiences of international students in the US highlights the unique challenges and opportunities these students face. From adjusting to different learning environments to navigating new social dynamics, the experiences of international students are deeply influenced by their cultural identities. These identities significantly impact their academic success, social integration, and overall well-being. The cultural differences manifest in the classroom have been examined, affecting communication styles, expectations of faculty and peers, and approaches to learning. These differences significantly affect their ability to adapt, succeed academically, and form meaningful social relationships. Understanding these academic experiences requires an appreciation of the diverse cultural perspectives that international students bring and the challenges they encounter as they transition into a new educational environment. Despite their obstacles, international students also bring invaluable perspectives that enrich US higher education. Their diverse experiences, ideas, and worldviews contribute to a global learning environment that benefits all students. International students serve as bridges between cultures, creating opportunities for cross-cultural dialogue, mutual respect, and shared learning experiences.

Educational institutions are critical in supporting international students as they navigate their academic journeys. Universities must go beyond merely acknowledging cultural differences and actively foster inclusive environments that celebrate and support this diversity. By embracing cultural competence in curriculum design and student support services, institutions can ensure that international students thrive academically and personally. Looking ahead, higher education institutions must continue to innovate and adapt to the evolving needs of international students. This includes but is not limited to incorporating more inclusive teaching practices, fostering stronger peer relationships, and providing accessible resources for mental health and social integration. Additionally, as the global landscape of higher education evolves, universities must remain conscious of addressing the changing demographics and needs of international student populations, ensuring that all students, regardless of their cultural backgrounds, have the tools they need to succeed.

In conclusion, there are many of us (international students) who have been part of the system for a longer period of time, yet have failed to make our space between the multiple cultural backgrounds of fellow international students, social expectations of the domestic students, and the read-between-the-lines attitude of institutions and policymakers. Although international students are part of the academic community for a shorter timespan, they are here to understand themselves, and make parents who are often hundreds and thousands of miles away proud of their accomplishments. To these international students, who sacrifice so much to create a unique path, an act of empathy or kindness can go a long way and help them find their people amid us and "others."

*This is my attempt to bridge the gap and create an inclusive environment rather than us and them or we and they.*

# Bibliography

Abu-Raiya, H., Pargament, K. I., & Mahoney, A. (2011). Examining coping methods with stress from a religious perspective. *Journal of Religion and Health, 50*(3), 743–761. https://doi.org/10.1007/s10943-009-9286-8

Adeoye, B. F. (2021). Learning styles and cultural differences in online learning environments in the twenty-first century. *Research Anthology on Developing Effective Online Learning Courses.*

Alakaam, A., & Willyard, A. (2020). Eating habits and dietary acculturation effects among international college students in the United States. *AIMS Public Health, 7*(2), 228–240. https://doi.org/10.3934/publichealth.2020020

Alanya-Beltran, J., & Panduro-Ramirez, J. (2021). Mobile learning in Business English: Its effect on South American students' learning styles in the COVID-19 pandemic era: Its economic implications. *Education and Economy, 39*(12). https://doi.org/10.25115/eea.v39i12.6394

Ali, R., & Sharma, P. (2017). Cultural adaptation and academic performance of international students. *Journal of International Education Research, 13*(4), 129-141. https://pmc.ncbi.nlm.nih.gov/articles/PMC5693765/

Ali, S., Yoenanto, N. H., & Nurdibyanandaru, D. (2020). The language barrier is the cause of stress among international students of Universitas Airlangga. *PRASASTI: Journal of Linguistics, 5*(2), 118-123. https://doi.org/10.20961/prasasti.v5i2.44355

Ammigan, R., Veerasamy, Y. S., & Cruz, N. I. (2022). 'Growing from an acorn to an oak tree': a thematic analysis of international students' cross-cultural adjustment in the United States. *Studies in Higher Education, 48*(4), 567–581. https://doi.org/10.1080/03075079.2022.2150757

Amoyaw, J., Pandey, M., Maina, G., Li, Y., & Nkrumah, D. O. (2022). Food insecurity among postsecondary international students: A scoping review protocol. *BMJ Open, 12*(10), e060952. https://doi.org/10.1136/bmjopen-2022-060952

Andrade, M. S. (2006). *International students in English-speaking universities: Adjustment factors. Journal of Research in International Education, 5*(2), 131–154. https://doi.org/10.1177/1475240906065589

Angelova, M., & Riazantseva, A. (1999). If you don't tell me, how can I know? A case study of four international students learning to write the US way. *Written Communication, 16*(4), 491-525. https://eric.ed.gov/?id=EJ592798

Ardila, C. M., & Gómez-Restrepo, Á. M. (2021). Relationship between physical activity, academic achievement, gender, and learning styles in students of a Latin American Dental School: A cross-sectional study. *Journal of Education and Health Promotion, 10*, 149. https://doi.org/10.4103/jehp.jehp_646_20

Ariastuti, M. D., & Wahyudin, A. Y. (2022). Exploring the academic performance and learning style of undergraduate students in English education program. *Journal of English Language Teaching and Learning, 3*(1). https://doi.org/10.33365/jeltl.v3i1.1817

Barkley, E. F., Cross, K. P., & Major, C. H. (2005). *Collaborative learning techniques: A handbook for college faculty.* San Francisco, CA: Jossey-Bass.

Battye, J., & Mak, A. (2008). Intercultural communication barriers, contact dimensions and attitude towards international students. *43rd Annual APS Conference.* Retrieved from researchprofiles.canberra.edu.au

Bekteshi, V., & Kang, S. W. (2020). Contextualizing acculturative stress among Asian international students in the US: A systematic review. *Journal of Social Work, 20*(4), 506–528. https://doi.org/10.1177/1468017319825806

Bennett, M. J., & Bennett, J. M. (2004). Developing intercultural sensitivity: An integrative approach to global and domestic diversity. In D. Landis, J. M. Bennett, & M. J. Bennett (Eds.), *Handbook of intercultural training* (pp. 147–165). Thousand Oaks, CA: SAGE Publications.

Berková, K., Pavlis, P., Klement, M., & Knápek, J. (2020). Learning style preferences of university and college students. *Problems of Education in the 21st Century, 78*(5), 752-765. https://doi.org/10.33225/pec/20.78.752

Berry, J. W. (1997). Immigration, acculturation, and adaptation. *Applied Psychology: An International Review, 46*(1), 5–34. https://doi.org/10.1111/j.1464-0597.1997.tb01087.x

Bethel, A., Ward, C., & Fetvadjiev, V. H. (2020). Cross-cultural transition and psychological adaptation of international students: The mediating role of host national connectedness. *Frontiers in Education, 5,* Article 539950. https://doi.org/10.3389/feduc.2020.539950

Bhaktivedanta Swami Prabhupāda, A. C. (2008). *The Bhagavad-Gita as it is: With the original Sanskrit text, Roman transliteration, English equivalents, translation and elaborate purports* (2nd rev. ed.). The Bhaktivedanta Book Trust.

Bianchi, I., & Martini, L. (2023). Academic and social integration of international students in higher education: A review of the literature and implications for practice. *International Journal of Research Publication and Reviews, 4*(5), 1502-1507. https://doi.org/10.55248/gengpi.234.5.39555

Bista, K., & Foster, C. (2016). *Exploring the social and academic experiences of international students in higher education institutions.* IGI Global. https://doi.org/10.4018/978-1-4666-9749-2

Boafo-Arthur, S., & Boafo-Arthur, A. (2016). Help seeking behaviors of international students: Stigma, acculturation, and attitudes towards counseling. In *Psychology and mental health: Concepts, methodologies, tools, and applications* (pp. 1368–1386). Information Science Reference/IGI Global. https://doi.org/10.4018/978-1-5225-0159-6.ch059

Boundless. (2023). International student numbers reach pre-pandemic levels in 2023. Retrieved from https://www.boundless.com/blog/international-students-increase-2023/

Bozdogan, K., & Comeaux, D. (2007). International students' experiences in US higher education: A review of the literature. *Journal of Studies in International Education, 11*(1), 1-28.

Brogden-Ward, A. J. (2021). *Experiences of international students studying in a UK university: How do international students studying in the UK's Higher Education sector build academic resilience?* [Unpublished doctoral thesis]. University of Chester. http://hdl.handle.net/10034/625612

Brunton, M., & Jeffrey, L. (2014). Identifying factors that influence the learner empowerment of international students. *International Journal of Intercultural Relations, 43,* 321-334.https://doi.org/10.1016/j.ijintrel.2014.10.003

Campbell, T.A. (2015). A Phenomenological Study on International Doctoral Students' Acculturation Experiences at a US University. *Journal of International Students, 5,* 285-299. https://files.eric.ed.gov/fulltext/EJ1060045.pdf

Cena, E., Burns, S., & Wilson, P. (2021). Sense of belonging and the intercultural and academic experiences among international students at a university in Northern Ireland. *Journal of International Students, 11*(4), 812-831. https://doi.org/10.32674/jis.v11i3.2541

Chauhan, L. R. (2023). Boosting English communication skills for international students. *Journal of Critical Reviews, 7*(8), 626-635. https://doi.org/10.48047/jcr.07.08.626

Chennamsetti, P. (2020). Challenges faced by Indian international students in the US. *Journal of Interdisciplinary Studies in Education, 9*(2), 259-273. https://doi.org/10.32674/jise.v9i2.2345

Constantine, M. G., Anderson, G. M., Berkel, L. A., Caldwell, L. D., & Utsey, S. O. (2005). A qualitative investigation of the cultural adjustment experiences of Asian international college women. *Cultural Diversity and Ethnic Minority Psychology, 11*(2), 162-175. https://doi.org/10.1037/1099-9809.11.2.162

Constantine, M. G., Okazaki, S., & Utsey, S. O. (2004). Self-concealment, social self-efficacy, acculturative stress, and depression in African, Asian, and Latin American international college students. *American Journal of Orthopsychiatry, 74*(3), 230–241. https://doi.org/10.1037/0002-9432.74.3.230

Cooper, C. M., & Yarbrough, S. (2016). Asian-Indian female international students: A photovoice study of health and adaptation to the immigration experience. *The Qualitative Report, 21*(6), 1035-1051. https://doi.org/10.46743/2160-3715/2016.2356

de Wit, H. (2016). *Global perspectives on international student mobility.* Routledge. https://doi.org/10.4324/9781315113456

Domínguez, D. G., & Cheng, H. L. (2022). Career barriers and coping efficacy with international students in counseling psychology programs. *The Counseling Psychologist 50*(6), 780–812. https://doi.org/10.1177/00110000221097358

Elhami, A., & Roshan, A. (2024). Religion and higher education migrants' acculturation orientation. *Intercultural Education, 35*(3), 283–301. https://doi.org/10.1080/14675986.2024.2348428

Ennin, F., & Manariyo, E. (2023). Language as communication barrier for foreign students: Evidence from Gujarat State Universities. *European Journal of Education and Pedagogy, 4*(6).

Erturk, S., & Nguyen Luu, L. A. (2022). Adaptation of Turkish international students in Hungary and the United States: A comparative case study. *International Journal of Intercultural Relations, 86*(2), 1-13. https://doi.org/10.1016/j.ijintrel.2021.10.006

Felder, R. M., & Silverman, L. K. (1988). Learning and teaching styles in engineering education. *Engineering Education, 78*(7), 674-681.

Filomeno, F. A., & Brown, C. (2022). Immigrant students and global education. *Journal of Global Education and Research, 6*(2), 166-180. https://www.doi.org/10.5038/2577-509X.6.2.1183

Flannery, M. E. (2025, January 22). Recognizing World Hijab Day, supporting Muslim women. *NEA Today*. National Education Association. https://www.nea.org/nea-today/all-news-articles/recognizing-world-hijab-day-supporting-muslim-women

Fleming, N. D. (1995). I'm different; not dumb. Modes of presentation (VARK) in the tertiary classroom. In A. Zelmer (Ed.), Research and development in higher education, proceedings of the 1995 annual conference of the Higher Education and Research Development Society of Australasia (HERDSA), HERDSA, 18, 308–313.

Forbes-Mewett, H., & Nyland, C. (2008). Cultural Diversity, Relocation, and the Security of International Students at an Internationalised University. *Journal of Studies in International Education, 12*(2), 181-203. https://doi.org/10.1177/1028315307308136

Gabriel, R. (2023). Correlations Between Learning Style Preferences and Arab-Speaking Gulf Region First-Year College Students' EFL Performance: A Literature Review. *Journal of Language Teaching and Research, 14*(3), 709-714.https://doi.org/10.17507/jltr.1403.18

Galperin, B.L., & Punnett, B.J. (2021). Designing Culturally Appropriate Training and Development Programs: A Learning Styles Approach. *Intercultural Management in Practice*. doi:10.1108/978-1-83982-826-320211009

Gartman, K. D. (2016). Challenges of international students in a university setting. *Journal of Adult Education, 45*(2), 1-10. https://typeset.io/papers/challenges-of-international-students-in-a-university-setting-2mpuzwes6y

Gay, G. (2010). *Culturally responsive teaching: Theory, research, and practice* (2nd ed.). Teachers College Press. https://www.design.iastate.edu/img Folder/files/Culturally_Responsive_Teaching_Geneva_Gay.pdf

Glass, C. R., & Westmont, C. M. (2014). Comparative effects of belongingness on the academic success and cross-cultural interactions of domestic and international students. *International Journal of Intercultural Relations, 38*, 106-119. https://doi.org/10.1016/j.ijintrel.2013.04.004

Gudykunst, W. B., & Ting-Toomey, S. (1988). *Culture and interpersonal communication*. Sage Publications.

Guo, S., & Chase, M. (2011). Internationalisation of higher education: integrating international students into Canadian academic environment. *Teaching in Higher Education, 16*(3), 305–318. https://doi.org/10.1080/13562517.2010.546524

Hall, E. T. (1976). *Beyond culture*. Anchor Books.

Han, Y., Li, W., Bao, M., & Cao, X. (2020). An investigation of the experiences of working with multilingual international students among local students and faculty members in Chinese universities. *Sustainability, 12*(16), 6419. https://doi.org/10.3390/su12166419

Hansen, H. R., Shneyderman, Y., McNamara, G. S., & Grace, L. (2021). Assessing acculturative stress of international students at a US community college. In R. Raby & E. Valeau (Eds.), *International students at US community colleges* (1st ed., pp. 118–132). Routledge. https://doi.org/10.4324/9781003121978-10

Hofstede, G. (2001). *Culture's Consequences: Comparing Values, Behaviors, Institutions, and Organizations Across Nations* (2nd ed.). Sage.

Holmes, P., Bavieri, L., & Ganassin, S. (2015). Developing intercultural understanding for study abroad: Students' and teachers' perspectives on pre-departure intercultural learning. *Intercultural Education, 26*(1), 16–30. https://doi.org/10.1080/14675986.2015.993250

Hounsell, D. (1984). The nature and quality of student learning. In F. Marton, D. Hounsell, & N. Entwistle (Eds.), *The experience of learning: Studies in experiential psychology* (pp. 201-226). Scottish Academic Press.

Hsu, C. (2019). Transitions and transformation: Lessons learned from educating international students in a globalized age. *What Next for Sustainable Development?*, 0, 0-0. https://www.amazon.com/Transitions-Transformation-Educating-International-Globalized/dp/3845443731

Hsu, C., Liu, Y., & Cheng, H. (2017). Are international students quiet in class? The influence of teacher confirmation on classroom apprehension and willingness to talk in class. *International Journal of Educational Research, 87*, 1-10. https://doi.org/10.1016/j.ijer.2017.06.006

Hussein, I., & Schiffelbein, K. (2020). University professors' perceptions of international student needs. *Journal of Applied Learning & Teaching, 3*(1). https://doi.org/10.37074/jalt.2020.3.1.8

Institute of International Education. (2015). *Open Doors Report on International Educational Exchange.* https://www.iie.org/news/2015-11-16-open-doors-data/

Institute of International Education. (2022). Open Doors Report on International Educational Exchange. Retrieved from https://www.iie.org/news/us-sees-strong-international-student-enrollment-rebounds/

Jiang, L., & Altinyelken, H. K. (2021). Understanding Social Integration of Chinese Students in the Netherlands: The Role of Friendships. *Journal of Intercultural Communication Research, 51*(2), 191–207. https://doi.org/10.10 80/17475759.2021.1877178

Jibreel, Z. (2015). Cultural identity and the challenges international students encounter. (Master's thesis). St. Cloud State University. https://repository.st cloudstate.edu/engl_etds/23/

Jin, L., & Schneider, J. (2019). Faculty views on international students: A survey study. *Journal of International Students, 9*(1), 84-96. https://doi.org/10.32674 /jis.v9i1.268

Johnson, R., & Kumar, R. (2010). The monsoon wedding phenomenon: Understanding Indian students studying in Australian universities. *Higher Education Research & Development, 29*(3), 215-227. https://doi.org/10.10 80/07294360903532008

Kara, A., Mintu-Wimsatt, A., Spillan, J., Zhang, L., Ruiz, C. (2020). A Cross-National Investigation of Students' Views of International Marketing/ Business Topics and their Preferred Learning Methods: An Abstract. *In: Pantoja, F., Wu, S., Krey, N. (eds) Enlightened Marketing in Challenging Times. AMSWMC 2019. Developments in Marketing Science: Proceedings of the Academy of Marketing Science.* Springer, Cham. https://doi.org/10.1007/978-3-030-42545-6_87

Karky, N. (2013). International students in an Indian technical university: Faculty perspectives on managing cultural differences. *Journal of Studies in International Education, 17*(1), 3-4. https://doi.org/10.1177/1028315312471455

Kaur, D. (2019). Academic experiences of Indian international students in US higher education. *American Journal of Creative Education, 2*(1), 1-12. https://doi.org/10.20448/815.21.1.12

Kolb, D. A. (1984). Experiential learning: Experience as the source of learning and development. Prentice-Hall.

Krsmanovic, M. (2022). Encountering American higher education: First-year academic transition of international undergraduate students in the United States. *Journal of Global Education and Research, 6*(2), 148-165. https://www.doi.org/10.5038/2577-509X.6.2.1164

Kushner, K. A. (2010). Indian international students in American higher education: An analysis of India's cultural and socioeconomic norms in light of the international student experience. *Journal of the Student Personnel Association at Indiana University, 38*, 17-25. https://scholarworks.iu.edu/journals/index.php/jiuspa/article/view/4999

Kwon, Y. (2009). Factors affecting international students' transition to higher education institutions in the United States. *College Student Journal, 43*(4). https://eric.ed.gov/?id=EJ872317

Lai, H., Wang, D., & Ou, X. (2023). Cross-cultural adaptation of Chinese students in the United States: Acculturation strategies, sociocultural, psychological, and academic adaptation. *Frontiers in Psychology, 13*, 924561. https://doi.org/10.3389/fpsyg.2022.924561

LaMontagne, A. D., Shann, C., Lolicato, E., Newton, D., Owen, P. J., Tomyn, A. J., & Reavley, N. J. (2023). Mental health-related knowledge, attitudes and behaviours in a cross-sectional sample of Australian university students: A comparison of domestic and international students. *BMC Public Health, 23*(1), 170. https://doi.org/10.1186/s12889-023-15123-x

Lee, J. J., & Rice, C. (2007). Welcome to America? International student perceptions of discrimination. *Higher Education, 53*(3), 381-409. https://doi.org/10.1007/s10734-005-4508-3

Leong, P. (2015). Coming to America: Assessing the Patterns of Acculturation, Friendship Formation, and the Academic Experiences of International Students at a US College. *Journal of International Students, 5*(4), 459-474. https://doi.org/10.32674/jis.v5i4.408

Li, J. (2016). A cultural hybridization perspective: Emerging academic subculture among international students from East Asia in US *Universal Journal of Educational Research, 4*(9), 2218-2228. https://doi.org/10.13189/ujer.2016.040934

Li, W. (2020). *2020 study on collegiate financial wellness: Key findings report.* Center for the Study of Student Life, The Ohio State University. Retrieved from: https://cssl.osu.edu/posts/632320bc-704d-4eef-8bcb-87c83019f2e9/documents/2020-scfw-key-findings-report-combined-accessible.pdf

Lin, M. (2012). Students of different minds: Bridging the gaps of international students studying in the US. *US-China Education Review, 3*(4), 333-344. https://files.eric.ed.gov/fulltext/ED532905.pdf

Lin, S. Y., & Scherz, S. D. (2014). Challenges facing Asian international graduate students in the US: Pedagogical considerations in higher education. *Journal of International Students, 4*(1), 16-33. https://doi.org/10.32674/jis.v4i1.494

Lorenzetti, D., Lorenzetti, L., Nowell, L., Jacobsen, M., Clancy, T., Freeman, G., & Oddone Paolucci, E. (2023). Exploring international graduate students' experiences, challenges, and peer relationships: Impacts on academic and emotional well-being. *Journal of International Students, 13*(4). https://doi.org/10.32674/jis.v14i2.5186

Lutfiana, L., Tono, S., & Mahmuda, A. (2020). Overseas Students' Language and Culture Barriers towards Acquiring Academic Progress: A Study of Thai Undergraduate Students. *International Journal of Current Science and Multidisciplinary Research, 3*(4), 107 – 114.

Ma, J. (2022). Challenges and strategies facing international students and faculty in US higher education: A comprehensive literature review. *GATESOL Journal, 32*(1), 18-38. https://doi.org/10.52242/gatesol.122

Markus, H. R., & Kitayama, S. (1991). Culture and the self: Implications for cognition, emotion, and motivation. *Psychological Review, 98*(2), 224-253. https://doi.org/10.1037/0033-295X.98.2.224

Maya, J., García, A., & Ríos, C. (2021). The relationship between learning styles and academic performance: Consistency among multiple assessment methods in psychology and education students. *Sustainability, 13*(15), 8193. https://doi.org/10.3390/su13158193

Merriweather, L. R., Howell, C. D., & Gnanadass, E. (2022). Cross-cultural mentorships with Black and Brown US STEM doctoral students: Unpacking the perceptions of international faculty. In 2022 IEEE Frontiers in Education Conference (FIE) (pp. 1–9). IEEE. https://doi.org/10.1109/FIE56618.2022.9962715

Mok, D. S. (2013). *The impact of student-faculty interaction on undergraduate international students' academic outcome* (Order No. 3609959). Available from ProQuest Central; ProQuest Dissertations & Theses Global; Publicly Available Content Database. (1497943867).

Moussa, N. M. (2021). International students' achievements and adaptation to the United States' culture. *Qualitative Research Journal, 21*(3), 212-225. https://doi.org/10.1108/QRJ-06-2021-0101

Mustapha, S. (2010). Understanding classroom interaction: A case study of international students' classroom participation at one of the colleges in Malaysia. *Asian Social Science*, 6(1), 135-145. https://doi.org/10.5539/ass.v6n1p135

NAFSA. (2019, November 1). Combatting hunger and homelessness on campus. *NAFSA: Association of International Educators.* Retrieved from https://www.nafsa.org/ie-magazine/2019/11/1/combatting-hunger-and-homelessness-campus

Naicker, A., Singh, E.S., & van Genugten, T. (2021). Collaborative Online International Learning (COIL): Preparedness and experiences of South African students. *Innovations in Education and Teaching International, 59*, 499 - 510. DOI:10.1080/14703297.2021.1895867

Naik, B., Tech, D., & El-Bendary, N. (2012). Does Culture Influence Learning Styles of Business Students? A Comparative Study of Two Cultures. *Faculty Research & Publications*. 254. https://scholar.dsu.edu/bispapers/254

Navarro, A. F., Arauco, S. E., Huamán, H., Carrión, R., & López-Cuadros, D. (2022). Strengthening of learning styles, applying a multiagent adaptive model. In 2022 XVII Latin American Conference on Learning Technologies (LACLO) (pp. 1-7). IEEE. https://doi.org/10.1109/LACLO56648.2022.10013481

Neto, F. (2021). *Loneliness among African international students at Portuguese universities. Journal of International Students, 11*(2), 397–416. https://doi.org/10.32674/jis.v11i2.1379

Ninnes, P., Aitchison, C., & Kalos, S. (1999). Challenges to stereotypes of international students' prior educational experience: Undergraduate education in India. *Higher Education Research & Development, 18*(3), 323-342. https://doi.org/10.1080/0729436990180304

Owusu Boateng, R. (2022). Exploring the Impact of the Academic Interactions and Social Relations of Graduate Black African Students on their Learning Experiences in Beijing. *Journal of International Students.* doi:10.32674/jis.v12i4.2563

Patel, N., Calhoun, D. W., & Tolman, S. (2024). Understanding the role of cultural competence in peer mentorship programs for international students: A student development theory perspective. *Georgia Journal of College Student Affairs, 40*(1), 62–80. https://files.eric.ed.gov/fulltext/EJ1416733.pdf

Poyrazli, S., & Lopez, M. D. (2007). An exploratory study of perceived discrimination and homesickness: A comparison of international students and American students. The *Journal of Psychology: Interdisciplinary and Applied, 141*(3), 263–280. https://doi.org/10.3200/JRLP.141.3.263-280

Rahman, O., & Rollock, D. (2004). Acculturation, competence, and mental health among South Asian students in the United States. *Journal of Multicultural Counseling and Development, 32*(3), 130-142. https://doi.org/10.1002/j.2161-1912.2004.tb00366.x

Rienties, B., Héliot, Y., & Jindal-Snape, D. (2013). Understanding social learning relations of international students in a large classroom using social network analysis. *Higher Education, 66*(4), 489-504. https://doi.org/10.1007/s10734-013-9617-9

Rivas, J., Hale, K., & Burke, M. G. (2019). Seeking a sense of belonging: Social and cultural integration of international students with American college students. *Journal of International Students, 9*(2), 687–703. https://doi.org/10.32674/jis.v9i2.943

Sawesi, G., & Tusch, G. (2023). From diversity to inclusion: Understanding learning styles and adjustment challenges of international students - A literature review. In EDULEARN23 Proceedings (pp. 3776-3783). IATED. https://doi.org/10.21125/edulearn.2023.1025

Shapiro, S., Farrelly, R., & Tomaš, Z. (2014). *Fostering international student success in higher education.* TESOL Press. https://eric.ed.gov/?id=ED627179

Shu, F., Ahmed, S. F., Pickett, M. L., Ayman, R., & McAbee, S. T. (2020). Social support perceptions, network characteristics, and international student adjustment. *International Journal of Intercultural Relations, 74*(1), 136-148. https://doi.org/10.1016/j.ijintrel.2019.11.002

Singh, H., Bailey, F., Eppard, J., & McKeown, K. (2021). Partners in learning: 'An exploration of multi-cultural faculty and Emirati students' perspectives of university learning experiences'. *Learning, Culture and Social Interaction.* DOI:10.1016/j.lcsi.2021.100564

Sodowsky, G. R., & Plake, B. S. (1992). A study of acculturation differences among international people and suggestions for sensitivity to within-group differences. *Journal of Counseling & Development, 71*(1), 53–59. https://doi.org/10.1002/j.1556-6676.1992.tb02171.x

Stojanović, M., & Robinson, P. A. (2021). Interculturality at a US university: International faculty's experiences with intercultural communication. *Journal for Multicultural Education, 15*(3), 225–238. https://doi.org/10.1108/JME-03-2021-0029

Tang, L., & Zhang, C. (2023) Intercultural friendships with international students in China. *Behavioral Sciences, 13*(10), 855. https://doi.org/10.3390/bs13100855

Taş, M. (2013). International students: Challenges of adjustment to university life in the US *International Journal of Education, 5*(3), 1-10. https://doi.org/10.5296/ije.v5i3.3481

Tatar, S. (2005). Classroom Participation by International Students: The Case of Turkish Graduate Students. *Journal of Studies in International Education, 9*(4), 337-355. https://doi.org/10.1177/1028315305280967

Thibault, N. (2024). Reducing the Gap: A Phenomenological Study of Student-Faculty Interaction Experiences of International Students in Korea. *The Qualitative Report, 29*(6), 1663-1688. https://doi.org/10.46743/2160-3715/2024.6558

Tinto, V. (1993). *Leaving college: Rethinking the causes and cures of student attrition.* University of Chicago Press. https://doi.org/10.7208/chicago/9780226922461.001.0001

Tochkov, K., Levine, L., & Sanaka, A. (2010). Variation in the prediction of cross-cultural adjustment by Asian-Indian students in the United States. *College Student Journal, 44*(3), 677-689. https://psycnet.apa.org/record/2010-21257-007

Tu, X. (2021). The role of classroom culture and psychological safety in EFL students' engagement. *Frontiers in Psychology, 12*, Article 760903. https://doi.org/10.3389/fpsyg.2021.760903

Tung, W. C. (2011). Acculturative stress and help-seeking behaviors among international students. *Journal of American College Health, 59*(5), 377-384. https://doi.org/10.1080/07448481.2010.513406

US Commission on Civil Rights. (2003, May). *Arab and Muslim civil rights issues in the Chicago metropolitan area post-September 11* (Chapter 1). Illinois Advisory Committee. https://www.usccr.gov/files/pubs/sac/il0503/ch1.htm

US Department of State's Bureau of Educational and Cultural Affairs. (2023). United States announced as leading destination for international students: Annual impact to US economy is $38 billion and 335,000 jobs. Retrieved from https://www.state.gov/united-states-announced-as-leading-destination-for-international-students-annual-impact-to-u-s-economy-is-38-billion-and-335000-jobs/

UNESCO Institute for Statistics. (2021). Global flow of tertiary-level students. http://uis.unesco.org/en/uis-student-flow

United States Citizenship and Immigration Services. (2015). *Definition of international students in the US.* https://www.uscis.gov/policy-manual/volume-12

Urban, E. L., & Bierlein Palmer, L. (2014). International students as a resource for internationalization of higher education. *Journal of Studies in International Education, 18*(4), 305-324. https://doi.org/10.1177/102831531 3511642

UWS-Promethean. (2019, November 5). International students and the challenges that they face: Housing and food. *Promethean.* Retrieved from https://uws-promethean.com/2019/11/05/international-students-and-the-challenges-that-they-face-housing-and-food/

Valdez, G. (2016). International students classroom exclusion in US higher education. In B. J. Irby, G. Brown, R. Lara-Alecio, & S. Jackson (Eds.), *Campus support services, programs, and policies for international students* (pp. 22-37). IGI Global. https://doi.org/10.4018/978-1-4666-9752-2.ch003

Vuong, Q., Nguyen, M., Quang-Loc, N., Nguyen, T. Q., & Le, T. (2021, October 23). A gender study of food stress and implications for international students acculturation. https://doi.org/10.31219/osf.io/d28xt

Wahyudin, A. Y., & Rido, A. (2020). Perceptual learning styles preferences of international master's students in Malaysia. Bahtera Jurnal Pendidikan Bahasa dan Sastra, 19(1), 100-108. https://doi.org/10.21009/bahtera.191.10

Wang, D. (2022). The cross-cultural academic adaptation of Chinese students in an American university: Academic challenges, influential factors, and coping strategies. *Research in Social Sciences, 5*(1), 43-53. https://doi.org/10.53935/26415305.v5i1.231

Wang, R. & BrckaLorenz, A. (2018). International Student Engagement: An Exploration of Student and Faculty Perceptions. *Journal of International Students, 8*(2), 1002-1033. https://doi.org/10.32674/jis.v8i2.124

Wang, H., Chang, C., & Li, Y. (2025). Chinese International Students in the U.S. Higher Education: Underserved & Marginalized. *International Education Studies, 18*(1), 56. https://doi.org/10.5539/ies.v18n1p56

Wang, X., & Sun, W. (2022). Unidirectional or inclusive international education? An analysis of discourses from US international student services office websites. *Journal of Diversity in Higher Education, 15*(5), 617–629. https://doi.org/10.1037/dhe0000357

Ward, C. (2001). The impact of international students on domestic students and host institutions. *Education Counts, 45*(2), 205-217. https://www.education counts.govt.nz/publications/international/the_impact_of_international_st udents_on_domestic_students_and_host_institutions

Wu, H. (2015). International student's challenge and adjustment to college. *Education Research International, 2015,* Article ID 202753. https://doi.org/10.1155/2015/202753

Wu, H., Garza, E., & Guzman, N. (2015). International student's challenge and adjustment to college. *Education Research International, 2015,* Article ID 202753. https://doi.org/10.1155/2015/202753

Wu, H.-p., Garza, E., & Guzman, N. (2015). International student's challenge and adjustment to college. *Education Research International, 2015*, Article 202753. https://doi.org/10.1155/2015/202753

Xu, W. (2022). Pedagogic affect and African international students' attunement to Chinese language learning. *Journal of Multilingual and Multicultural Development.* doi:10.1080/01434632.2022.2049803

Yee, T., & Ryan, K. (2023). Examining international students' help-seeking intentions utilizing the theory of planned behavior. *International Journal for the Advancement of Counselling, 45*, 370–384. https://doi.org/10.1007/s1 0447-022-09491-z

Young, M. Y. (2017). Confucianism and the academic environment: The influence of Confucian values on East Asian students. *Journal of International Education Research, 13*(2), 45-54. https://doi.org/10.19030/jier.v13i2.10000

Yousef, D. A. (2021). Learning style instruments in Arab countries: An analysis of existing literature. *European Journal of Training and Development, 45*(4/5), 449–468. https://doi.org/10.1108/EJTD-06-2020-0112

Zhai, L. (2004). Studying international students: Adjustment issues and social support. *Journal of International Students, 4*(1), 16-33. https://doi.org/10.326 74/jis.v4i1.494

Zhang, Y. (2022). Rethinking internationalization at home from a system perspective: Evidence from China's higher education institutions. *International Journal of Chinese Education, 11*(1), 1–15. https://doi.org/10.1177/2212585X 221095881

Zhang, Y., & Mi, Y. (2010). Another look at the language difficulties of international students. *Journal of Studies in International Education, 14*(4), 371–388. https://doi.org/10.1177/1028315309336031

# Index

www.ingramcontent.com/pod-product-compliance
Lightning Source LLC
Chambersburg PA
CBHW050521280326
41932CB00014B/2403

# Acknowledgments

I AM GRATEFUL TO THE MANY PEOPLE WHO HELPED ME WRITE THIS BOOK. FIRST, I THANK Professor Forrest Colburn who provided especially thorough and constructive criticism as the manuscript was being written. Moreover, I profited from Professor Colburn's suggestions for improving the manuscript once it was completed. The manuscript has also been strengthened by the critical readings of other colleagues and friends. I wish to thank Nancy López, Jorge Duany, José Luis Rénique, Segundo Pantoja, Xavier Totti, Laird Bergard, César Ayala, and Michaeline Crichlow. They read the manuscript and provided many insightful comments. Simona Acosta and Vicky Rodríguez helped me with computer software. Assistance in the libraries of the City University of New York was provided by Professor Susan Voge. I am also grateful to Professor Roger Sanjek, a great teacher and friend, for sharing with me his ethnographic skills.

Two institutions in New York City provided me with the resources to conduct research and write: The Community Development Research Center at the Milano School of Urban Policy of the New School, and the City University of New York.

I especially thank all the people who gave me their time and their trust during my fieldwork in Queens, the Bronx, and Manhattan.

Finally, I am indebted to Félix, my husband, and my sons Miguel, Andrés, and Fernando. I could not have done this work without their support and patience.

# DOMINICANS IN NEW YORK CITY

# CHAPTER 1

# Introduction

THIS STUDY EXPLORES THE DIVERSE STRUGGLES OF INCORPORATION PURSUED BY immigrants from the Dominican Republic to one city in the United States—New York City. The Dominican Republic, the second largest country of the Greater Antilles in the Caribbean Sea, was the nation that sent the most immigrants to New York City during the 1980s and 1990s. This study chronicles the lives of Dominicans in New York City: their difficulties, their courage, and their boldness to incorporate themselves into American politics. Their political success makes Dominicans an emerging ethnic community in New York City. Indeed, Dominicans are the first group of new immigrants—those people migrating to the United States after 1965—who have gained electoral representation in both the New York City Council and the New York State Assembly. Despite their immigrant status and their poverty, Dominicans have managed to become an ethnic political force in New York.

Ethnic studies have gained renewed vigor in the wake of accelerating immigration after the 1965 immigration act. Unlike the earlier immigration wave, composed primarily of Europeans, contemporary immigrants come mostly from Latin American and Asia. The process of adaptation to America society by this new group of immigrants poses many practical and theoretical questions. New immigrants live in a different socioeconomic environment, processes of migration are continuous, and they are of different races, which can alter significantly processes of incorporation.

Ethnic studies in the past took for granted that incorporation was part of acculturation into the values, norms, and practices of American society. Today this assertion is problematic. I argue that incorporation does not mean the acquisition of a new culture (American) at the expense of the "old" culture (Dominican) as proposed by assimilation theories. Instead, incorpora-

3

tion today evolves in the midst of a multiplicity of allegiances, and a reconstituted identity where both old and new cultures are reshaped.

But ethnicity also complicates the politics of incorporation of Dominicans. The Dominican community includes long-established and even second-generation Dominicans who push and practice incorporation. But other Dominicans have their identity and loyalties torn between two places—the Dominican Republic and the United States. Still others see themselves as exiles and foreign nationals. Dominicans have diverse, and sometimes even multiple, ethnic identities. The "identity" of Dominicans is spread out on a wide continuum, one that complicates their "incorporation" into the United States.

Just where on this continuum individual Dominicans reside depends on a number of considerations. Clearly, as has been the case with previous immigrant groups, length of residence in the United States is an important determinant of assimilation. However, a proposition of this study is that the barriers to successful integration that many Dominicans confront lead many Dominicans to cling to their ethnic identity as a social, political, and even a cultural strategy to improve their individual and collective welfare. Ironically, the route to the full panoply of benefits to life in the United States may entail—at least for Dominicans—foregoing assimilation (at least for a while) and banding together as an ethnic community for the purpose of being politically recognized. Thus, deciding on one's "identity," of where to place oneself on the continuum stretching from Dominican to Dominican-American to "American," depends at least in part on a political calculus. The choices individual Dominican immigrants make depends in part, too, on the institutional parameters: what does the United States—and New York City in particular—offer Dominicans who quietly assimilate and what does it offer to Dominicans who press claims as "Dominican-Americans."

Dominicans' decision about how to shape—or choose—their identity are also determined in part by gender and their own particular household structure. Gender strongly influences the major parameters of life—including of career opportunities—and so it shapes, too, decisions made by men and women about where to settle on the continuum of Dominican, Dominican-American, American. Similarly, household structures differ, thus offering different opportunities and incentives for ethnic identification, social involvement, and political participation. Clearly, decisions about "assimilation," about social, cultural, and political incorporation into the United State, are complex, being much more than simply a function of length of residence in the United States.

Dominicans varying perceptions of themselves and of their place in the United States are suggested by the following answers to questions I posed in interviews:

• Rosa: We are a community that has roots here. The tree has already grown and already bears fruit: the second generation of Dominicans, those born here. If we are already rooted here it is not that we are going to survive. No, we are going to construct something better for ourselves.

• Gustavo: If you are in a place only for the time being you don't care how the place looks, but if suddenly you realize that you are going to stay you start to change the place to your own taste. The same happens with us Dominicans in New York City. We are going to stay and we already want to change the city to satisfy our own preferences.

• Woman at the Dominican-Americans round table in Providence, Rhode Island in 1999: We won't wait five more years to get a Dominican in Congress.

• Fausto: This is home. I grew up listening to the elevated train running in Roosevelt Avenue and eating hamburgers. I carry this city in my blood.

• Juana: I was born here. My children were also born here. Now my granddaughter was also born here—third generation. I know I will be buried here.

• Josefina: I have worked pretty hard here. I am 51 years old and as soon as I reach retirement age I am returning to my country, to the Dominican Republic.

• Marcos: I am here waiting for good luck. Otherwise I would be in Santo Domingo.

• José: I am here physically but my mind is there.

• Luis: I identify myself as in between the United States and the Dominican Republic. I belong here, but I also belong in the Dominican Republic.

The kinds of identifications expressed in my interviews reflect multiple ethnic identities.

There are three different yet interconnected identities in the Dominican community. Dominican-Americans are a group of individuals that are becoming aware that they are a permanent community in New York City. Dominican Americans are second-generation Dominicans, naturalized individuals, and adults who migrated to the United States as children who feel they belong in New York City. They do have an identity of being Dominican, but more commonly—and more accurately—of being Dominican-Americans. Not all Dominicans, however, share this identity. Many Dominicans are "new immigrants," Dominicans who have less than five years of residency in the United States. New immigrants usually have more loyalties to the Dominican Republic than the United States, and they still dream of returning to their homeland. Other immigrants are those who have more than five years of residency in the United States, yet aspire to maintain a dual identity, with loyalties to both the Dominican Republic and the United States.

These three groups may be somewhat different, yet they are connected to a continuous and overlapping process of ethnic identification, due to continuous immigration from the Dominican Republic to the United States. Both groups influence community development and political incorporation of Dominicans in New York City. Dominican-Americans develop strategies to push Dominicans with loyalties to the Dominican Republic and with a dual identity to legalize their status in the United States, to "naturalize," to exercise their voting rights, and to mobilize their communities for social and economic vindications. This book explores these differences in ethnic identification and how they affect Dominicans politics of incorporation.

This study also analyzes the social forces shaping Dominican multiple identities. These forces include the migration of Dominicans to New York City, which have been constant and increasing, allowing for the emergence of many identities. Consideration is given to the social factors produced by the host society—in the United States—which shape ethnic formation, such as residential concentration and segregation, structural economic changes, and state and federal policies toward the immigrant community.

This book also looks at community issues, such as the work of social service agencies and the politics of community control. Both are also central to ethnic identification and the politics of incorporation. For example, social service agencies, directed by Dominican-Americans, have paved the way for Dominican political participation through both community empowerment programs, naturalization, and voter registration drives. Social service organizations are essential agents in the process of community development and immigrant political incorporation. Moreover, social service organizations, as well as other community organizations, play other roles, such as building bridges between newer immigrants and the institutional, economic, and social life of established Dominicans. These agencies have been key to Dominican political incorporation, which is important in the formation of a more permanent community, with more roots in the host society, and more powerful politically. These Dominican agencies follow earlier patterns of African-American and Puerto Rican organizations in New York City.

The politics of community control also play a central role in ethnic formation and the politics of social and political incorporation. The politics of community control have evolved in the Dominican community since the 1970s. During the late 1970s and throughout the 1980s, Dominican leaders successfully targeted Community Planning Board 12, then Community School Board 6, and the democratic party district leadership in Manhattan. Later, in the 1990s, that same leadership also successfully targeted the City Council and the New York State Assembly, winning one seat in each of these bodies. This study looks at the social processes occurring from mid 1960s to 1990s that make possible some degree of political empowerment.

There are other issues I will address in this book, too. One of my main interests is to see how gender complicates ethnicity, community development and politics of incorporation. So often scholars offer only quantitative analysis of immigrants and provide little insight into the internal dynamics of their community. In contrast, I will devote time explaining how ethnicity emerges in the Dominican community, taking into consideration how men and women build their identities and relate to politics in different ways.

I am also interested in looking at Dominicans who share their residential space with other immigrants from Latin American. Although there are exceptions, there exists a tendency in the literature on recent immigrants to focus only on a single ethnic group. Most neighborhoods in New York City, however, are multi-national neighborhoods. Is there collaboration or conflict? I will explain what happens when Dominicans share their residential and workspaces with other Latin Americans. How does this mingling of Latin American nationalities affect ethnicity formation and the politics of incorporation? This question is important and I provide at least a tentative answer.

Finally, I will weave through the text the argument that the political momentum experienced in the Dominican community decreased in mid-1990s due to competition over scarce resources, political fragmentation, individualism, and gender biases. Moreover, I argue that in spite of some electoral success, the Dominican community remains significantly isolated from other minorities, such as the African-American, Asian, and other Latino communities in New York City, and consequently has little impact on major social transformations in the United States.

## THEORETICAL ROOTS

More important than describing a community's struggle to gain political power are larger questions about the incorporation of new immigrants. Studies of ethnicity and community development have been important in understanding immigrants at the beginning of the twentieth century. American urban sociology has explored ethnic, working-class neighborhoods, posing questions such as how do earlier immigrant communities, for example Italians, face economic, political, and demographic changes and how those affected quality of life, social behavior, culture, class, and ethnicity. Scholars such as Gans (1962), Whyte (1943), Kornblum (1974), and Suttles (1968) examined European immigrant communities, posing the above questions. Ethnicity was important in these studies and some of their questions and answers offer a good point of departure for my study.

A century later, though, there are new immigrants communities in the United States. Unlike the earlier immigrant waves, composed primarily of Europeans, these new immigrants come basically from Latin American and Asia. For example, in the Dominican case there are major differences. It is a community of working class, service and informal workers, as well as unemployed people of *color* made up by new immigrants who started to come during the 1960s and have never stopped migrating to the United States. Structural changes, race, gender, as well as increasing and uninterrupted migration affect the construction of ethnicity and incorporation processes in the Dominican case.

The concept of transnationalism offers a way to understand the formation of immigrant communities such as the Dominican case. In contrast to classic perspectives, transnationalism argues that immigrants are not in the host society to stay and adapt. Instead, immigrants "develop networks, activities, patterns of living, and ideologies that span their home and the host society" (Basch et al. 1994: 4). Although what I have observed in Dominicans in New York City partially fits the definition of transnationalism, other issues of identity are not explained well by this approach. Many individuals in the Dominican community are in an "in-between" status, torn between here and there, or find it very difficult to determine where they belong. But there are still other individuals shifting their loyalties to the host society. Finally, some individuals are fully engaged in incorporating themselves into U.S. society and polity. As Basch et al. argue, transnational theories invite scholars to rethink "our conceptions of the migration process, immigrant incorporation, and identity" (1994: 3). My theoretical purpose is to present a community within the framework of conceptual developments in transnational studies. It permits me to see the phenomena of the politics of incorporation of recent diasporas in the United States in a new light and to advance propositions about their future course.

## METHODOLOGY

I have conducted ethnographic fieldwork in the Dominican community of New York City for fourteen years, from 1986 to 2000. In 1986, I became part of the "New Immigrants and Old American Project" of Queens College, directed by Roger Sanjek of Queens College. The goal of the project was to understand the social, cultural, and political life of an urban neighborhood that was experiencing the impact of substantial new immigration. The project addressed these concerns through intensive ethnographic fieldwork, and through interviews using a household interview form, covering social and demographic characteristics, migration and work histories, and community involvement.

I moved into Corona, Queens and lived there from 1986 to 1988. During this time I interviewed 50 women—33 housewives and "working women," and 17 community leaders, church pastors, social service agencies directors, and appointed officers. Twenty of the 50 women were Dominicans. The New Immigrants and Old American Project's outcomes include several dissertations (Chen 1990; Park 1990; Ricourt 1994), a master thesis (Danta 1989a), several articles (Danta 1989b; Gregory 1992, 1993; Sanjek 1988, 1992; Ricourt 1989), books (Chen 1992; Park 1997; Sanjek 1998), and other works. I have continued to return to Corona, most recently in 1994, when Ruby Danta and

I conducted ethnographic research on small grocery stores in Corona. Most of these stores are Dominican-owned. From 1994 to 1998, I re-interviewed many community activists and conducted interviews with leaders of organizations created after I finished research with the "New Immigrants and Old Americans Project." During 1999 and 2000, I participated in many different activities organized by Dominican activists in Washington Heights and Queens. During visits to the Dominican Republic in the summers of 1999 and 2000, I had the opportunity to interview Dominicans who have returned to the Dominican Republic after many years of residing in New York City.

My desire to write this book, however, can be traced to the summer of 1994. That summer, I attended a youth conference organized by *Alianza Dominicana*. Before that event, I knew Washington Heights only as a place to buy Dominican products, eat in Dominican restaurants, and dance in Dominican nightclubs. Washington Heights was also a place where I felt nostalgic among so many Dominicans, some of them even from my hometown in the Dominican Republic, San Cristóbal. Or I conceived of Washington Heights as a place, as one of my college students once told me, where one must wear a bulletproof jacket to visit. But the youth conference showed me a Washington Heights I never imagined.

That morning I entered "*La Plaza,*" located at Public School 143 in the corner of Amsterdam and 184th Street, where the conference was being held. At the entrance I encountered a long registration table and behind it five teenagers, both male and female, registering attendants. One of the young ladies wrote my name in a list and gave me a bag full of flyers announcing community activities; booklets explaining Mario Cuomo's campaign against drugs and teenage pregnancy, and additional information about AIDS, and safe sex; condoms; and a clapping hand. The young lady showed me the way to the auditorium. The entrance to the auditorium was packed with people and tables exhibiting pictures and more information. The auditorium itself was full. There were about eight hundred people sitting and about two hundred standing by the aisles and the back of the auditorium. From the elevated entrance, I could see the stage, decorated with both Dominican and American flags. A young fellow was rapping. Then Moisés Pérez, the executive director of *Alianza Dominicana*, addressed the audience. Later on Guillermo Linares, the Dominican councilman spoke, encouraging youth to finish school. Congressman Charles Rangel also addressed the audience, talking about the numerical power of the Dominican community. After each presentation, plastic clapping hands filled the air with noise.

At about 1:00 P.M., the show ended and everybody was invited to a reception in the school cafeteria. About fifteen different Dominican dishes were offered to the guests: roasted pork, rice and *guandules* (pigeon peas), white rice, rice with black beans, stewed beans, roasted chicken, pork chops, stewed beef, potato salad, pasta salad, green salad, beef patties, fried eggplant and fried yellow plantains, boiled green plantains, and yucca. Miriam Mejía, the *Alianza Dominicana* project director and an old friend, told me that *Alianza*

*Dominicana* paid women from the community to cook. During lunch, I met almost everybody from Washington Heights' political leadership.

The youth conference presented the image of a highly sophisticated ethnic community. Together were Dominican women and men, who were second and third generation "New Yorkers," ordinary community residents, community leaders, political activists, and elected officials. This experience awakened my academic interest in the Dominican community of New York City. I requested a grant at the Graduate Center, City University of New York, to start conducting research in the neighborhood. I received a summer grant that allowed me to interview executive directors and staff members of the major social service organizations in Washington Heights. Later on, in 1995, I continued to conduct participant observation and further interviews as part of my responsibilities as a post-doctoral fellow at the Community Development and Research Center of the Milano School of Urban Studies at the New School for Social Research. Members of the *Alianza Dominicana* and the Dominican Women's Development Center introduced me to women and youth of both sexes in Washington Heights, who agreed to being interviewed. Through them, I met still other women and men. *La Unión de Jóvenes Dominicanos*, a Dominican student organization at City College, the City University of New York, also helped me contacting Dominican students.

Representatives of two Dominican Parties, the *Partido Revolucionario Dominicano* (Dominican Revolutionary Party—PRD) and the *Partido de los Trabajadores Dominicanos* (Dominican Workers' Party—PTD), granted me interviews. Further participant observation in their headquarters and activities were helpful, too. Both Guillermo Linares, the first Dominican elected to the New York City Council and Adriano Espaillat, the first Dominican to be elected to the New York State Assembly, allowed me to visit their offices and granted me interviews. From 1994 to 1996, I resided in a neighborhood adjacent to Washington Heights, in the Grand Concourse area of the Bronx. There the Dominican population was increasing. During that period, I expanded my research area to the Bronx, where I started to interview both women and men. My prior contact in Corona, a traditionally Dominican community, allowed me to use some of the interviews conducted among both women and men while I conducted research in that community from 1986 to 1998. During the course of my research, I interviewed 98 Dominicans residing in New York City, whom I asked questions regarding time of migration, attachment to the Dominican Republic, United States citizenship, political affiliations, voting participation, and community activism, among other questions. Of those interviewed, 56 were women and 42 were men. I complement this sample with aggregate data from the census and other surveys.

In summary, this study is based on long-term ethnographic fieldwork in Washington Heights, Queens, and the Bronx. It documents the processes of community formation from four interrelated perspectives: ethnic identity formation, community development, politics of incorporation, and gender relations. My methodology included participant observation of the whole social and political tissue of Dominican New York. This collection of observations and interviews supports my qualitative portrayal of Dominican New York.

During the course of my research, and mostly during the course of making sense out my interviews and field notes, I discovered myself in many of the Dominicans talking about their lives and expectations. I saw myself torn between *here* and *there; here*, in the United States: teaching, writing, being a wife and a mother; *there*, in the Dominican Republic, walking the eternal streets of my hometown, contemplating the seashores of *El Malecón*. There was a lot of nostalgia in this thought. But this discovery did not stop me from looking beyond my own personal experience to discover the experiences of other Dominicans in the Diaspora. These are individuals who might think similar to me, or different, but together we belong to an emerging community in the United States. Learning about this emerging Dominican community did not help me to solve my own dilemma about *here* and *there*. Still my own personal experience and my Dominican background gave me a greater access to the community and stimulated me to ask more thought provoking questions.

## ORGANIZATION

Chapter two centers around three continuous and overlapping ethnic identification tendencies in the development of the Dominican immigrant community in New York City. Chapter three discusses Dominicans in the context of recent immigration to the United States, in general, and New York City, in particular. It also looks at the effects of labor market transformation in New York on Dominicans that have placed them economically at the margins of society. Chapter four argues that the geographical concentration of Dominicans in specific neighborhoods in New York City has facilitated Dominican ethnic solidarity and civic involvement in the city. Data show that ethnic solidarity and residential clustering have been essential in the advancement of the Dominican community in New York City, through social service organizations, clubs, women organizations, and student groups.

Additional chapters explore the processes of Dominican ethnicity, community development, and political incorporation. Chapter five deals with the instrumental role of social service organizations building strategies of community empowerment and development. Chapter six explores the formation of a Dominican-American identity, as reflected in the construction of a political community with strong roots in the American political system and distance from the Dominican Republic. Politics, within this scheme, have been central to the process of transformation from newer immigrants' ties to the country of origin and established immigrants—second generation—identification with the receiving country.

Chapters seven and eight discuss gender politics. Dominican women are instrumental in community construction through activism in buildings and block associations. They are important in organizing neighborhood protests against police brutality and other issues affecting community residents. Dominican women also participate in electoral politics. However, both the city bureaucracy as well as the predominantly Dominican male leadership limit their participation. Despite of women's involvement in the social construction of their communities, they are still excluded from mainstream politics and decision-making bodies.

Chapter nine looks at how Dominican ethnic identification is affected when Dominicans share residential space with other Latino groups. Corona, a neighborhood that houses people from every nation of the Spanish-speaking Caribbean, Mexico, Central and South America, is a site where these interactions occur and it is used to offer both generalizations and descriptive detail about an important issue in the United States—the interactions and community formation of Latinos from different national backgrounds.

An examination of the politics of incorporation of the Dominican community in New York City offers insights into why ethnicity continues to be important in the quest for power by recent immigrants and racial minorities. Through the process of building their organizations, creating a voice, and empowering community residents, the Dominican leadership in New York City consciously constructs an ethnic community. Despite differences of ethnic identification, Dominican-Americans rally together politically. Political culture and capable leadership enable Dominicans in New York City to appropriate power from the margins of society.

# CHAPTER 2

# Ethnic Identity of Dominicans in New York City

HE ETHNIC IDENTIFICATION OF THE DOMINICAN COMMUNITY OF NEW YORK CITY raises many questions. How do Dominicans identify themselves in the Diaspora? Do Dominicans have a transmigrant behavior? What is the role of second-generation Dominicans in politics of incorporation? What is the impact of Dominican ethnic identification on community development and political empowerment?

On May 16, 2000, the day of Dominican presidential elections, more than 7,000 Dominicans living in New York City traveled to the Dominican Republic to exercise their right to vote and elect the country's new president (*El Diario/La Prensa* May 16, 2000). For the previous five months, Washington Heights had been a center of heated political arguments about Dominican elections. Caravans, walks, betting, and arguments in almost every corner of the neighborhood, were part of the Dominican political agenda during the electoral process. At the same time, New York City became a successful fund raising center for Dominican candidates.

However, the entire Dominican community was not involved in this electoral campaign. Many, including the Latino newspaper *El Diario /LaPrensa*, argue that those who went to vote in the Dominican Republic were a minority relative to those who were "resigned and accustomed to live in the United States." Some Dominicans did not care about the elections. Carmen, a librarian at one of the City University of New York campuses, said, "I am too busy to follow this show." Some of my students, mostly second-generation Dominicans, had never read Dominican newspapers in New York City and did not know much about the elections, but were thrilled by the upcoming NBA playoff season.

Many scholars have argued that Dominicans live between two islands— Manhattan and Hispaniola (Grasmuck and Pessar 1991). Dominicans have a

13

foot here—the United States—and another there—in the Dominican Republic. The literature on transmigration posits that immigrants live across borders and maintain their ties home, even when their countries of origin and settlement are geographically distant (Appadurai 1991, Duany 1994, Sutton 1987, Glick Schiller et al. 1992, Portes 1996). According to this perspective, "transmigrant communities are characterized by a constant flow of people in both directions, a dual sense of identity, ambivalent attachments to two nations, and a far-flung network of kinship and friendship ties across state frontiers" (Duany 1994: 2).

In other words, transmigrants take actions, make decisions, and feel concerns within a field of social relations that link together their country of origin and their country or countries of settlement. Transnationalism is also a multifaceted, multi-local process (Smith and Guarnizo 1999: 6). For Portes (1996), small capitalists expressed their transnationalism as a social resistance that might erase all national boundaries. In the study conducted by Peggy Levitt in a semi-urban village in Baní, Dominican Republic, she found out that "connections between sending and receiving countries strengthen and become widespread, a transnational public sphere emerges" beyond national boundaries (Levitt 1998: 928). There is no doubt that transmigrant behaviors expand across national frontiers. Locality is both here and there.

But are all immigrants and, specifically, are all Dominicans in New York City involved in transnational practices? If local subjects embedded in the contingencies of issues reproduce their neighborhoods (Appadurai 1996: 185), how then do Dominicans construct and reproduce their neighborhoods in terms of identity?

If one examines immigrant communities, transnationalism tells only a partial story. One discovers other processes that occur along with this transmigrant behavior. As the immigrant community develops transmigrant processes of the type described above, other processes related to community formation and community politics complicate its outcome (Basch et al. 1994). The following story is illustrative.

Angel Tavares is the son of immigrant parents from the Dominican Republic. He graduated from Harvard University cum laude in government and from Georgetown University Law School. According to Angel, Dominicans are making their mark and establishing themselves like never before in this country. He said: "Still much work remains to be done, and that is why today, I am working to continue our progress by taking an important step in a new direction: I am running for the United States Congress in my home state of Rhode Island."[1]

These processes are important in the formation of a more settled community with permanent roots in the host society. Many Dominicans care about the Dominican Republic, still others care more about the Dominican community in the United States. Thus, transnationalism holds different meanings for new, established immigrants, and second-generation of immigrants. New immigrants are typically between two countries—the country of origin and the receiving society, with perhaps more loyalties to the sending nation. People who have lived longer in the United States are both torn between here and there and/or live within a process of *distanciamiento*/separation from their countries of origin. Second-generation Dominicans usually search for meaning in an immediate environment that for them is home.

## VARIABLES AFFECTING DOMINICAN ETHNIC IDENTIFICATION

Variables such as migration, unemployment, geographic concentration, length of residency in the United States, and discrimination affect the process of ethnic formation.[2] Gender also shapes ethnicity. These variables help to forge ethnic solidarity and mobilization. There is an additional variable, however, that prominently shapes ethnic identification in the case of Dominicans. This variable is the continuous and increasing immigration from the Dominican Republic to the United States. Dominicans came to New York City in large numbers after 1960. Since then, they have continued to come to New York. Is the identity of Dominicans who have been in the United States since the 1960s similar to those who came in later years? With who do the offspring of Dominicans identify?

The continuous immigration of Dominicans for over forty years affects how Dominicans engage in the process of identity formation. Dominicans who came in the 1960s entered the process of ethnic identification over 40 years ago. Many of them have children, who are second-generation Dominicans. Some of these second-generation are now the parents of third-generation Dominicans. Other Dominicans entered the process of ethnic identification twenty, ten, five, one year or less than one year ago. In that way, the Dominican community exhibits different layers of ethnic identification.

## THE EFFECTS OF CONTINUOUS IMMIGRATION ON ETHNIC IDENTIFICATION

During the course of my research, I interviewed ninety-eight individuals. Their answers helped to craft my argument that there are three main tendencies in the development of Dominican immigrant community identity due to continuous immigration. Chart 1 illustrates the effects of continuous immigration on ethnic identity.

I have identified three major groups in the Dominican community of New York City: new immigrants, established immigrants and Dominican-Americans.

### Chart 1: Process of Continuous Immigration

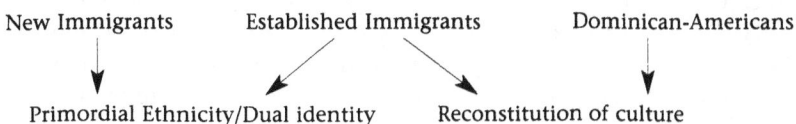

| New Immigrants | Established Immigrants | Dominican-Americans |
|---|---|---|

Primordial Ethnicity/Dual identity     Reconstitution of culture

## NEW IMMIGRANTS

A group of Dominicans exhibits an approach to ethnicity that emphasizes group ties, physical affinity, common language, common religion, and historical commonalities.[3] These are the new immigrants. In typology, new immigrants are Dominicans who have ten or less years of residency in the United States. Some are legal residents. Some do not have legal papers to live here. None are naturalized. They have strong feelings toward their native country, and consider themselves *birds of passage*. They call a relative or a friend in the Dominican Republic weekly. They send money to the Dominican Republic at least twice a week. They listen only to Dominican or Caribbean music (salsa). They read Dominican newspaper, such as *El Listín Diario, Hoy, El Siglo, Ultima Hora* or/and *El Nacional* almost daily, and some of them are affiliated to a political party in the Dominican Republic. They do not speak English at all, and most are here to make money and return in a better economic condition to the Dominican Republic.

New immigrants feel no tension between the United States (here) and the Dominican Republic (there). Their loyalties lie with the Dominican Republic. They perceive themselves as Dominicans whom economic circumstances have placed in a foreign country momentarily. The following testimony talks about the nostalgia, the desire to go back to the Dominican Republic, and the lack of attachment to the United States. Julio describes his position in the United States.

> I came in 1993. A friend helped me to get a passport and a residency card in New York City and I got a *machete*[4] in the Dominican Republic. . . . I came through Mayagüez, Puerto Rico. But there the immigration officer took my papers because I forgot my father's name well, the real passport owner's father's name. But he let me go asking me to report myself the next day at the Aguadilla INS office. Of course I did not. I went to my aunt's house on the other side of the island, until I was ready to travel to New York. . . . In May 1993, I came. I did not have any trouble in Puerto Rico's airport. . . . I came here to work hard because I am not staying here. I hate New York. Apartments are like prisons infested with roaches. The cold weather is like hell. You don't trust anybody, not even your relatives. I already sent my little car there and I am saving money and I am giving myself two more years here. I am going back.

Margarita, a Dominican who came to the United States in 1997 at the age of 27 said: "My mind is in the Dominican Republic, my body is here. I haven't traveled there since I came two years ago." As Julio and Margarita, the newest Dominican immigrants exhibit more loyalties to the home country. New York City is a place to work and save money to return to the Dominican Republic economically solvent. When I asked about their feelings about New York City and the Dominican Republic, twenty-five of my interviewees (out of ninety-eight) identified themselves as "true" Dominicans who came here because of economic circumstances and expressed their desire to return.

A primordial ethnicity emerges among new immigrants. The Spanish language, religion, foods, music, among other cultural traits become self-conscious after immigration. New immigrants embrace these values with a fervor that makes them "more Dominican than Dominicans themselves" (Guarnizo 1997: 167). Social and sports clubs, baseball leagues, churches, kinship networks, and workspaces provide a sense of togetherness and recreate what they have left behind. At the same time, new immigrants evolve ways of relating to other Dominicans in these social environments where they ventilate nostalgia and share information about the homeland. In so doing, new immigrants span themselves into two localities, New York and the Dominican Republic, exhibiting more loyalties to the Dominican Republic.

## ESTABLISHED DOMINICANS

I call established Dominicans those immigrants who have between ten and forty years of residency in the United States. On average, these Dominicans commonly phone the Dominican Republic once a month or less. They send money to the Dominican Republic from regularly to almost never. They listen to both American and Dominican/Latin music. They read both United States and Dominican newspapers, but they read more United States newspapers. Most of them do not belong to any political party in the Dominican Republic. Some of them are affiliated with both Dominican and American political parties. All of them are documented United States residents and most of them are naturalized. Some experience a transitional identity, having loyalties to both the sending and the receiving countries. In some cases, loyalties are stronger for the host society. Some others are immersed in a process of physical and emotional separation from the sending country. Some have learned to speak English and adapted to the United States ways.

Some established Dominicans still dream of returning to the homeland. They have been in the United States for the longest time since Dominican migration started in the early 1960s. They have worked here, saved money, and returned to the Dominican Republic. Mireya, for example, came to the New York City in 1967 from the Dominican Republic. She worked initially in a belt factory on 38th street. While working in this factory, she took English classes and eventually went to college where she finished an associate degree in psychology in 1977. She started to work as a counselor in a senior citizens center in upper Manhattan in 1979. She worked there for 17 years until her retirement in 1996. During those years she built a house in the Dominican Republic and planned for her retirement, which she finally accomplished in 1997. She left behind a daughter and a granddaughter who plan to visit at least once a year.

For others, the tension between here and there is significant. However, they are also in a process of *distanciamiento*/separation from the Dominican Republic. Pedro speaks of this experience.

> When I first came here in 1971, I felt my heart bled of pain from being separated from my land and from my family. I just dreamed of returning. But in 1973, my wife finally came. We had two daughters. They are now 22 and 23 years old. They are both in college. Yeah, you asked me where do I belong now and I have to tell you that I don't know. That's a contradiction I haven't solved but to be sincere I believe I belong here more than there.

Ana also portrays her experience.

> I was planning to repair my house back in the Dominican Republic but I would rather buy a house here. My first daughter is married here. She gave me a beautiful granddaughter. My second daughter is going to college this year. What is the use of having a house in the Dominican Republic when my life is here?

Both Pedro and Ana experience a tension between there and here. However both individuals seem to care more about the United States. Family attachments such as children born here make both of them to bind more to the host society.

For others, the tension does not exist and they live between two places without apparent conflicts. These Dominicans are usually naturalized Americans but hold Dominican citizenship. They own homes both in the United States and the Dominican Republic. They travel at least once a year. Their loyalties are both here and there. They belong to both U.S. and Dominican political parties. They are generally men.

An example of a transmigrant Dominican is the case of the well-known community leader, Dr. Rafael Lantigua. Dr. Lantigua is a naturalized immigrant who influenced politics both in the United States and the Dominican Republic. He is a leader of the Dominican Revolutionary Party (*Partido Revolucionario Dominicano*—PRD) and a leader of the Democratic Party in Washington Heights. Indeed, he might be considered the ideologue of Dominican politics of incorporation in New York City. But at the same time is the liaison between Dominican politics and Dominican-American politics.

## FROM TRANSMIGRANT BEHAVIORS TO POLITICS OF INCORPORATION

The multiplicity of allegiances exhibited by Dr. Lantigua as well as the emergence of a political Dominican-American identity is rooted in three factors. First, it is the political conditions in the Dominican Republic. Second, it is the presence of political parties in the Diaspora. Third, it is the political capital of Dominican immigrants.

The 1960s and 1970s witnessed a flow of Dominican migrants into the United States for political reasons. Those years were marked by political upheavals after Trujillo's death, the 1963 coup d'etat against the incumbent Juan Bosch, the 1965 U.S. military invasion, and the twelve years of Balaguer's semi-authoritarian regime (1966–78). These immigrants continued with their political activism in the receiving society, but with views and interests deeply rooted in the Dominican Republic. This activism permeated second-generation Dominicans and other Dominicans who came to the United States with their parents at a very early age.

Dominicans, who migrated to the United States to escape political repression during the turmoil that followed Trujillo's death in 1961 and during Balaguer's presidency, maintained their political activism in the United States. For instance, during the 1970s, a significant group of Dominicans in New York City used to parade from 125th Street to Dyckman Street in Washington Heights, every 28th of April to commemorate the 1965 United States military invasion of the Dominican Republic. They also created political parties that belonged to those in the Dominican Republic and commemorated Dominican historical events here in New York City. That kind of activism changed during the late 1970s.

In 1978, major political changes occurred in the Dominican Republic with the electoral triumph of the Dominican Revolutionary Party (*Partido Revolucionario Dominicano*—PRD). With the advent of a democratic government, it was expected that a significant return migration to the Dominican Republic would follow. But migration from the Dominican Republic to the United States continued unabated. However, the late 1970s marked a change in the political vision of the Dominican community, and two different political trends emerged. First, Dominican political parties, both from the right and left, but basically those parties that during the 1960s and 1970s were involved in political struggles against Balaguer's regime, assumed a dual political position. Among these parties is the PRD of which Dr. Rafael Lantigua became a liaison between Dominican politics in the Dominican Republic and Dominican-American politics in New York City. These political parties supported the political activities developed by Dominican-Americans in New York, and at the same time supported political activism back in the Dominican, publicly accepting their dual political commitment.

The second trend was that a group of Dominicans, some part of a second generation born in the United States, and others brought to the United States at a very early age, started to identify themselves as Dominican-Americans and started considering New York City as their home. These Dominicans started a conscious process characterized by two interconnected dimensions. One was the struggle to obtain political representation in the formal political structure of New York City. The second was the commitment to create influential community-based agencies that could provide services to empower the community.

## DOMINICAN-AMERICANS

Dominican-Americans are both established immigrants and second-generation Dominicans who have grown roots in the United States and identify themselves as Dominican-Americans or Dominican New Yorkers—holding an ethnic Dominican identity grounded in the host society. Moisés Pérez, executive director of Alianza Dominicana identify himself as a Dominican-American. This is his definition of the Dominican-American identity:

> I think we're becoming aware we're a permanent community in New York City. The younger kids don't have the linkages that older people have. They're urban creatures. They have an identity of being Dominicans, but New York Dominicans.

Dominican-Americans are a segment of the Dominican community who are basically, second-generation and Dominicans who migrated at a very early age. Many still identify themselves as Dominicans, but say that New York City is their home. Some of them, mostly the younger ones, visit the Dominican Republic once a year in the summer. They seldom call anyone in the Dominican Republic. They seldom send money to the Dominican Republic. They listen to both American music and Dominican/Latino music. They seldom read the Dominican newspaper. None of them belongs to a Dominican political party. Some of them, however, have an affiliation with the Democratic Party. Some belong to Parent Teacher's Association (PTAs), school boards, building and block, women, or youth organizations. Some others are community activists. They are United States citizens. Most of them are fluent in the English language and are comfortable in New York City urban environment. Some of them want to be buried in the United States.

How do second-generation Dominicans perceive themselves ethnically? When I asked Alexandra, a young Dominican college student with political aspirations, she told me that she was a Dominican-American. To learn she was a Dominican-American took her a long time. First, she thought she was Dominican and she went back to the Dominican Republic in search of her roots. One day, while in the Dominican Republic, she put on her jeans, a T-shirt, and her backpack because she was going to the beach. Her aunt stopped her, asking, "Where do you think you are going?" She thought she had lost her freedom. From that moment on, she understood she did not belong there and she came back to New York City to continue her search. Here she found herself and discovered she was a black Dominican woman, born in the United States, bilingual, raised in West Harlem and with a political attitude to change for the better her community. She was not like her sister, who in her own search, found herself into the African-American community, and so acting, dressing, and dancing as an African-American. Alexandra found something that she called "unique, different, the new *Dominicanidad.*"

During the course of my research, I found other second-generation Dominicans like Alexandra. They were also in search of their identities. Some have traveled to the Dominican Republic and like Alexandra, found out that their lives belong in New York City. Others are still searching.

Many Dominicans, especially Dominican community activists, also identified themselves as Dominican-Americans. One of them was very categorical when she told me she never read Dominican newspapers. "What for?" She added, "If the struggle is here. Besides, they don't understand us there." Another said that he never got involved in Dominican politics in the Dominican Republic. "Politics is here, we need to create a political niche here," he added.

Rosita Romero, the executive director of the Dominican Women's Development Center, Dominican-born, but residing in the United States since she was a child, knows that her place is in the United States. Even though she refuses to call herself a Dominican-American, she understands she belongs here and leads an organization to mobilize an important segment of the Dominican community, its women.

## NEW IMMIGRANTS, ESTABLISHED DOMINICANS, AND DOMINICAN-AMERICANS' INTERACTIONS

New and established Dominican immigrants, as well as Dominican-Americans, melt into the everyday life of Dominican New York, making it difficult to acknowledge these differences. Moreover, continuous immigration tends to obscure the political role of established immigrants and Dominican-Americans. In one single block along Broadway, one encounters the nostalgic feeling of the newly arrived, the duality of the established immigrant, and the activism of the Dominican-American.

During my research in Washington Heights, I observed these groups from an ethnographic perspective. One of the observations that struck me the most was the experience in the elevator at the 181st Street subway station. That summer afternoon in 1995, during the rush hour, the elevator was crowded. In the back of the elevator, next to me, two Dominican men, in their thirties, were talking in perfect English commenting on the candidacy of the Dominican-American Adriano Espaillat to the New York State Assembly. One of these men was holding the *Daily News.* Two young girls, also speaking English and probably returning from school, were laughing and looking at another group of boys standing next to them. A man and a woman, accompanied by two children, were speaking Spanish with a heavy *Cibaeño* accent. Another Dominican man, holding the *Listín Diario,* a Dominican newspaper, looked distant and thoughtful. That elevator was a micro-representation of Dominicans different experiences of migration, adaptation, and ethnic identity formation.

## COMPLEXITIES OF DOMINICAN ETHNIC IDENTITY

Issues of gender, social mobility and assimilation complicate Dominican ethnic identification in the United States. Gender is important in the creation of
identity. Women grow roots faster than men in the Diaspora as Chart 2
shows. For example, more women than men are naturalized, and have fewer
attachments to the Dominican Republic, such as plan to buy a house or fewer
levels of return migration.

Chart 2: Levels of Duality and *Distanciamiento/* Separation from the Dominican
Republic

|                                                    | Women | Men |
| -------------------------------------------------- | ----- | --- |
| Have U.S. Citizenship                              | 10    | 2   |
| In the process of obtaining U.S. Citizenship       | 8     | 2   |
| Own house in New York                              | 3     | 0   |
| Planning to buy a house in New York                | 6     | 2   |
| Have voted in the United States                    | 10    | 4   |
| Intend to vote in the United States in the future  | 15    | 4   |
| Participate in Dominican political party           | 0     | 6   |
| Send money to the Dominican Republic               | 10    | 6   |
| Own house in the Dominican Republic                | 1     | 1   |
| Plan to buy house in the Dominican Republic        | 0     | 4   |
| Plan to return to the Dominican Republic           | 5     | 6   |

In my interviews, the majority of Dominicans who fell into the primor-
dial/transmigrant identity are men. Only five women out of twenty-five considered themselves *birds of passage* in the United States. These women were
single. But when women were married and/or with children, they were
beyond the primordial/transmigrant immigrant ideology.

Sonia illustrates the case. Sonia and her daughter came to the United
States in 1996, following her husband. She overstayed her tourist visa. Even
though she was ineligible to work, she took free courses in English as a
Second Language, enrolled in a data entry class at a community center
Montefiore Hospital, and became a member of her daughter's school PTA.
Her husband filled out INS applications for her and his daughter. She got her
work permit in 1999 and started to work for Montefiore Hospital accounting
department. Her husband, a taxi driver, wants to return to the Dominican
Republic. In 1998, he shipped a car to the Dominican Republic to prepare for
the day when he goes for good. Sonia told him she was not going back. She
has a nice job. Her daughter is doing very well in school. She feels she
belongs here. Sonia is convinced that she is not coming back to the
Dominican Republic.

> There is a constant tension between my husband and me. I don't
> believe I have any future in the Dominican Republic. But he only

dreams of coming back.

The issue of return migration is the source of heated arguments between married couples in the Dominican community. As one of my informant told me:

> I want to stay here. He wants to go back. I won't give up. If he insists there is not solution but to separate.

Gender is a critical point for transmigrant theories. Women develop roots faster than men in this country. Women's allegiances switch faster to the host society. Why do women move faster than men to adapt? There are two reasons. First, women have more work, opportunities, and freedom in the United States than in the Dominican Republic. To this respect, Rosa argues:

> When I was in the Dominican Republic I was a teller in a bank. I made RD$2,000 a month less than US$200. Here even though I am unemployed at present I always manage to invent something such as selling clothing, perfumes, cleaning apartment off-books to have money in my pocket.

Many other of my interviewees, were not as lucky as Rosa. They were unemployed in the Dominican Republic, although some have completed four years of college.

In terms of freedom, Pessar and Grasmuck (1991) found that Dominican women enjoy more freedom here in the United States than in the Dominican Republic, having Dominican women weaker return migration than men. There are more laws—penalizing domestic violence and sexual harassment— and ways of enforcing them here in the United States than in the Dominican Republic. Freedom, however, goes beyond a legal system benefiting women. For many women, this freedom is translated into the liberty to escape the male figure, to discover their true self, to create their own spaces. Viviana's comments are illustrative.

> I came to the United States at the age of 27, widowed, and with two small children. I moved into my parents' apartment. And they were checking on me all the time. They wanted to control my life. I went to college, got a part-time job and moved into my own apartment. Now I am on control of my own life.

I asked Viviana if she could not achieve the same level of personal freedom in the Dominican Republic. "Well yes and no. Yes, if I had a good job, a house, money to pay my children private school and so on. No, if I were poor like I was there. But even if I had money in Dominican Republic, there is always your neighbor, your cousin, your mother's friend checking on you, if you came late, etc. Here I don't have to worry about that."

The stories of Sonia, Rosa, and Viviana tell about three Dominican women who fell well here than in the Dominican Republic. For reasons such as job and education opportunities, as well as personal freedom, these women have more allegiances to the United States.

Second, there is a gender difference in the ethnicity of Dominicans. In my sample men thought more about returning to their homelands and saving money to do so. Women, on the other hand, thought about their children and worked to provide them with all the privileges that United States society can offer. They, more than men, desired to learn English, both to help their children with homework and to communicate with their teachers. Women fought for bilingual education for these reasons, and also more likely than men to further their education here. My sample, also show that women were serious about becoming United States citizens and participating in politics. Women, in general, are led by a maternal instinct to better their community.

Temma Kaplan (1982), writing about early twentieth century women of Barcelona, Spain, identified a "female consciousness" that accepted the gender system of its society which assigned women the responsibility of "preserving life." Working class women shopped for necessities, secured fuel, and guarded their neighborhoods, mates, and children from danger, and saw these duties as their right. When external forces pressures intensified, they organized collectively and mobilized their communities to fulfill these obligations and protect their rights. A similar "female consciousness" was evident in the testimonies of many Dominican women, and also marked the activities of many women I describe later in this book.

Social mobility also complicates the ethnic identification of Dominicans. While women independently of upward social mobility move faster to an identification with the host society, men are different. Many men with a college education who speak English and who have steady jobs regardless of marital status and children are distant immigrants. I mean by distant immigrants that they start to identify more with the host society. Typically, men with less than college education, not speaking English, are transmigrants with more inclinations to the sending society.

Standards indicators of incorporation, such as knowledge of the English language, education, and political participation in the host society, bring established Dominican immigrants closer to the values and norms of the United States. Assimilation, however, does not "melt" immigrants into the mainstream society. Scholars have argued in the past that when immigrants try to enter mainstream society, they learn about their true status in this society. In this case, ethnicity is translated into ethnic mobilization to lobby both political, economic, and social vindications for the immigrant community. Another group of Dominicans have advanced primordial ethnicity to a mobilizationist perspective. Here ethnicity is created in the context of adjustment to the host society. Ethnic ties and solidarity are crucial to mobilize the ethnic community for economic, social, and political vindications.[5]

## THE RECONSTITUTION OF ETHNIC CULTURE: THE NEW *DOMINICANIDAD*

I traveled with about fifty Dominican youths from New York City to Rhode Island in the summer of 1999. The youths belonged to the Alianza Dominicana Folkloric Group. They were going to perform in the Dominican American Roundtable to be held in Providence. This event was hosted by dozens of Dominican organizations from New York City, Providence, Boston, and Miami.

Outside the bus, Iván Domínguez, the folkloric group director, shouted, *"jóvenes, jóvenes, jóvenes* stop that and get in the bus."　They just finished putting in the bus trunk the costumes, drums, masks, and other items for their presentation. *Bachata* music was blasting and a few youth were dancing in the sidewalk outside Alianza Dominicana. Finally, after Iván's remarks they all went into the bus. Inside, one listened to the shifting from Spanish to English and vice versa; merengue and *bachata* music. Then, they tuned one single radio to "El Vacilón de la Mañana."[6] People laughed at the jokes they were telling on the radio. Minute later, American music—hip-hop, reggae, and rapping— started to blast the air until we arrived in Rhode Island. In the meantime, people passed salami, *mangú*,[7] fried white cheese, and crackers from one seat to the other. Two youths danced to hip-hop music in the bus aisle. In Providence, at the roundtable, I saw these youths dancing to the most traditional Dominican music with an elegance and skill I never dreamed of observing outside the Dominican Republic. Some of them have never returned to the island after they migrated ten or eleven years ago. Some were born here. On our way back to New York City, I spoke to them.

Rosa Ventura is a 17-year-old who perceives herself as Dominican-American and who sings typical Dominican folk songs such as *salves, pregones, coco, palos, décimas,* and meregues and also plays the *güiro, pandero and valsié* for the folkloric group. She came to the United States when she was 10 years old, eats hamburgers, dresses hip-hop style, and listens to soft rock. She will graduate from high school in 1999 and is planning to go to college and become a physical therapist. She also wants to write short stories based on her diary.

Dario Hernández came here when he was five years old, in 1985. He also perceives himself as Dominican-American. He is in his third semester in college majoring in liberal arts. He likes to speak English, listens to rock and roll, and watches American television. He also dresses in hip-hop style. He joined the Alianza Dominicana Folkloric Group in 1996. Dario comments that the group kept him away from trouble, taught him discipline, and is fun. He is a great dancer of Dominican typical dances.

Many other youths belonging to the Alianza Dominicana folkloric dance group identified themselves as Dominican-American. What makes them American? Most answered that it was the language, the music, food, and clothing. Girls added to this list the way of American thinking, more freedom, and opportunities for women. What makes them Dominican? Most answered that it was the culture, such as the language, the food, the music, the history, and skin color. Another woman told me that what makes her American are the rights of an American citizen, and what makes her Dominican is the food at her mother's house, and the Dominican accent, "the way we speak Spanish." When I asked Arelis Figueroa if she was a Dominican-American, she answered:

> Am I a Dominican-American? I don't know. First of all, I am very skeptical about the use of that term because it reinforces the misconception that the United States is in fact America, when we all know that America is the continent, including South, Central, and North America. Now, if by Dominican-American you mean a person that is involved and concerned with the political and social life in this country, a person who pays taxes and fulfills her duties and rights to the best of her knowledge then I am a Dominican-American.

When I listen to these youths, I could not place them in the Dominican Republic. They were different from Dominicans in the Dominican Republic. They dress, talk, eat, and think differently from other teenagers in the Dominican Republic. But I could not say they were unhyphenated Americans either. "American" is such a vague label if is not related to race and social class. There is not a single definition of American. The values and norms of white middle class Americans are significantly different from the values and norms of the white working class or white unemployed, not to mention the void between the norms and values of African-Americans and whites in general. They were not white Americans; they were not African-Americans. They are Americans who retain cultural, ethnic and linguistic differences, struggling to avoid becoming second-class citizens. They were Dominican-Americans, new Dominicans.

Certain theories pertain to explain hyphenated identities, or what Blauner calls the reconstitution of ethnic culture. According to Blauner (1972), the rejection experienced by immigrants and their descendants in their attempts to become fully assimilated constitutes a central element in the reconstitution of ethnic culture. This culture is not a mere continuation of that originally brought by immigrants, but is a distinct, emergent product. It is forged in the interaction of the group with the dominant majority, incorporating some aspects of the core culture and lending privilege to those aspects from the past that appear most suited in the struggle for self-worth and social mobility. David Vicente defines this reconstituted *dominicanidad*.

I am a bilingual/multicultural individual. I feel I don't belong there
but I am looking for a cultural and existential integration here in the
United States because I am here, both my mind and my body. It is not
enough that our body is here and our mind there. We need to integrate our bodies and our minds so we can stand up and contribute to
the development of our Dominican community here.

David Vicente has appropriated the language of the host society but has
retained his mother tongue. For him, multiculturalism works as an integra-
tional identity important to the development of the Dominican community
in the Diaspora.

## ETHNIC IDENTIFICATION AND THE DOMINICAN COMMUNITY

Ethnic identification is a social construction that starts only after migration.
In this sense, "identities brought to the United States are reassembled into
'ethnicities' within the contemporary forced-field of the majority culture and
its others" (Davis 2000: 16). A common sense of ethnicity emerges only when
ones leaves the homeland and arrives in a different nation. In the homeland
individuals never thought of themselves as an ethnic group or as foreigners.
The process of identifying themselves as an ethnic group occurred only when
they came to a foreign land and shared their space with people of different
nationalities and races. They become "a segment of larger society whose
members are thought, by themselves and/or others, to have a common origin and to share important segments of a common culture and who, in addition, participate in shared activities in which common origin and culture are
significant ingredients" (Yinger 1985: 151–180). Yinger's definition fits Dominicans
in New York City.

However, there are different categories and levels of identification
among Dominicans. In the Dominican community converge new immigrants, established immigrants, and Dominican-Americans. The following
chart 3 defines the allegiances and identification of each Dominican group in
the United States.

**Chart 3: Levels of Dominican Ethnic Identity**

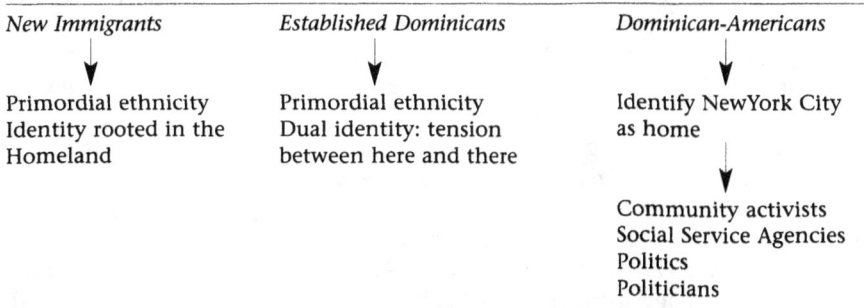

| *New Immigrants* | *Established Dominicans* | *Dominican-Americans* |
|---|---|---|
| ↓ | ↓ | ↓ |
| Primordial ethnicity | Primordial ethnicity | Identify New York City |
| Identity rooted in the | Dual identity: tension | as home |
| Homeland | between here and there | |
| | | ↓ |
| | | Community activists |
| | | Social Service Agencies |
| | | Politics |
| | | Politicians |

This ethnic identification affects the process of community formation and
political mobilization. While new immigrants navigate in the illusion of

returning home (the Dominican Republic) and old immigrants struggle to solve the dilemma of here or there, Dominican-Americans mobilize all Dominicans to empower their community. When Dominicans identify New York City as home, they start organizing themselves to create a voice and influence the political arena in the city and nationwide.

Becoming aware of social afflictions and discrimination creates the conditions for both a discovery of immigrant otherness and the will to be organized. In the late 1970s, a group of Dominican parents identified a series of anomalies in their school district in Washington Heights. They organized and in the next school board elections they took control of the school board directive. In 1985 a group of Dominicans, mostly women, in Washington Heights, found out their landlord's intentions to raise the rent, even though they were lacking heat and the apartments were roach-infested. They called for a tenant meeting, crafted a directive that went to New York City Housing Authority. Eventually, the tenants became owners of the building.

Ethnic identification is central to social change in immigrant communities. When Dominicans reach the stage of identifying New York City as home, they become activists. Ethnic identification is the catalyst shifting an entire community from settlers to political selves. Cruz (1998) portrayed a group of Puerto Rican migrants who settled in Hartford and acquired an ethnic awareness. Ethnicity led them to collective behavior and eventually to political empowerment, transforming the political landscape of Hartford. According to Portes and Rumbaut (1990: 95), the first foreign-born generation lacks "voice." Descendants of the first immigrants, however, have gained voice and have used it to reaffirm identities and to empower themselves. In the Dominican case, identity formation beyond transmigrant behaviors influences the formation of a Dominican political community rooted in the United States, supplying the understanding Dominicans are in New York City to stay.

**NOTES**

1. Angel Taveras lost the Democratic primary by a very small margin.

2. William Yancey, Eugene Ericksen, and Richard Juliani, "Emergent Ethnicity: A Review and Reformulation, *American Sociological Review*, 76 (1976): 391–403, accept the concept of "emergent ethnicity," where residential segregation, occupational concentration, and other structural factors in the host society are the sources of ethnicity. Other authors have expanded this ethnicity perspective, including economic competition and the level of discrimination against a group, as factors also explaining emergent ethnicity (Michael Banton, *Racial and Ethnic Competition*, New York: Cambridge University Press, 1983; Frederick Bath (ed.) *Ethnic Groups Boundaries*, Boston: Little Brown, and Company, 1969; Edna Bonacich and John Modell, *The Economic Basis of Ethnic Solidarity: Small Business in the Japanese American Community*, Berkeley: University of California Press, 1980; Susan Olzak and

Joane Nagel (eds.) *Competitive Ethnic Relations*, New York: Academic Press, 1986).

3. Social scientists emphasize primordial ethnicity as fundamental in the process of ethnic identity formation yet recognize that minority groups whose members share many commonalities in physical characteristics, culture, religion, etc. are likely to maintain a higher level of ethnicity that other groups with fewer commonalities (Harold Abramsom, *Ethnic Diversity in Catholic America*, New York, John Wiley, 1973; Andrew Greely, *Ethnicity in the United States: A Prelimanary Reconnaissance*, New York: John Wiley, 1976).

4. A machete is the picture in a passport with a stamped visa or a residency card that is replaced with the picture of the person trying to enter the United States illegally.

5. The assimilation viewpoint as presented by Milton Gordon in *Assimilation in American Life: The Role of Race, Religion, and National Origin*, New York: Oxford University Press, 1964, is that contact between a new foreign minority and an established majority will lead, through a series of stages, to an eventual merging of values, symbols, and identity. This integration into a single society offers the minority the possibility of access to positions of higher prestige and power. Several quite different theories view immigrant adaptation from other perspectives. For instance, Michael J. Piore's *Birds of Passage: Migrant Labor and Industrial Societies*, New York: Cambridge University Press, 1979 argues that greater knowledge of the core language and culture by immigrants and greater familiarity with members of the dominant group do not necessarily lead to more positive attitudes and more rapid assimilation. Such conditions can lead precisely to the opposite, as immigrants discover their objective economic position and are exposed to racist ideology directed against them. According to Piore, immigrant groups may learn the language, become thoroughly familiar with the values and life styles of the majority and be completely integrated into the economic structure, but still not abandon their distinct cultural traits and self-identities and may even resist further assimilation. Nathan Glazer and Daniel P. Moyniham (*Beyond the Melting Pot*, Cambridge: MIT Press, 1968) emphasize ethnic consciousness and the ethnic resilience of ethnic culture as instruments of political resistance by minorities.

6. "El Vacilón de la Mañana" is a radio program in "La Mega," a New York radio station broadcasting in Spanish.

7. *Mangú* is a typical Dominican food made of mashed plantain.

CHAPTER 3
# Dominicans at the Margins

A COMMON TOPIC OF CONVERSATION BETWEEN DOMINICANS IN NEW YORK CITY, even inspiring merengues lyrics, is the hard economic life in the city. As Ramón, a taxi driver, would put it:

> The situation in New York City is tough. Things are not as they used to be when the first Dominicans came thirty years ago. There are not jobs. Apartment rents are very high. One spends one hundred pesos [dollars] in two or three small bags in the supermarket. For nothing, they shoot and kill you. New York is not the same as yesterday. Opportunities are gone.

A scholarly, yet similar, view is presented by John Mollenkopf and Manuel Castells in their introduction to *Dual City*:

> Wall Street may make New York one of the nerve centers of the global capitalism system, but this dominant position has a dark side in the ghettos and barrios, where a growing population of poor people lives. (1991: 3)

New York is a city of both opulence and poverty. Most Dominicans live with its poverty. Unemployment, underemployment, welfare dependency, poor quality public schools, expensive food prices, crime, and high rents, among others factors plague many New York City neighborhoods, including Dominican neighborhood. Even though these social afflictions have always been present, the United States labor market has historically been able to employ most immigrants and alleviate the situation by providing for future generations. Today, there are fewer employment opportunities.

31

But in spite of adverse social conditions, Dominicans continue to migrate to the United States and create and re-create their ethnic community. Why do Dominicans continue to migrate to the United States? I point to several reasons. The living conditions in the Dominican Republic are very precarious not comparable to the economic situation in New York City. Biased information about the United States portrayed by immigrants and the media distort reality and create the illusion of a country where the streets are paved with gold. The process of migration and settlement in the new society is problematic. Immigrants learned the truth about the hardship of this country. Many work very hard to save money and come back to the Dominican Republic. Others feel deceived. Many others learned that by adapting—learning the English language, pursuing an education, involving into politics—may be the key of success.

This chapter narrates the economic changes in the United States that affect migratory flows and labor market conditions. Specifically, it places the socioeconomic position of Dominicans in New York City in historical perspective. It looks at the transformation of the labor market, the persistence of poverty, and lack of education as the major factors contributing to the structural position of Dominicans at the bottom of the socioeconomic ladder and placing them at the margin of society. The understanding of these social factors is central to the development of an ethnic political consciousness among Dominicans. In a society with limitations to advance economically, ethnic politics is one of the doors still open for immigrants to achieve power.

This analysis is underlined with a comparison between the immigration waves of Italians, Jews, and Poles at the end of the nineteenth century and of Mexicans, Puerto Ricans, and Dominicans during the post World War II period.

## IMMIGRATION TO THE UNITED STATES: THEN AND NOW

The United States is a nation of immigrants. Since pre-colonial times, immigrants have come to this land in search of freedom and economic advancement. The British came as colonizers. African-Americans were forced into slavery, providing much of the labor needed at the time. English, Dutch, French, Swedish, Welsh, Scottish, Irish, Jewish, German, Scandinavian, Japanese, and Chinese immigrants also came to the United States in significant numbers searching for economic advancement and religious and political freedom. Toward the end of the nineteenth century and during the capitalist boom and labor shortage, large numbers of Italians, Russian Jews, Poles, Czechs, Hungarians, Bulgarians, Austrians, and Greeks began to arrive for the same reasons. Chinese and Japanese also came as labor immigrants to the United States in the latter part of the nineteenth and early twentieth century.

Between 1881 and 1890, more than five million European immigrants from England, Ireland, Germany, France, and the Scandinavian countries arrived in the United States. From 1890 to 1910, close to nine million new immigrants arrived. Two-thirds of these came from East-Central and Southern Europe (Kennedy 1964: 5). Scholars have pointed out that the increase in immigration from Europe to the United States coincided with shifts in the structure of the American economy. "The powerful drive toward industrial consolidation and monopoly displaced agriculture as the dominant sector of the economy . . . and the new urban-based industries generated a strong demand for manual labor" (Portes and Bach 1985: 30). According to these scholars, what the new industries required was a mass of unskilled workers who could be hired cheaply. Labor demand grew due to large railroad and canal construction projects. Domestic labor scarcity was met by European labor.

European immigrants witnessed tremendous economic growth in the United States during this period. By the 1920s, per capita income in the United States was the highest of any industrialized country (Muller 1993: 75). According to Muller, in the ten most affluent states in 1920, one of every four residents was an immigrant. The wealthier industrial states, which included Connecticut, Illinois, Massachusetts, New Jersey, and New York, attracted a high proportion of the second wave of Eastern and Southern European immigrants, who became primarily factory workers. New York State, for example, which absorbed more immigrants than any other state, increased its per capita income 3.7 times between 1880 and 1920.

World War I altered the structure of the American economy and the role of immigrants in it (Portes and Bach 1985: 48). European immigration ceased to be the prime supplier of low-wage labor and had to be replaced by other, primarily domestic sources, such as African-American. During the 1930s, immigration dropped drastically. This fall can be attributed to the Depression and the final implementation of the national origins system.[1] While economic depression reduced the demand for labor, the National Origins System restricted migration from European countries and other foreign sources of labor.

After World War II, immigration to the United States accelerated due to the industrial and agricultural boom of the Cold War period.[2] In the 1940s, the United States fostered the immigration of Mexicans to work in the agricultural sector of the economy. Some Mexicans, however, lived in the United States long before the 1940s. Large numbers of Mexicans became United States subjects in the mid-1800s when California, Arizona, New Mexico, Texas, and Colorado were annexed to the United States after the conclusion of the Mexican-American War in 1846–47.[3] Another large wave of Mexicans came to the United States through immigration between 1880 and 1929. After World War II, the American agricultural sector benefited from Mexican immigrants who came through the Bracero Program.[4] Since then, millions of Mexicans have continuously migrated to the United States.

The United States also attracted thousands of Puerto Ricans to work in the booming manufacturing sector in the New York region. Puerto Ricans came to the United States during the 1940s and the 1950s to supply the labor for a booming industrial sector on the East Coast of the United States and elsewhere.[5] In 1959, the United States witnessed the immigration of thousands of Cubans fleeing the island after Fidel Castro came to power.

After 1965 a new flow of immigrants arrived in the United States. The Immigration Act of 1965 opened the door to people from Asia, Latin America, and even from Africa and the Middle East. Among these groups were Dominicans. This act established an annual quota of 290,000 for each country, plus family reunification provisions (Yang 1995: 15). Indeed, the major source of immigration shifted from Europe to countries colonized by Europe. From 1955 to 1965, one-half of the new immigrants were born in Europe, but in the next decade the figure declined to less than one-third.

During the period between 1901 and 1997, the highest level of migration from southern Europe to the United States was in 1901. The year 1991 was another peak year for immigration to the United States, when the Dominican Republic sent the larger number to New York City, and Mexico was the point of origin for most immigrants to the United States in general (United States Immigration and Naturalization Service, 1999a).

## DOMINICAN MIGRATION

The Dominican Republic has been the top country sending the most immigrants to New York City (see Map 1).

**Map 1: The Caribbean Region Showing the Domican Republic.**

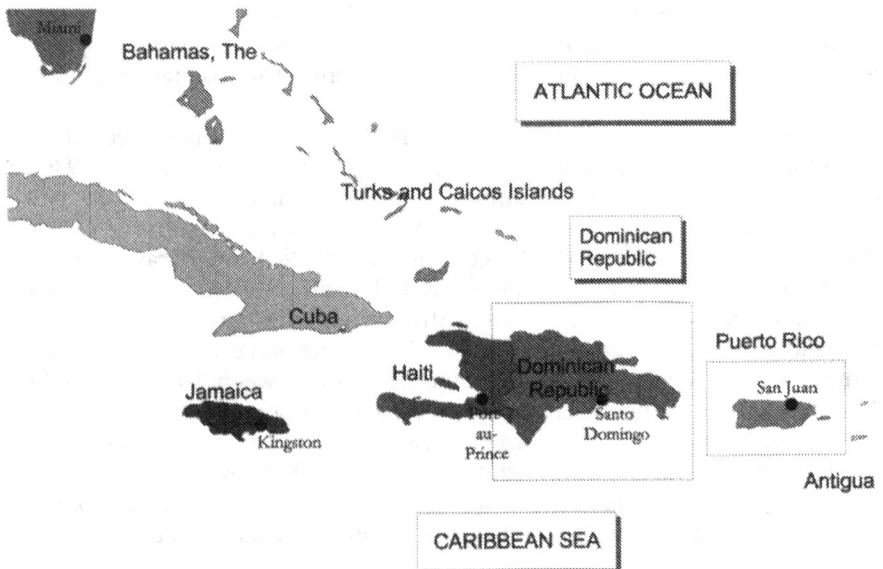

As Table 1 shows, the Dominican Republic was the number one source of immigrants to New York City in the 1970s and 1980s, and maintained that position in the early 1990s. In 1995 the former Soviet Union became the major source of immigrants to the city.

**Table 1: Immigrants by Country of Birth to New York City—Annual Average**

|  | 1972–79 | 1982–89 | 1990–94 |
|---|---|---|---|
| All Immigrants | 78,477 | 85,602 | 112,598 |
| Dominican Rep. | 9,997 | 14,470 | 22,028 |
| Former Soviet U. | 2,664 | 1,347 | 13,260 |
| China | 5,190 | 8,985 | 11,960 |
| Jamaica | 6,636 | 9,043 | 6,584 |
| Guyana | 3,244 | 6,705 | 6,153 |
| Poland | 897 | 985 | 3,907 |
| Philippines | 1,927 | 1,692 | 3,476 |
| Trinidad and Tobago | 3,501 | 1,690 | 3,176 |
| Haiti | 3,602 | 5,102 | 2,991 |
| India | 2,857 | 2,505 | 2,897 |
| Ecuador | 2,793 | 2,241 | 2,796 |
| Ireland | 351 | 534 | 2,481 |
| Colombia | 2,579 | 2,851 | 2,262 |
| Bangladesh | 123 | 416 | 1,911 |
| Korea | 1,741 | 2,514 | 1,725 |

Source: New York City Department of City Planning, The Newest New Yorkers, 1990–1994. New York City Department of City Planning, December 1996: 10–11.

Part of the decline in flows to New York City was a result of a two percent decline in Dominican flows to the United States as a whole. But the primary reason was the increasing propensity of Dominicans to bypass New York City. States such as Rhode Island, Massachusetts, and Florida are attracting more Dominicans. In the 1980s, 61 percent of Dominicans coming to the United States settled in New York City; 55 percent came in the early 1990s and 50 percent in 1995 and 1996 (New York City Department of City Planning 1999: 19). Dominican migration has been continuous and has increased from the early 1960s to the early 1990s, as Chart 4 illustrates.

**Chart 4: Dominican Migration to the United States, 1981–2000**

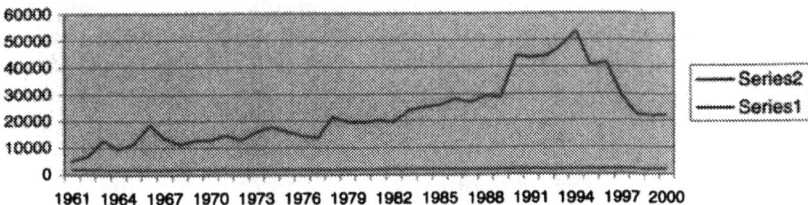

Dominicans migrating to the United States during the 1960s have been identified by earlier studies as migrants of predominantly rural origins. Hendricks
(1974), for example, identified Dominican immigrants in New York City as
mostly peasants from a mountain village in the province of Santiago, in the
northern Cibao region. Other studies have demonstrated that Dominican
migrants were more urban and middle class at least during the 1970s
(Grasmuck 1983; Ugalde, et al. 1979). Yet, other scholars later argued that
even those rural international migrants originated primarily in the sector of
medium and large farmers (Pessar 1982).[6]

Several studies showed Dominican international migration during the
1960s and 1970s to be the result of capitalist penetration and the modernization of the Dominican state. Bray (1984: 219) argues that capitalist development neglected the improvement of a nascent middle class in the Dominican
Republic, a class that eventually found the opportunity to achieve a better life
through international migration. From another perspective, migration from
the Dominican Republic to the United States has occurred because of the
linkages with the United States that were formed during the U.S. invasion of
1965 (Sassen 1992: 15) or the permanent presence of the United States in the
Dominican Republic during the last two centuries (Torres-Saillant and
Hernandez 1998). On the other hand, the recomposition of capitalism that
allowed a great number of factories to move into the Caribbean islands,
Mexico, and Southeast Asia, and the increase of the service sector in the
United States have encouraged migration processes to cities such as New York
(Sassen 1992:19 ).[7] Dominicans have also migrated to countries such as
Venezuela in the 1970s and European countries during the 1980s and 1990s.

## SHIFTING GROUNDS: THE IMMIGRANT FLOWS AND THE LABOR MARKET

When new immigrants entered the United States in 1965, the United States
economy had begun to shift. Manufacturing started to leave en masse the
New York region in the 1960s, leaving thousand of Puerto Ricans and
Dominicans unemployed and a new wave of immigrants condemned to work
in dead-end jobs in the service sector and in the leftovers of the manufacturing sector. In spite of a major transformation of the United States economy
that created fewer opportunities in industrial employment, immigration to
the United States continued to grow. However, new immigrants contribution
to the United States labor force was much smaller than at the turn of the century. Portes and Bach (1985: 53) argue that even if all adult immigrants aged
16 to 44 were considered to have joined the labor force, this proportion represents about one-tenth of the annual average between 1900 and 1914 and is
even lower than during the 1920s.

Labor market transformations reflected the process of deindustrialization
in the United States.[8] Industries were moved from the United States to Third
World countries in search of boosting profits. Part of the manufacturing sec-

tor moved to the southern United States, Mexico, Southeast Asia, and the Caribbean, and a new sector emerged in the United States: the service sector.

It has been calculated that during the five years between January 1981 and January 1986, nearly eleven million workers lost their jobs as a result of plant closing (Kamel 1990: 20). Plant closings hurt Latinos very especially. Puerto Ricans were concentrated in the Northeast, where employment opportunities in the garment and textile industries have declined sharply (Bean and Tienda 1987: 286). Similarly, the declining employment opportunities in many large, industrialized cities in the Midwest (Michigan, Ohio, Indiana, and Illinois) during the 1970s and 1980s also explains rising unemployment rates for Mexican men because of their concentration in these labor markets. After deindustrialization, the United States economy experienced an expansion that improved the availability of certain kinds of jobs in the nation. Over ten million jobs were gained nationwide by 1993 (Sanjek 1998: 122).

In New York City, these economic changes went through different stages. First, the city practically went bankrupt due to mismanagement by politicians, bankers, and unions in the 1970s (Tabb 1982: 1). Second, this fiscal crisis occurred in the context of the decline of the industrial Northeast and the transformation of its cities to suit the purposes of major corporations and service industries. Third, federal expenses cut the budget for social issues such as education and health in the urban setting. According to Tabb (1982) and Lankevich (1998), the federal government decreased its interest in the older cities. Government emphasis was placed on plant modernization and office construction for the corporate elite. Economic and political concerns were accompanied by declining real wages, higher taxes, unemployment, and fewer public services for working people. The long default, as William Tabb explains, was the process by which providing tax incentives and infrastructural investment for private capital, the government financed its own crisis (Tabb 1982: 4). This model fostered further social service cutbacks and continued redistribution from the poor to the wealthy.

Fourth, the movement of white people—largely the descendants of Irish, Italian, and Jewish immigrants-second-and third-generations— from the city to suburbia had a great impact on New York during the 1950s, 1960s, and 1970s. White flight from the city to the suburbs accelerated urban social afflictions. Thousands residents left the city and took their jobs with them. The number of commuters from Westchester County to Manhattan has risen 50 percent since 1950, and the percentage of New Yorkers traveling northward to jobs increased an amazing 500 percent from 1950 to 1970 (Lankevich 1998: 210). All of these structural changes increased unemployment rates in New York City. For example, manufacturing employment in New York City reached a peak of 1,073,000 workers in 1947 and had declined 12 percent by 1960. By 1970, a further 121,000 manufacturing jobs had been lost, and by 1977 another 287,000 (Tabb 1982: 75). Sanjek (1998) argues that contemporary New York City has three economies: the speculative-electronic economy, the real economy, and the underground economy. The speculative-electronic economy is based on global trading in currency and security values. This type of employment has shrunk over the last few decades. For example, in 1995 New York had 13,000 fewer jobs in the securities business (Sanjek 1998: 123). The real economy of goods and services provides the basics of daily life: food, clothing, machinery, housing, transportation, health care, and repairs. Its decline as a source of employment for New Yorkers between 1980 and 1996 was due in part to job dispersal to the suburbs and other regions of the United States as well as abroad, and in part to new productive technologies and downsizing policies that required fewer workers (Sanjek 1998: 119). An underground economy expanded as a consequence of diminishing opportunities in the real economy. Through the underground economy, a vast army of unemployed New Yorkers managed to survive. Some people received public assistance, others begged on the streets, still others labored in the unreported, unrecorded, underground cash economy (Sanjek 1998: 131). More than other groups, Latinos have been adversely affected by labor market changes in the city. Many Latinos and especially Dominicans in New York City hold on to the underground economy to survive economically.

## DOMINICANS IN A TRANSFORMED ECONOMY

Dominicans, as part of the new wave of immigrants, were affected by labor market transformations in the United States. In 1970 and for about ten years after the first major wave of Dominicans came to New York City, the city suffered a dramatic economic shift that plummeted the socioeconomic standards of Dominicans in the city.

In the 1960s and 1970s, a significant number of Dominicans in New York City were blue-collar and service workers, mainly employed in light manufacturing, particularly in the garment industry (Pessar 1987, Grasmuck and Pessar 1991). But Dominicans lost nearly half of the positions they held in this sector, reducing their labor force participation from 48.6 percent in 1970 to 25.7 percent in 1980 (Torres-Saillant and Hernández 1998: 71).

Much academic work on Dominicans in the United States has concentrated on the migrants incorporation into the U.S. labor market. Gurak and Kritz (1987) compared Dominican and Colombian women in New York City, stressing their major sociodemographic and labor market characteristics, and concluding that Colombians were better educated, had a more urban background, and were more skilled than Dominicans. Following the same argument, Pessar (1987) argued that the majority of Dominicans in New York City were blue-collar and service workers, mainly employed in light manufacturing, particularly in the garment industry. Later, Grasmuck and Pessar (1991) again concluded that Dominicans were basically blue-collar and service workers.

Both studies correctly stress that Dominican labor was basically employed in light manufacturing during the 1970s. During the 1980s, however, Dominicans suffered the consequences of structural transformations in

New York City, which affected the labor force in three ways. First, Dominicans reduced their participation in the manufacturing sector, which provoked increasing unemployment. Second, Dominicans were inserted in the service sector of the economy. Third, Dominicans explored new possibilities for making a living in the informal sector of the economy.

Despite high rates of unemployment, many Dominicans have become self-employed, developing their own businesses. Studies have shown that Dominicans have created a network of small businesses to serve the needs of the Dominican community. Portes and Guarnizo (1991) estimated that during the 1980s, Dominicans owned more than 20,000 businesses in New York City, particularly grocery stores (*bodegas*), taxi cab companies, sweatshops, travel agencies, and restaurants. Another study found an average of 12 Dominican businesses per block between 157th and 191st streets in the Washington Heights neighborhood (Mahler 1989). However, contrary to these studies, some other research (Hernández et all. 1995), has portrayed Dominicans as one of the poorest groups in the city, and challenged earlier studies claiming that significant proportions of Dominicans were self-employed. While Portes and Guarnizo (1991) and Mahler (1989) relied on ethnographic research, Hernández et al. (1995) based their study on census data. Census data tend to overlook the daily reality of a large numbers of individuals who often rely on income outside the formal economy. They are in the underground economy.

The case of one of my interviewees in Washington Heights illustrates the shortcomings of census data in explaining the reality of immigrants income. Luz is a single mother of three. According to the census count, she and her children live below the United States poverty line. They receive less than $500 in cash and food stamps every month from public assistance. However, besides receiving public assistance, Luz sells Avon and Amway products among neighbors and friends. She also babysits for her working neighbors. These income-generating activities allow this woman and her children to improve the quality of their lives. This example indicates the shortcomings of relying exclusively on official data. More studies are needed that combine both quantitative and qualitative research to address the position of Dominicans in the United States economy. Furthermore, the distinction between beings self-employed—which Luz was—and being a business owner—which she was not—should be made for analytical purposes.

## ECONOMIC RESTRUCTURING, EDUCATION AND POVERTY

The United States labor market has become highly competitive. Education attainment is essential to compete for the good jobs. Latinos and Dominicans in particular lack education. In spite of a relatively long presence in this country, Latino immigrants continue to be at the bottom of American society. This inequality is explained by a multiplicity of factors, such as the lack of fluency in English language and educational limitations, as well as the growth of an urban underclass, and residential segregation.

In terms of educational attainment, Latinos have shown improvement, but they continue to lag behind blacks and whites. In 1997, the Population Reference Bureau reported that Latinos have the lowest rates of high school and college graduation of any major group (Population Reference Bureau 1997: 4). Dominicans do not escape this reality. Research has portrayed Dominicans as one of the least educated groups in New York City, having the highest numbers of persons twenty-five years of age who had not completed high school and the smallest numbers of people who had completed college (Torres-Saillant and Hernández 1998: 72). For instance, at Uptown High School, with a student population that is 90 percent Dominican, only 25 percent of students graduate (López 1998: 85).

According to William Julius Wilson, the underclass and the persistence of poverty for African-Americans is a consequence of the economic restructuring of the 1970s and 1980s that left million of workers jobless (Wilson 1990). What is the meaning of the underclass and persistent poverty to the Latino community of the United States? Joan Moore and Raquel Pinderhughes (1993) argue that even though economic restructuring for Latinos also provokes the same social afflictions as in African-American neighborhoods, social processes in the Latino community are different. First, the Latino community does not suffer from higher rates of unemployment but from the quality of jobs Latinos get. Most of the expanding low-wage service and manufacturing industries, like electronics and garment manufacturing, employ Latinos ... and some depend almost completely on immigrant labor working at minimum wage (Moore and Pinderhughes 1993: xxvi). Second, and similar to Sanjek's argument, the role of the informal sector and illicit economies also impact Latinos as well as other minority communities differently. Velez-Ibañez (1993: 173–194) explains that the underclass debate has neglected the significant income-generating informal and illicit activities that are part of survival strategies and an important part of community life.

These structural factors have left Dominicans with few opportunities for economic advancement. According to a study conducted by Hernández et al. (1995), the income of the Dominican population is one of the lowest in New York City, and the poverty rate of Dominican households is over 36 percent, making them one of highest in the city. The unemployment rate of Dominicans was close to twice that of the overall population in New York.

## CONCLUSION

The interplay of social conditions, especially economic restructuring, has shaped Dominicans' socioeconomic status and their communities in New York City, leaving them in poverty. Poverty and unemployment are pervasive in the Dominican community of New York. A comparison to immigrants who came to the United States at the end of the nineteenth century shows a different pattern. European immigration slowed down significantly after the passage of the National Origin Acts, and second-generation Europeans benefited from the boom during War World II and the postwar economic bonanza. Latino immigration to the United States has been continuous and increasing since the 1950s. Dominicans, in particular, have experienced continuous and increasing records of migration to the United States from the 1960s to the present. Moreover Dominicans have disproportionately suffered from the transformation in the United States labor market that brought unemployment and poverty to the Latino population.

Labor market shifting from an industrial to a service economy left millions of workers jobless. Latinos and specifically Dominicans suffered the highest figures of unemployment and underemployment because they lacked the education to compete in the newly structured labor market. These socioeconomic indicators explain the location of Dominicans at the other extreme of the "dual city" and at the margins of society.

Structural constraints, however, are important in shaping Dominican identities in the diaspora. Adverse social and economic conditions fuel ethnicity. On one hand, immigrants learned that a venue of advancement is through education and learning the English language. As a response to economic limitations, they experience a desire to belong, to learn the skills to succeed in the new environment. In another word, assimilation is viewed as a weapon to better their conditions. But fully assimilation is never achieved. Rather Dominicans experience a reconstituted ethnicity.

On the other hand, ethnic politics is another venue to achieve power and to transform the social conditions affecting Dominicans. The Dominican-American leadership awareness of the importance of both politics of empowerment and electoral politics is demonstrated in the role of social service agencies empowering Dominicans and processes of community control in Washington Heights. In summary, the incorporation of Dominicans is stimulated by the social conditions generated by postindustrial New York City.

Indeed, Dominicans are poor, but socially, culturally, and politically are an active population—in complex ways. In spite of major structural limitations, many Dominicans have chosen to develop their own ethnic organizations and to incorporate as a way to advance in American society. Dominicans have developed dozens of organizations shaping the social, cultural, and political Dominican community in New York City. The literature on Dominicans in the United States, however, provides little information about a community that has developed neighborhood activism and has engaged in city, state, and transnational politics. Few studies analyze the processes of local community activism and organizational life. Georges (1984), focusing on Washington Heights and using data collected during the late 1970s, shows the importance of the local Dominican political structure. Sassen-Koob (1979) compared Dominican and Colombian ethnic associations and concluded that Dominicans had less sophisticated organizational structures than Colombians. When Georges and Sassen-Koob conducted their research, the Dominican community was more engaged in transnational politics than it is today when there is a process of incorporation to American politics. Other study shows that even politics of incorporation are permeated by transmigrant behaviors (Graham 1998). Ricourt (1998) looks at the social capital generated by social service agencies. Duany, on the other hand, presents a transnational community looking at issues of Dominican ethnic identity in New York City

A recent work attempts to explore both the migration process and the rise of the Dominican community in the United States. Torres-Saillant and Hernández (1998) cover the complete process of migration, from the structural forces pushing Dominicans to migrate, and the process of migration, to settlements, labor market insertion, and community development. They look at voluntary associations, political empowerment, and education empowerment as well as the definition of what they call the "diasporic identity," an identity that melts both Dominican and American experiences. They also show the impact of macro-structural process, such as the labor market, education, and race relations in the Dominican Republic on the lives of Dominicans in the Diaspora. The work of Torres-Saillant and Hernández is an important start in entering into the dynamics shaping the Dominican community in the United States. But one must go beyond definitions and take a closer ethnographic look into the neighborhood. I examine community social interactions, weaving these interactions with other social facts such as labor market transformation, continuous immigration, residential concentration, gender, and ethnicity, to have a broader picture of the Dominican community of New York City.

## NOTES

1. The National Origins System is part of the development of the U. S. immigration policies. From the founding of the Republic through the late nineteenth century (1776–1882), the United States opened its doors to immigrants of all nations. This period is called the open-door era. Discrimination against certain groups on the basis of nationality began with the passage of the Chinese Exclusion Act in 1882. The Immigration Act of 1921 set the first immigration quotas in the nation history. It marked the beginning of restrictions on immigration to the United States from Southern Europe, Africa, Asia, and Oceania. The Immigration Act of 1924, popularly known as the National Origins System, was enacted to replace the temporary Immigration Act of 1921 with a national origin quota. This act favored Northern and Western European nations and reduced quotas to Southern European, Asian, and African countries. The immigration reform movement of 1965 abolished the discriminatory national origin quota system and established the principle of equal treatment for immigrants from all nations. Recent immigration

reforms have set restrictions to the 1965 Immigration Act, such as family reunification provisions.

2. During World War II the United States and its satellites (many Third World countries) produced both agricultural and industrial commodities for the rest of the world. The traditional European industrial nations were fighting within their own territories. The United States was the only powerful nation that did not get involved directly in the conflict until the very end, and none of those battles were fought in its own territory (except Pearl Harbor in Hawaii), leaving its productive infrastructure intact.

3. Authors argue that Mexican entry into the United States came about through conquest and subordination. Frank Bean and Marta Tienda in *The Hispanic Population of the United States* (1987) argue that the social conditions of Chicanos in the United States have roots in the history of subordination that Chicanos confronted after annexation. They argue that after the territories of California, Arizona, New Mexico, Colorado, and Texas were conquered, and the Southwest was opened for Anglo settlement. "Chicanos lost their land, their social mobility became blocked, and this eventually led to a deterioration of their position vis-à-vis Anglos." (18)

4. The Bracero Program, which lasted from 1942 to 1964, was a contract labor system between Mexico and the United States. It was conceived as a temporary solution to the labor shortage in agriculture.

5. Puerto Rico, which has been a U.S. territory since the culmination of the Spanish-American War in 1898, became a United States Commonwealth in 1952. This confers Puerto Ricans the following: United States citizenship and currency and common defense. But Puerto Ricans are not allowed to vote in the United States presidential elections, are not represented in the United States senate, and have a non-voting resident commission in the House of Representatives. Unrestricted migration from Puerto Rico to the United States mainland occurred during the 1940s and accelerated after 1950. Concomitant with migration was industrialization on the island. Operation Bootstrap (1948–65) could not absorb the available workers, many of whom were leaving the countryside and establishing in the urban center due to the failure of the plantation system. Migration to the mainland provided a temporary solution to the unemployment problem.

6. Most of these studies were completed during the late 1970s or early 1980s and do not explain more recent Dominican international migration. The 1980s and 1990s witnessed a large Dominican migration to the United States and other international destinations fostered by a deep economic crisis in the Dominican Republic. It has been suggested that illegal immigration was even larger than legal migration. After these two developments, is it correct to characterize Dominican migration to the United States as an urban middle-class phenomenon?

7. These studies have been important in explaining the process of migration from the Dominican Republic to the United States. However, they portray the United States as the sole recipient of Dominican migrants.

Dominican international migration to Europe, for example, has been significant during the 1980s and 1990s. Dominican international migration has also been to urban centers that are not considered "world cities," such as Caracas, Madrid, Athens, Rome. Moreover, the reasons for migration have revolved around the deep economic crisis that afflicted the Dominican Republic during the 1980s. A more global analysis is necessary to reconsider Dominican international migration during the last two decades.

8. The deindustrialization of the United States was much discussed during the 1980s. For example, Barry Bluestone and Bennett Harrison in their book *The Deindustrialization of America* (1982) offer a comprehensive study of the disappearance of the U.S. manufacturing and its effects on local communities. The same authors in 1986 published *The Great U-Turn* in which here they discuss the impact of corporate mergers and the global factory on the U.S. economy. Other authors have also looked at this phenomenon from different angles. For example, Ellen Israel Rosen (1987) explores women workers in declining industries in New England. María Patricia Fernández-Kelly (1983) analyzes the *maquiladoras* industry and its effects on Mexican women. All of these studies conclude with the ill effects of deindustrialization of the United States on both local and foreign workers.

# CHAPTER 4

# Neighborhood Change and Ethnic Solidarity

I HEARD THE ROAR OF CELEBRATION WHEN I WAS CLIMBING THE STAIRS OUT OF THE SUB-way station at 137th Street and Broadway. Outside there was a group of young men standing on the corner opposite the park. They were talking loudly. A *bachata* rhythm blasted from a car parked around the corner from 137th Street. The corner grocery store had placed plastic tanks filled with ice and beers, soda, fruit salad, and water. The park across the street had five tables where men surrounded domino players. I could hear the heated arguments of the players from across the street. Their voices resounded above the young men's chatter in the opposite corner, the *bachata* music, and the rest of the noise coming from every single space along Broadway, not to mention the hundreds of vehicles passing by. Mothers with their children, men by themselves, elders, walked by obliviously. One man shouted from the middle of the avenue to another man on the sidewalk who shouts back, establishing a conversation. A passing bus and a dozen cars did not stop these two men from talking to each other. From grocery stores, bakeries, liquor stores, Korean miscellaneous stores, clothing stores, and restaurants people came in and out, talking and laughing. The tall buildings stopped the breeze coming from the Hudson River, but not the pollution from the sewage treatment site built below the park.

Most of the people I observed were Dominicans, clustered in West Harlem, New York City, a neighborhood adjacent to Washington Heights.[1] There they share apartment buildings, doctors' offices, supermarkets, Laundromats, parks, streets, corners, grocery stores, beauty parlors, restaurants, pollution, night-clubs, churches, and life. In sharing they also create their own social environments, naming their stores after places they left behind in the Dominican Republic, selling and buying yucca from Moca, a town in the Cibao region of the Dominican Republic, or cassaba, a bread made out yucca flour, or home-

45

made remedies for a varieties of illnesses. They also share information such as the location of the next apartment where the parish priest is going to take the image of the Virgin of La Altagracia, the national patroness of the Dominican Republic, to be venerated by the entire community. Where a mother can buy a dress for her daughter's First Communion. Which Dominican merengue orchestra is performing at Studio 84. There are many other advantages in the neighborhood, such as inexpensive phone services to the Dominican Republic. There one can talk for less than 10 cents a minute. Places are available where one can wire money and in return receive a few minutes free to call someone in the Dominican Republic.

Sharing a locality fosters ethnicity. Thus the residential concentration of immigrants is one of the factors that contribute to the emergence of ethnicity as well as reinforces preexisting ties of solidarity among immigrants.[2] Sharing the same residential and occupational space is crucial to the formation of ethnic group solidarity, producing common interests, lifestyles, and friendships. This chapter explores neighborhood change in the midst of heavy immigration from the Spanish-speaking Caribbean, and particularly the Dominican Republic, into New York City and how residential segregation catalyzes the social process of ethnic construction.

Historically, many New York City neighborhoods have experienced the arrival of new ethnic groups while older groups moved elsewhere. The migration of African-Americans from the South to the North of the United States during the late 1800s and early 1900s turned New York into a more racially diverse city, while the arrival of Europeans turned it into a more multiethnic setting. More recently, with the advent of newer immigrants from Latin America, Southeast Asia and other Asian regions, New York City has acquired the characteristics of a "beautiful mosaic."[3] Yet the living conditions of new immigrants were never good. The neighborhoods' racial and ethnic turnover perpetuated segregation, discrimination, and poverty (Alba et al. 1995: 651–653; Massey and Denton 1993: 87).

Washington Heights, for example, has experienced a transition from a basically white neighborhood to a racially diverse neighborhood since late 1950s and 1960s. Latinos, and specifically Dominicans, are now prevalent in this neighborhood and are contributing to the formation of a new minority neighborhood (Ricourt 1998). New York City neighborhoods have been experiencing great changes, contributing to the reshaping of the city's landscape. Dominicans in New York City, for example, have added a new piece to New York City's mosaic of people, music, food, parades, politicians, and organizations. This neighborhood's demographic transition has been important for the formation of a new ethnicity in the city. Along with these transformations, Dominicans fight social afflictions: poverty, unemployment, drug addiction, illnesses, and other forms of "institutional discrimination" (Massey and Denton 1993:142). In the midst of community struggle, Dominicans make contributions to New York City's ethnic and racial mosaic.

## THE GEOGRAPHIC DISTRIBUTION OF DOMINICANS IN NEW YORK CITY

The number of Dominicans in New York City is 593,777, a figure that is 186,304 higher than the census bureau official count, according to John Logan (2000). Logan adds that there is more than 50 percent growth of Dominicans in New York City in the last decade. Moreover, in providing information on specific Hispanics and Asia nationality groups (such as Chinese and Asian-Indians, Mexicans and Dominicans) show that almost all of these groups are more segregated from the white majority. "Each group has its own distinctive residential pattern, and this suggests that their separate group identities remain strong in their American setting." (Logan 2000).

During the 1990s the number of Dominicans in the United States was also a much-debated issue. The 1990 United States census reported 500,000 Dominicans living in the United States. Many challenged these official numbers. The media, for instance, estimated the number of Dominicans residing in the United States at between 400,000 and over a million. Scholars, on the other hand, stated that the number of Dominicans residing in the United States "cannot be reported with any degree of accuracy" because one needs to take into account illegal immigration and the lack of reliable sources of information (Hernández and Torres-Saillant 1996; Larson and Sullivan 1987). Dominican community activists claimed that the numbers of Dominicans surpassed Cubans, placing Dominicans as the third Latino group in numerically importance in the United States.

Table 2: Dominican Population in New York City Compared to Other Ethnic and Racial Groups 1980-1990

| Ethnic and Racial Group | 1980 | % | 1990 | % |
|---|---|---|---|---|
| Total Population | 7,071,639 | 100 | 7,322,564 | 100 |
| Dominicans | 125,380 | 1.8 | 332,713 | 4.5 |
| Other Latinos | 1,406389 | 19.9 | 1,783,511 | 24.4 |
| African Americans | 1,694,505 | 24.0 | 1,847,049 | 25.2 |
| Asian | 239,338 | 3.4 | 489,851 | 6.7 |
| White | 3,703,203 | 52.4 | 3,163,125 | 43.2 |

Source: New York City Department of City Planning, Socioeconomic Profiles, City of New York Department of City Planning, March 1993.

Nevertheless, New York City has certainly been the main recipient of Dominican migration from the 1960s to the present. The Dominican Republic sent the most immigrants to New York City in the 1970s, 1980s, and first half of 1990s. According to the City of New York Department of City Planning (1993), the Dominican population of New York City grew from 125,380 in 1980, to 332,713 in 1990, representing 4.5 percent of the entire city's population (see Table 2) and 19 percent of the Latino population of New York City.

In 1996, over 39,000 Dominicans settled in New York City (City of New York Department of City Planning 1996). The same source revealed that from 1995 to 1996, 38 percent of Dominican immigrants to the city settled in Manhattan, 31 percent in the Bronx, 17 percent in Brooklyn, and 14 percent in Queens.

## THE GEOGRAPHIC CONCENTRATION OF DOMINICANS IN MANHATTAN, BROOKLYN, THE BRONX, AND QUEENS

The concentration of Dominicans in New York City's five boroughs in relation to other ethnic and racial groups is larger in Manhattan, as Table 3 shows.

**Table 3: Distribution of Dominicans in New York City Five Boroughs Compared to Other Ethnic and Racial Groups 1990**

|                  | Bronx     | Brooklyn  | Manhattan | Queens    |
|------------------|-----------|-----------|-----------|-----------|
| Total Population | 1,203,789 | 2,300,664 | 1,487,536 | 1,951,598 |
| Dominicans       | 87,261    | 55,301    | 136,696   | 52,309    |
| Other Latinos    | 523,111   | 462,411   | 386,630   | 381,120   |
| African Americans| 369,113   | 797,802   | 261,120   | 390,842   |
| Whites           | 272,503   | 923,229   | 726,755   | 937,557   |

Source: New York City Department of City Planning, Socioeconomic Profiles, City of New York Department of City Planning, March 1993

In these boroughs, Dominicans are concentrated in specific areas as Table 4 shows.

**Table 4: Highest Population of Dominicans in Specific Community Districts in the Bronx, Brooklyn, Manhattan, and Queens**

| Borough   | Dominican Pop. | Community Districts |          | %    |
|-----------|----------------|---------------------|----------|------|
| Bronx     | 87,261         | (CD 4, 5)           | 62,214   | 71.3 |
| Brooklyn  | 55,301         | (CD 1, 4, 5)        | 32,860   | 59.4 |
| Manhattan | 36,696         | (CD 9,12)           | 108,041  | 79.0 |
| Queens    | 52,309         | (CD 3, 5)           | 27,018   | 51.6 |

Source: New York City Department of City Planning, Socioeconomic Profile, March 1993

These data show both the high levels of demographic concentration of Dominicans and their numerical importance in New York City.

Manhattan's community districts 9 and 12, correspond to the neighborhoods of West Harlem and Washington Heights. Both house 79 percent of the borough's Dominican population. During the late 1960s and early 1970s, Washington Heights was still a predominantly white neighborhood. Other groups, such as Irish, Greeks, and Cubans also settled in the area in large numbers. For example, when Diana, one of my informants, came to

Washington Heights, New York City, in 1969, her husband had rented an apartment for her at 170th Street and Amsterdam Avenue. She moved into a building where the majority of tenants were white and there were few Latinos, both Cubans and Dominicans. At present, the same building, which has 18 apartments, is all Dominican except for an Ecuadorean family.

In Washington Heights, even though the German-Jewish population declined from about 24,000 in 1960 to about 15,000 in 1970 and 10,500 in 1980, the more traditionally religious and culturally conservative remained in Washington Heights. Thus, two different communities have survived in Washington Heights. The German-Jewish population is crowded behind the high ground around Fort Tryon Park on upper Fort Washington Avenue in adjacent areas, mainly west of Broadway and north of the George Washington Bridge. The Dominican population begins in West Harlem and continues to the end of northern Manhattan.

Washington Heights suffered a larger scale demographic change beginning in the late 1950s. It is estimated that between the late 1950s and 1980s the size of the German-Jewish community fell by 50 percent (Lowenstein 1989). The arrival of new immigrants, however, did not trigger "white flight" in Washington Heights. Prior to the arrival of Dominicans in the early 1960s, the Jewish population was already dropping in numbers for several reasons. First, the increased prosperity of many members of the second generation led them to move to suburban or more prestigious urban areas where some of them bought houses. Second, many members of the immigrant generation had died. Finally, there was a wholesale change in the ethnic composition of Washington Heights, with the substantial immigration of Hispanics and (to a lesser extent) blacks and a proportionately substantial decline in the white non-Hispanic population.

Nor can the decline of the socioeconomic status of Washington Heights be attributed solely to the arrival of Dominicans. The decline in the social status of Washington Heights started as early as 1951, long before the arrival of Dominicans. According to Lowenstein (1989: 213), in 1954 Washington Heights was a "downhill residential area." Washington Heights was experiencing social deterioration before Dominicans started to come to the United States. New immigrants cannot be held responsible for neighborhood deterioration. They only inherited the social consequences of the "white flight." Neighborhoods formerly inhabited by old Americans were left abandoned, and new immigrants were lumped together in these segregated neighborhoods.

In Washington Heights, Lowenstein acknowledged that the relationship between German-Jewish and Dominicans has been typically distant and cold. In the 1960s and 1970s, several clashes between Jews and Dominicans occurred, and were different from earlier clashes between Jews and Irish. Jewish and Dominicans, however, avoided each other and "viewed each other with suspicion" (Lowenstein 1989: 215). Like members of the other older immigrant groups, Jewish resented the fact that Hispanics were allowed to use Spanish for official purposes while Jewish had been forced to learn English. Jews organized themselves in three different areas to confront Dominicans and African-Americans. They set up the Washington Heights-Inwood Safety Patrol (WHISP) to protect the Jewish neighborhood from crime. They also established control of the local school board. They started to organize politically to defend themselves from the newcomers. A slate dominated by the mainly Jewish Fort Tryon neighborhood controlled the school board during the entire decade of 1970s. The Jewish Community Council was designed to sit council members in the local community planning board. These attempts to control the neighborhood by Jews, however, did not last long. At the end of the 1970s, Dominicans were already fighting to control the school board and the community board. By the mid-1980s, Dominicans controlled both institutions.

In the Bronx, community districts 4, 5, and 7, located along the Grand Concourse and Kingsbridge area of the Bronx contained 71.3 percent of the borough's Dominican population. The presence of Dominicans in the Bronx became visible during the 1980s and 1990s. The case of Ramona, another interviewee, illustrates the story of the first Dominicans in the Bronx.

Ramona moved into the Bronx in mid-1968. When she first came to New York City in 1962 from the Dominican Republic, she rented a furnished room around 96th Street in Manhattan. When her husband came after she filed his immigration papers, they moved to the Bronx at Morris Avenue between Mcleland and 167th Street. One of her sisters also found an apartment on Sheridan Avenue, and her other sister moved into McClelland Street, where her husband got a job as the building superintendent. Ramona always longed to live on the Grand Concourse, the wide avenue above Morris Avenue. But for many years, building owners in that area were very reluctant to rent apartment to Latinos. Some buildings had ads saying, "No Puerto Ricans Allowed."[4] During the 1960s and 1970s, Spanish-speaking persons in New York City were treated as Puerto Ricans. Ramona managed to bribe the super at the building located at Grand Concourse and the corner of 167th Street. In 1977, she finally made her dream come true by being the first Dominican to move into that building. Her sister also moved into the same building soon after. At present, the same building is mostly Dominican and Puerto Rican. A few Indians, Pakistanis, Bangladeshis, and Yugoslavians started to move into the building in the 1990s.

The Bronx, meantime, suffered one of the most drastic occurrences of white flight in the nation. As Lowenstein (1989: 216) explains, "Ethnic and racial change in the West Bronx was far more rapid than change in Washington Heights. Within a few years a solidly Jewish area became almost exclusively black and Hispanic." In terms of housing, Lankevich (1998: 209) shows how in the mid-1960s, 200,000 existing housing units in sound buildings were either abandoned by their owners or fell prey to fire or vandalism. "Arson for insurance profit emerged as one of the most prevalent crimes in the city; the early 1970s saw fire transform the South Bronx into a national symbol of urban decay (Lankevich 1998:209)." The Hispanic population in the Bronx was and still is basically Puerto Rican. Although small groups of Dominicans were present in the Bronx during late 1960s and 1970s, the Dominican presence in the Bronx and specifically in the West Bronx is a relatively new phenomenon.

Queens' community districts 3 and 4, corresponding to Jackson Heights and Corona, contain more than 51 percent of the borough's Dominican population. The following statement reflects the arrival of the first Dominicans in Corona, Queens:

> Twenty years later, after their arrival to the United States at the beginning of the 1950s, Amado Corona and his wife Mercedes (Sila) and his three children, as well as other relatives and friends, started to move into Corona, whose residents resisted to accept people of color in the southern part of the neighborhood, separated from the northern part (which was becoming a middle-class African-American sector), around Northern Boulevard. Neither Amado, nor Simón Corona, nor Juan Abreu, nor Zoilo Díaz, nor Enrique, nor Benito Lugo and his people had any problem purchasing homes in a white neighborhood, because they looked white. But Roman Lugo, Enrique and Benito's brother, were denied the right to buy any property in the neighborhood. . . . In that way, during the 1950s, a small group of Dominicans started to develop a small corner in a neighborhood that was named like some of these Dominicans' last names: Corona. (Source: Francisco Rodríguez de León, El Furioso Merengue del Norte, New York, 1998. [My translation from the original version in Spanish.])

Mireya, my interviewee, came to Corona, Queens from the Dominican Republic in 1966. When she first moved into the neighborhood in Corona Heights, she said she was the only Dominican and the second Latina in the neighborhood. Her next-door neighbor was Puerto Rican. The rest of the neighborhood was Italian, Irish, and Polish. During the 1970s and 1980s, Mireya witnessed major transformations in her neighborhood. At present, Mireya's block still houses a few Irish, Polish, and Italian residents, but other ethnic groups have joined them. There are also Chinese, Korean, Indian, and Latin American residents, including Dominicans, Puerto Ricans, Colombians, and Bolivians.

Glenn Hendricks' *The Dominican Diaspora* (1974) stated that the first Dominican immigrant from the country's northern region of El Cibao moved into Corona (probably referring to the Corona family). Corona is called by Dominicans "Sabana Church," because most Dominicans in the area originally came from the northern town of *Sabana Iglesias*. According to census figures, the white population of Corona, which corresponds to community district 4 (Elmhurst-Corona), declined from 45,000 persons in 1950 to 10,000 in 1990, while the Latino population increased from zero in 1950 to over

45,000 in 1990. Confrontations between Italians and Latinos in Community District 4 have taken many different forms throughout the years. In 1974, for example, Community Board 4 leaders started what Sanjek (1998: 70) calls The Great Illegal Aliens Panic of 1974. Members of the board were concerned with the emergence of overcrowded buildings, off-books jobs, turning schools into Spanish-speaking schools. They requested immediate actions from the INS and city officials to deport Hispanics. But soon more Latin Americans, including Dominicans, became part of the community board's leadership. However, Latino participation in decision-making bodies did not stop conflict. For example, in 1991, Manuel Mayí, a Dominican-Puerto Rican, 19 years old, was chased and murdered by an Italian gang. A Queens's court acquitted the Italians.

## ETHNIC SOLIDARITY

Residential concentration of minorities is largely the result of racial segregation, and ends in impoverished neighborhoods afflicted with crime, unemployment, and the worst schools. In the past, European immigrants also confronted segregation. Irish, Italians, Greeks, Poles, Jews were clustered in poor inner-city neighborhoods. Italians, for instance, initiated their own ethnic associations in order to challenge discrimination (Portes and Bach 1985). As Glazer and Moyniham (1968) argue, ethnicity is a weapon that immigrants use to improve their political, economic, and social status in the host society. For many European immigrant groups, significant generational improvements in education, income, and white collar employment, however, have accompanied declines in residential concentration. The race factor also played an important role in the advancement of European immigrants. According to Lieberson (1980), European economic improvements during the Cold War lead to a decline in segregation while, for African-Americans, the same did not lead to a decline in residential isolation.

In the case of Latinos, the second largest minority group in the United States, residential segregation also persists and may have increased over the last few decades. In New York City, for example, Latinos continue to cluster in specific neighborhoods, such as northern Brooklyn, northern Manhattan, and central Queens. Residential segregation as well as unemployment influences the socioeconomic position of Latinos in New York City. In 1989, one out of every five-city resident lived in poverty. Between African-American and Hispanic New Yorkers, the proportion was 25 percent and 33 percent, respectively (Torres 1995: 4). A 1995 report showed that the poverty rate of Dominican households was one of the highest in New York City. Unemployment rate of Dominicans was close to twice that of the overall population in New York. Moreover, the Dominican population in the city had comparatively low educational attainments at both the high school and college levels (Hernández et al. 1995).

The demographic patterns of Dominican settlements reflect that more and more neighborhoods in New York City contain multiple minority neighborhoods; fewer and fewer are ethnically or racially homogenous (Denton and Massey 1991: 41). However, most of the studies conducted on neighborhood transition do not address the complexities of ethnic and racial change that occurred after these new ethnic groups arrived in the neighborhood. None of these studies have taken into consideration the role of newer Spanish-speaking immigrants in neighborhood transformation.

The concentration of Dominicans in specific neighborhoods in New York City and the experience of segregation, however, have facilitated Dominican civic and political involvement in the city. Residential concentration creates a source of integration among Dominicans important to the formation of ethnic group solidarity. "Ethnic ties provide a ready system of support for groups that are readily distinguishable by race, national origin, and/or language" (Bean and Tienda 1987: 12).

The Dominican community has one of the largest numbers of ethnic associations in New York City. Cultural and sport clubs, student associations, professional organizations, women's groups, political parties, baseball leagues, domino clubs, and many other associations have flourished in Dominican New York since the first Dominican group arrived in the city. Many other institutions such as social service agencies are also present, providing benefits to community residents.

## NOTES

1. West Harlem corresponds to Community District (CD) 9 in Manhattan, New York City. Even though, Community District 9 population has been traditionally considered African-American, Dominicans represents more than 25 percent of the Community District population.

2. The work of Yancey, W. E. Erickson, and R. Juliani, "Emergent Ethnicity: A Review and Reformulation" *American Sociological Review* 41 (1976): 391–403, offers a useful theory of the social construction of ethnicity. Starting with the notion that the expression of ethnicity is a variable, these authors identify several factors that contribute to the emergence of ethnicity among European immigrant groups. Among these factors is the ecological configuration of urban areas. Geographical concentration of immigrants is crucial to the formation of ethnic group solidarity.

3. Andres Torres' work *Between Melting Pot and Mosaic: African Americans and Puerto Ricans in the New York Political Economy*, Philadelphia: Temple University Press, 1995, refers to the metaphor of the "mosaic," defining the term as a rainbow terminology that exalts the idea of racial diversity as central to American society. Moreover, the term "mosaic" included all minorities in the political process. Torres, however, points out that one of the limitations of the mosaic approach is the continuing problem of poverty among minority groups.

4. During that period of time all Spanish-speaking people were considered to be Puerto Ricans.

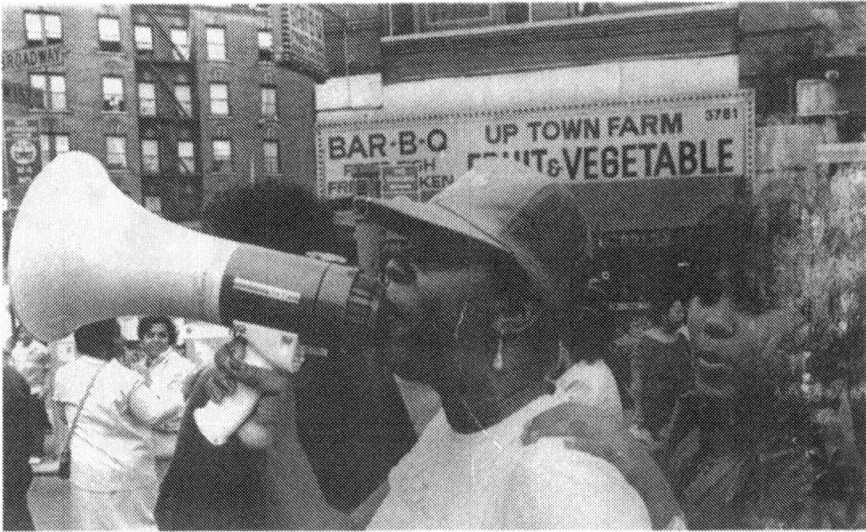

1. Mireya Cruz stirs the crowd with slogans against domestic violence in Washingt--
Heights. 1986. Courtesy of Dominican Women's Development Center archives.

2. Mireya Cruz, Rosita Romero, and Zenaida Méndez among other women gather out-
side the Dominican Women's Development Center to protest against the murder of
Gladys Ricart by her former boyfriend. 1999. Courtesy of Dominican Women's
Development Center archives.

3. Picket in front of Dyckman Income Maintenance Center to protest against Congressional attacks on welfare. 1996. Courtesy of Dominican Women's Development Center archives.

4. The Dominican Women's Development Center participates in the Immigrants and Poor People March in Washington, D.C. 1996. Courtesy of Dominican Women's Development Center archives.

5. Corner of Broadway and 138th Street in West Harlem, a neighborhood adjacent to Washington Heights populated significantly by Dominicans.

6. *Alianza Dominicana* Folkloric Dance group, directed by Iván Domínguez, performs during a street festival. 1999. Courtesy of *Alianza Dominicana* archives.

7. Guillermo Linares stirs the masses during his first political campaign. 1991. Courtesy of *Alianza Dominicana* archives.

8. The Bronx Borough President Fernando Ferrer with Ydanis Rodríguez and Alexander Rodríguez, leaders of the *Unión de Jóvenes Dominicanos* (Dominican Youth Association). Courtesy of *Alianza Dominicana* archives.

9. Congressman Charles Rangel (*center*) poses with Dominican leaders (*from left*, Moisés Pérez, Rafael Lantigua, and Guillermo Linares). Courtesy of *Alianza Dominicana* archives.

10. Guillermo Linares (*l.*) and Moisés Pérez (*r.*) pose with New York City Comptroller Alan Hevesi during the mayoral electoral campaign in 1993. Courtesy of *Alianza Dominicana* archives.

11. Rosa Lavern, co-founder of the Dominican Women's Development Center, and Arelis Figueroa. Courtesy of Dominican Women's Development Center archives.

12. The *Colectivo de Mujeres Dominicanas* (The Dominican Women's Collective) walks during the Dominican Parade along Sixth Avenue, Manhattan, in 1986. Courtesy of Dominican Women's Development Center archives.

13. The *Caucus de Mujeres Dominicanas* (The Dominican Women's Caucus) protests police brutality in Washington Heights. Courtesy of Dominican Women's Development Center archives.

# CHAPTER 5

# The Role of Social Service Agencies in Washington Heights

EMOGRAPHIC CHANGES IN NEW YORK CITY HAVE MOLDED THE ETHNIC AND racial composition of the city. In this chapter, I argue that the concentration of Dominicans in specific neighborhoods in New York City has facilitated Dominican ethnic and social capital formation. Dominican geographic concentration fueled an ethnic awareness that led to collective actions. In this sense, Dominicans develop associations, organizations, agencies, and political groups, and so on to channel their actions. These organizations are an expression of social capital. By social capital, I mean the benefits gained from relations of mutual trust and collaboration, which resides in the relations between members of a group (Coleman 1990: 300–321). The concept of social capital lies in identifying the role of community organizations, such as social service agencies, in community development. These community organizations emerged when a group of Dominicans came together in a collaborative manner, advancing their identity to mobilize, to create a voice, to bring resources, and to empower the community. This chapter examines the benefits generated by social service organizations and their impact on the development of the Dominican community in New York City. I argue that Dominican organizations experienced different phases from the 1970s to the 1990s, in which, they reached a political momentum during late 1980s and early 1990s that vanished during mid-1990s. Furthermore, I argue that organizations in the Dominican community reflect the wide continuum of ethnic identification of Dominicans in New York City.

The role of associations, clubs, and social service organizations has been instrumental in building strategies for the immigrant community's empowerment and development. In the past, other immigrant groups who were geographically concentrated experienced ethnic solidarity, developing organizations to benefit the community. Italians, for example, initiated their own ethnic associations in order to challenge discrimination (Portes and Bach, 1985; Glazer and Moyniham, 1963). Early Puerto Ricans settlers in New York City also showed a "significant degree of group involvement which reinforced and redefined the community image of the Spanish-speaking neighborhoods....Associations formed which acclimated incoming immigrants to their new environments, allowed them to participate in group activities based on common interests and represented the *colonias* before the host society .... Some groups concerned themselves with education, culture, or social service needs" (Sánchez-Korrol, 1983: 131). The case of Dominicans is similar to Puerto Ricans. For instance, both groups have benefited from mutual collaboration, and social capital to build their communities.

## SOCIAL CAPITAL AND COMMUNITY DEVELOPMENT

Social capital is important for community development. More specifically social capital is considered an important element in the reconstruction of inner city neighborhoods.

> Social capital is not itself sufficient to turn around inner-city neighborhoods. However, without social capital to sustain problem solving with a distressed community and to link community residents to the broader society, efforts to address specific problems of the neighborhood, individuals, and families will make little progress against urban distress.
>
> (The Committee for Economic Development's Report, "Rebuilding Inner-City Communities: A New Approach to the Nation Urban Crisis," 1995: 7.)

Scholars have addressed the importance of social capital not only to community development but also to international and national development and democracy. Putnam (1993), for example, argues that social capital embodied in norms and networks of civic engagement is a pre-condition for economic development. However, Walton (1993) states that "social trenches" or grassroots organizations nurture democracies in former socialist societies and poor countries. Other social scientists have moved beyond political and economic analysis, concentrating on specific age groups. Coleman (1990) has studied how social capital impacts positively the creation of human capital among youth, helping them to have a more positive attitude toward life and society. Loury (1987) also states that social capital constitutes an important advantage for children and adolescents in the development of their human capital.

Recent research, however, points to the decline in social capital in the United States. Putman (1998: 68) argues that the rates of joining voluntary associations, citizens' trust in one another, and citizens' rate of voting are decreasing in the United States. This decline, according to Putnam, is a threat to the successful maintenance of American democracy. In her critique of Putnam's thesis, Paxton (1999: 122) argues that there has been a decline in trust in individuals, but the level of participation in voluntary and formal associations remains the same in the United States. Rethinking Paxton's argument about trust, one suggests that trust as well as informal tie of solidarity, is a critical phenomenon in the Latino community. Mahler (1995), for example, argues that distrust, egotism, competition, and resentment of each other were the norms among Central American immigrants in Long Island, New York.

I have not explored "trust," however; the many organizations in the Dominican community of New York City suggest trust exists among Dominicans. The high numbers of ethnic associations in the Dominican community of New York City have interested social scientists. For example, Sassen-Koob (1979) counted thirty-six ethnic associations in Washington Heights in 1976. Both Sainz (1990) and Georges (1984) counted ninety associations in Washington Heights during the mid-1980s. Torres-Saillant and Hernández (1998: 80–81) offer a historical overview of voluntary and instrumental associations in Washington Heights. These studies portray the numerical strength of ethnic associations in the Dominican community of New York City. But it is important to go beyond numbers, and to look at the social capital generated by these associations and how it influences community development.

Similar to other immigrant communities, Dominicans' group building has not only been essential in neighborhood transformation but has also created a political, social, and cultural niche in the city. Washington Heights' associations, social service agencies, and social and sports clubs have been successful in bringing people together, creating political citizens with a political voice, and generating resources such as educational, training, and employment programs among others.

## DOMINICAN ASSOCIATIONS AND ETHNIC IDENTITY

Associations in Washington Heights reflect the ethnic identity trends present in the Dominican population of New York City. I argued earlier that Dominicans, according to their time of migration, generation, and gender, have different ethnic identities. Simply put, new immigrants tend to have a transnational identity with more loyalties to the home country, established immigrants are usually torn between *here* and *there,* and second generations immigrants typically espouse a Dominican-American identity. Social, political, cultural, and sport organizations in Dominican New York reflect these differences. I have divided these organizations into three different categories. First, transnational organizations are primarily rooted in loyalties to the sending country. One example is the type of organization emerged when Dominicans came to New York City in large numbers in the 1960s. Torres-Saillant and Hernández (1998: 80) comment that the two oldest "surviving formal voluntary associations of Dominican date back to the 1960s," namely the *Centro Cívico Cultural Dominicano* and *Club Juan Pablo Duarte*, also known as *Instituto Duartiano*. Also, the social and sports clubs continue a tradition in the Dominican Republic, still proliferate in New York City and especially in Washington Heights. Some of these clubs are named after a town or city in the Dominican Republic, such as the *Club Tamboril* (a town in *el Cibao*), a political hero such as Juan Pablo Duarte (the father of the Dominican nation), or Maria Trinidad Sánchez (the woman who sewed the first Dominican flag). Many of these clubs also served Dominican political parties in New York City, besides promoting dominoes, baseball leagues, and organizing parties.

Second, transitional organizations reflecting a dual identity have contributed enormously to the formation of Dominican-American identity. The Revolutionary Dominican Party (Partido Revolucionario Dominicano—PRD), for example, takes a dual political approach in New York City. The PRD supports political development in the Dominican Republic, but at the same time favors the politics of incorporation of Dominican-Americans in New York City. For example, the PRD encourages the naturalization of Dominicans and has supported voter registration campaigns in New York City. Other political parties, such as the Dominican Workers' Party (Partido de los Trabajadores Dominicanos—PTD), also have a dual approach to politics. The PTD organizes events about political and economic conditions in the Dominican Republic. It also organizes fundraising campaigns for political candidates in Dominican elections, and also supports Dominican candidates in elections in the United States. For example, The Dominican Workers' Party (PTD) organized the first electoral campaign of councilman Guillermo Linares.

Third, Dominican-American organizations are rooted in the host society and deal with issues created in the host society such as political empowerment. All these associations and organizations create a culture of civic involvement and community networking in Washington Heights. Chart 5 illustrates the different organizations of Dominicans in Washington Heights.

All these Dominican organizations play an important role in the construction of the Dominican community in New York City. Some of them recreate in the Diaspora what was left behind after migration. A social club is an example of this cultural recreation. A transnational group of men playing dominoes from the same hometown in the Dominican Republic shared valuable information about both Dominican political development in the Dominican Republic and job availability in New York City on a cool afternoon in April 2000. Another transnational group calling itself the New Quisqueyanos organized a festival, Quisqueya on the Hudson, with the objective of maintaining Dominican traditions in the Diaspora and to ensure that Dominican children and Dominican youth know their roots. Dominican social service organizations are among what I call Dominican-American organizations. These organizations provide resources to community residents

**Chart 5: Dominican Associations and Ethnic Identity Associations**

| TRANSNATIONAL | TRANSITIONAL | DOMINICAN-AMERICAN |
|---|---|---|
| *Sports, Domino, Bingo, Parties Cultural Groups* | *Sports, ESL, US Citizenship* | *Community Empowerment* |
| Centro Cultural Ballet Quisqueya | Asociaciones Dominicanas | Alianza Dominicana |
| Centro 27 de Febrero | Quisqueya for a Better New York | Dominican Women's Development Center |
| Centro Luz del Caribe | Asociación de Baloncesto | |
| Liga Deportiva Hijos del Monte | Centro Comunal Tamboril | Asociación Dom. Progresistas |
| Club Deportivo Dominicano | General 2000 Dominicana | Northern Manhattan Coalition |
| Alianza Maeña | Washington Heights Tennis Asso. | Washington Heights Inwood Coalition |
| Centro Deportivo Elpidio Jiménez | PRD | HACER/Parents in Action |
| Los Bravos Community Center | PTD | CERC Center P.S. 173 |
| Instituto Duartiano | New Quisqueyanos | Manhattan North Community Center |
| Centro Cívico Cultural Dominicano | Centro Social La Esperanza | Washington Heights and Inwood Development Citizens Advice Bureau |
| | | RENA COA Multi Service Center |
| | | Dominican Women's Caucus |
| | | Dominican Women United |
| | | Dominican Women Against Violence |
| | | Asociación de Mujeres Progresista |

and incentive for the civic involvement of Dominicans in becoming United States citizens, voting, and running for elections.

## MODELS OF SOCIAL SERVICE AGENCIES IN WASHINGTON HEIGHTS

Social service agencies emerged in the Dominican community of New York City during late 1970s with the expressed purpose of empowering Dominicans. Dominican leaders envisioned community empowerment. They wanted to obtain the following goals. First, activists wanted to bring resources into the community to alleviate social afflictions. Second, they wanted to raise awareness among community residents to the issue of community political control. They implemented programs to help Dominicans to legalize their immigrant status in the United States or to naturalize. Third, community leaders also wanted to provide a source of employment with the creation of social service agencies.

When David Norman Dinkins took office in 1990 as the first African American mayor of New York City, million of dollars were allocated to promote inner city community development. The Dominican community benefited from these funds. Moreover, after the Washington Heights rioting in 1992,[1] additional funds were allocated to implement youth development programs in Washington Heights. During this time, social service organizations in the Dominican community did not have to fight over resources. During the year (1994) of my research with Dominican social service agencies, most of these organizations, with the exception of the Community Association for Progressive Dominicans, share members in their board of directors, and I witnessed trust and cooperation among them.

In 1994, I identified three major social service agencies in the Dominican community of Washington Heights, namely the Northern Manhattan Coalition, the Community Association for Progressive Dominicans, and Alianza Dominicana.[2]

The Northern Manhattan Coalition for Immigrants' Rights was the first Dominican service organization in Washington Heights. It started in 1977, before the end of Balaguer's twelve years (1966–78), and is illustrative of a Dominican-American organization in the Dominican community of Washington Heights. Julio Hernández, acting director of the coalition in 1993, co-founder of the organization, and a well-known community leader, spoke to me about the origins of the coalition. According to him, by 1977 there was already a group of Dominicans in Washington Heights seeking to provide community residents with legal advice, with the express purpose of building community political empowerment.

For over two decades, the coalition has been assisting Dominicans and other immigrants in Washington Heights to become United States citizens in order to achieve more political power. During the period of my research, I visited the organization several times to conduct participant observation and carry out interviews. In each of my visits, I observed dozens of people, mostly Dominicans, but also from other Latin American countries, waiting to be assisted by coalition-trained personnel on immigration legal issues. Many of these people were applying for green cards for themselves and/or relatives. Others were interested in obtaining United States citizenship.

The coalition offered workshops to assist those seeking United States citizenship. They filled out the INS application, photocopied marriage and/or divorce certificates, passports, and other documentation required by the INS, took the applicant's fingerprints and pictures, and prepared the envelope to be sent to the INS. The applicant needed only to pay for the fingerprints and pictures, and include a money order with the INS application fees. The coalition does not charge for the services rendered.

The Community Association for Progressive Dominicans (Asociación Comunal de Dominicanos Progresistas—ACDP) is one of the oldest Dominican organizations, along with the coalition, in Washington Heights. During the late 1970s, a group of Dominican Americans, among them Guillermo Linares, built this organization to provide political leadership to Dominicans in the community. Many of today's Dominican community leaders were involved in creating, developing, and directing the ACDP. For example, Guillermo Linares, who in 1991 was elected New York City councilman and was re-elected in 1994, was one of the founders of this organization. The ACDP, according to the vision of its founders, would be a complement to the Northern Manhattan Coalition. While the coalition prepared the legal base to incentive the political participation of Dominican community residents, the ACDP was creating a base for political leadership. Victor Moriseti, ACDP executive director, told me "Dominicans like to participate in politics. Even first-generation Dominicans understand that only through participation and involvement in politics can a better future be built for Dominicans in New York City."

The ACDP is also an organization providing social services to community residents, specifically children and youth. ACDP's free after-school program includes karate, painting, swimming, and tutoring free classes in English as a second language, and mental health programs for family group's and children.

Alianza Dominicana, one of the largest Latino service organizations in the city, started to operate in Washington Heights during the 1980s. It is funded by both private and public sources. Moisés Pérez, the executive director of Alianza and a well-known leader in the community, says that the main objective of Alianza was to heal the community of major social afflictions. "How can we talk about empowerment in a community that is suffering from crack addition, unemployment, lack of proper housing, and school failure among other issues?" Moisés added, "We need to get rid of social illness in order to have a better community and in order to give people an incentive to participate." To accomplish this purpose, Alianza has opened sixteen programs to heal and empower the community.

The provision of social services such as drug addiction and AIDS prevention and rehabilitation, job training programs, and after-school programs was almost non-existent in Washington Heights when Alianza began to develop programs to fill these needs in the community in the late 1980s and early 1990s. The best example of a program aimed at "healing community social afflictions" is a drug addiction rehabilitation program for women in Washington Heights (CREO), created by Alianza. This program provides women with methods of rehabilitation and also offers women a day care facility and recreation.

I had the opportunity to examine the program several times during the summer of 1994 and 1995. CREO operates from a big office located on Amsterdam Avenue and 180th Street. A nursery is located in a room decorated with toys and dolls, cribs, baby furniture, rocking chairs, and strollers, neatly arranged inside the room. In the rear side of the main room are offices in cubicles. There are also other rooms where women receive acupuncture and attend classes. While conducting an interview with one of the Alianza program officers, I heard loud Dominican merengue music. My interviewee told me that at the end of the day, they played music for the women to enjoy themselves. I saw several of them dancing while picking up their children or leaving the room. The space and materials were clearly organized to help these immigrant women feel comfortable and "at home," not just as clients with a drug problem in need of rehabilitation but as women and mothers.

Alianza has targeted other community needs through different programs. It runs a job development program, which trains high school, graduates in different skills and then offered help to obtain jobs. Alianza has GED classes for young adult dropouts (under 21), and an after-school program. Alianza has also developed the Holistic Orientation Prevention and Education Program (HOPE), located in its Family Center at Fort Washington Avenue and 179th Street. HOPE was established in 1989 as an AIDS education and prevention program targeted to adolescents and young adults.

## SOCIAL SERVICE POLITICS AND NEIGHBORHOOD TRANSFORMATION

Washington Heights is a community plagued with crime, unemployment, overcrowding, and school desertion, among other social afflictions. Networking and collaboration, however, foster associations and organizations willing to transform the community, provide drug rehabilitation centers, after-school programs, English as a second language classes, leadership training, legal advice, naturalization classes, voter registration campaigns, and other resources. According to the Hispanic Federation's annual survey on leadership and civic responsibility, social service agencies conducting massive voting registration campaigns impacted the growing numbers of the

Hispanic electorate in New York City. Programs developed by social service agencies keep thousands of youth off the street with after-school programs in both the ACDP and Alianza Dominicana. The social capital generated by associations and organizations in Washington Heights motivates participation, civic involvement, and brings solutions, albeit partial, to social problems in the neighborhood.

Moreover, the numbers of associations and the different social service agencies and organizations described above have helped develop new individual and community identities more rooted in the host society than in the sending country. A group of leaders, such as Moisés Pérez from Alianza, Victor Moriseti from the ACDP, and Julio Hernández, have developed and/or directed organizations that serve as transitional bridges between newer and older immigrants. they help newer immigrants become familiar with the new system encountered in the United State and active participants in the creation of a strong community able to vote, to work, and at some point to define its own political future as an ethnic community in New York City.

The financial bonanza enjoyed by Dominican social service agencies vanished when in 1994 Rudolph William Guiliani became the new mayor of New York City. Mayor Guiliani lowered projected spending by 7.8 million to alleviate the 2.2 billion deficit of Dinkins' administration. He lowered the budget through a series of cost cutting measures among them were the funds allocated to social service agencies around the city. Many Dominican organizations were forced to terminate some of their programs. More significantly, competition over scarce resources emerged between the different social service agencies in the Dominican community.

These organizations still develop programs to empower the community. In the past, collaboration between these organizations was instrumental to the cohesion of the Dominican community, supporting the social service agencies program, responding to citizenship drives, and being part of the incorporation of Dominicans. Competition hampered the political enthusiasm in the community and people trust in community leaders weaken. Many community residents have voiced their disenchantment in newspaper articles, television programs, and writing graffiti in neighborhood walls.

## NOTES

1. In the summer of 1992, Washington Heights erupted in riots, protesting the assassination of a young man—by a police officer—who was identified as a drug dealer.

2. I also identified other social service and voluntary associations working with women. Among them is The Dominican Women's Development Center, The Dominican Caucus, Dominican Women Against Violence, and Dominican Women United. I analyze these organizations in Chapter 8.

CHAPTER 6

# Dominicans' Politics of Community Control

THIS CHAPTER NARRATES THE EXPERIENCE OF THE POLITICAL INCORPORATION OF Dominicans. This political incorporation required the collective action of individuals who have acquired a mobilizationist ethnic consciousness. I argued that factors such as political ethnic awareness, ethnic and racial coalitions, the gains of the civil right movements, and the dual citizenship of Dominicans, interplay in the process of Dominican politics of incorporation. The political awareness of Dominicans in the United States has been ignored and underestimates by scholars. For example, in 1981 Ira Katznelson wrote:

> Yet, for a variety of reasons, it was impossible for the Hispanic population to have any but a subordinated role in the political bloc of "new" Washington Heights-Inwood. (Katznelson 1981: 131)

In 1998 Silvio Torres-Saillant and Ramona Hernández, two leading figures in Dominican studies in the United States, wrote:

> At present, however, the [Dominican] community suffers from a political invisibility that is hardly justifiable in light of the great size of the Dominican population. (Torres-Saillant and Hernández 1998: 96)

By the year 2000, it seems that Dominicans have overcome this subordinated role and political invisibility and have taken control of Washington Heights' politics. Dominicans are the first group of new immigrants to the United States after the 1965 Immigration Act to have gained electoral representation in both the New York City Council and the New York State Assembly. Dominicans knew New York City was home and they started a conscious process to take control of their largest community, Washington

73

Heights. By community control, I mean decentralization, participation, power sharing, and neighborhood government (Navarro 1998: 11). German Jews, who held the majority on the community board, the school board, and the political machinery, politically controlled Washington Heights. But during the late 1970s and the 1980s, Dominican leaders successfully targeted Community Planning Board 12, then Community School Board 6, and the Democratic Party district leadership. Later on, in the 1990s, that same leadership successfully targeted the City Council and the New York State Assembly, winning one seat in each of these bodies.

Many factors have played into the process of community control. These factors include a will for community control, and ethnic and racial coalitions. Another factors are both domestic and foreign processes, which I call political catalyzers of the process of incorporation of Dominicans. Domestic catalyzers are the political actions occurring in the United States that pave the way for ethnic political participation and incorporation, such as the political gains of the civil rights movement. Foreign catalyzers are the political actions taken by the Dominican government that facilitate the political involvement of Dominicans in the Diaspora, such as granting dual citizenship to those Dominicans that might acquire foreign citizenship.

## POLITICAL CATALYZERS

A major political event in the Dominican Republic impacted Dominicans in the Diaspora: in 1994 the Dominican Congress amended the Constitution to include the right to dual citizenship. This was the result of the *Pacto por la Democracia* (Pact for Democracy), an agreement signed by the three main political parties in August 1994, after a post-electoral crisis lasting over two months. Any Dominican could be naturalized with another citizenship without losing Dominican citizenship. This constitutional change impacted Dominicans in the United States in major ways. First, it addressed the concerns of many Dominicans in the United States who did not want to become U.S. citizens for fear of losing their Dominican citizenship. As a result, the numbers of naturalized Dominicans increased considerably during the mid-1990s. Second, many Dominican political parties, including the leading Revolutionary Dominican Party (Partido Revolucionario Dominicano—PRD), also assumed a dual political position in New York City. They supported political activities developed by Dominican-Americans and at the same time supported political activism back in the Dominican Republic, accepting publicly their dual political commitment. This dual position helped Dominican-Americans attract more Dominicans to vote and to create a political voice city, state, and nationwide.

An important domestic catalyzer to push Dominicans to become United States citizens and exercise their political rights was the anti-immigrant campaign developed in the United States in the mid-1990s. United States House Speaker Newt Gingrich's exacerbated attacks on immigrants created the base for changes in the Immigration and Naturalization Service, Welfare, and other political measures that affected immigrants negatively. In 1994, Governor Pete Wilson's Proposition 187 was passed in California. In 1996, a new welfare law was approved, making very difficult for legal residents to obtain social service benefits. Also in 1996, the Immigration and Naturalization Service enacted a law jeopardizing family reunification, and President Clinton approved the anti-terrorist law that demanded the deportation of any legal or illegal immigrant who participated in any criminal act in the United States.

The unintended consequences of all these negative measures was that millions of Latinos became United States citizens during this period, and a very high percentage of them went to the polls in future elections. Even though naturalization rates declined steadily from 1965 to 1993, falling from 63 to 38 percent, in the mid-1990s, naturalization rates increased substantially. According to the INS, a total of 598,225 persons were naturalized in fiscal year 1997. The number of naturalizations in 1997 was the second highest in U. S. history, following the all-time record of 1,044,698 in 1996.

Until 1994 the annual number of persons naturalized had never exceeded 400,000, except during World War II in 1944. Mexico was the leading country of birth of persons naturalized in 1997, with 142,569 or 23.8 percent of the total. Other major countries naturalizing citizens were Vietnam (36,178), the Philippines (30,898), India (21,206), the Dominican Republic (21,092), the People's Republic of China (20,947), and Jamaica (20,253).

Even during the time of low naturalization rates, in New York City, more Dominicans than any other Latino group in New York City were naturalized from 1982 to 1989, as table 5 shows.

**Table 5: Persons Naturalized by Selected Country of Birth, New York City and the United States, 1982-1989**

|  | Number | | Percent | |
| --- | --- | --- | --- | --- |
|  | NYC | U.S. | NYC | U.S. |
| All persons naturalized | 229,681 | 1,777,847 | 100.0 | 100.0 |
| NYC's Top Source Countries | 178,043 | 1,099,373 | 77.5 | 61.8 |
| Dominican Republic | 27,581 | 43,333 | 12.0 | 2.4 |
| China | 25,009 | 138,444 | 10.9 | 7.8 |
| Jamaica | 17,457 | 42,802 | 7.6 | 2.4 |
| Soviet Union | 17,349 | 49,351 | 7.6 | 2.8 |
| Guyana | 13,532 | 21,646 | 5.9 | 1.2 |
| Haiti | 9,567 | 19,986 | 4.2 | 1.1 |
| Greece | 6,763 | 23,947 | 2.9 | 1.3 |
| Philippines | 6,505 | 198,936 | 2.8 | 11.2 |
| Colombia | 6,263 | 32,627 | 2.7 | 1.8 |
| Korea | 6,186 | 115,967 | 2.7 | 6.5 |

Source: New York City Department of City Planning, The Newest New Yorkers, June 1992: 132.

According to these data, naturalization rates were low for all national groups in the United States, but Dominican naturalization rates were among the highest ones nationwide and the largest in New York City from 1982 to 1989, and 1997. In the same manner, Dominicans are having high rates of voting. In New York City, Dominicans represent 25 percent of Hispanics registered to vote. This voting population is geographically concentrated in areas that have made significant impacts in the election of Linares and Espaillat to the New York City Council and the New York State Assembly.

Another domestic catalyzer was the impact of the civil rights movement on the political incorporation of minorities in the United States since the 1960s. African-Americans have influenced the development of minority political incorporation fundamentally. The struggle of African-Americans for civil rights created a favorable political platform for other minorities to launch their political aspirations. Latinos, Asian-Americans, and American Indians benefit from constitutional amendments, judicial decisions, laws, and administrative practices that originally came into existence to protect African-Americans, as do many other minorities, including groups not defined by race and ethnicity such as women, the aged, and the handicapped (Glazer 1981:23). Affirmative action, desegregation, the Voting Rights Act of 1965, the adoption of a single-member district system, among other political vindications of the civil rights movement, have facilitated the political incorporation of minorities in the United States. "As a result of the implementation of the Voting Rights Act of 1965 by the United States Department of Justice, many cities covered by the act re-adopted the single-member district system to promote the election of blacks to the city council" (Zimmerman 1992: 5). This trend gave Dominicans a favorable legal system for their politics of incorporation.

## THE IMPACT OF THE CIVIL RIGHTS MOVEMENT IN THE POLITICAL CAREER OF DOMINICANS

During the 1990s, Guillermo Linares and Adriano Espaillat were elected to the New York City Council and State Assembly, respectively. Both seats are based in districts that were reformed in the early 1990s under the mandate of the Voting Rights Act. In 1990 and 1991, the City of New York underwent a redistricting process for the city council. The reorganization of local political institutions led to the expansion of the council from 35 to 51 seats. The New York City Districting Commission, which oversaw the process, focused on improving the changes for the representation of previously under-represented groups. The districting commission as such a group identified Dominicans.

The geographic concentration of Dominicans was essential in the creation of these two new electoral districts. In the 1980 census, upon which the existing districts were based, Hispanics, mostly Dominicans made up 62 percent of the voting age population in District Six, Washington Heights, while non-Hispanic whites and non-Hispanic blacks accounted for 21 percent and 15 percent, respectively. Hispanics made up only 32 percent of the registered voters in this district, while non-Hispanic white voters were almost 40 percent of registered voters. Within District Five, in West Harlem, African-Americans formed the largest minority group, representing 77 percent of registered voters (Graham 1998: 51). Thus, creating a district to maximize Hispanic voting power required merging and re-dividing districts Six and Five and parts of eight. The districting commission finally approved the final plan for District Ten, or the "Dominican district," in June 1991 (See Map 2.)

The new District Ten contained 43 percent Hispanic registered voters, compared to 32 percent non-Hispanic, white registered voters, and 23 percent non-Hispanic Black registered voters (Graham 1998: 52).

Redistricting for the New York State Assembly took place in 1992 and resulted in 11 majority-Latino districts (out of a total of 61 districts) in the state. The previous District 72 was 65 percent Latino and the new one was 78 percent Latino in 1990 (Graham 1998: 55). As in the case of the city council districts, new lines were drawn that help to maximize the chances of the election of Latino candidates. (See Map 3.)

## ETHNIC COALITIONS

Inter-racial coalitions were vital for the electoral political success of Dominicans. Peggy Sheppard, an African-American activist in West Harlem and co-founder of West Harlem Environmental Action, stressed during interviews the importance of creating coalitions between the local African-American and Dominican communities. Although she resented the low level of cooperation between the two communities, she acknowledged that Dominican leaders in Washington Heights had succeeded in building inter-racial coalitions and how that has been instrumental in the neighborhood's political development. According to Sheppard, Guillermo Linares owed much of his political success to connections he established outside the Dominican community. During interview, Linares himself acknowledges the importance of ethnic coalitions in his political career.

> Before I was a councilman, I had been a community activist for more than fifteen years in the Dominican community of Upper Manhattan, specifically in the area of education. Since the very beginning, I understood the importance of making alliances and connections with other communities. I also recognized that the group that is pushing you ahead is your own ethnic group at the immediate level. But you also have potential allies with whom you are struggling together and whom you unite efforts and promote collective agendas. The results are more effective and viable solutions and with a wider outreach.

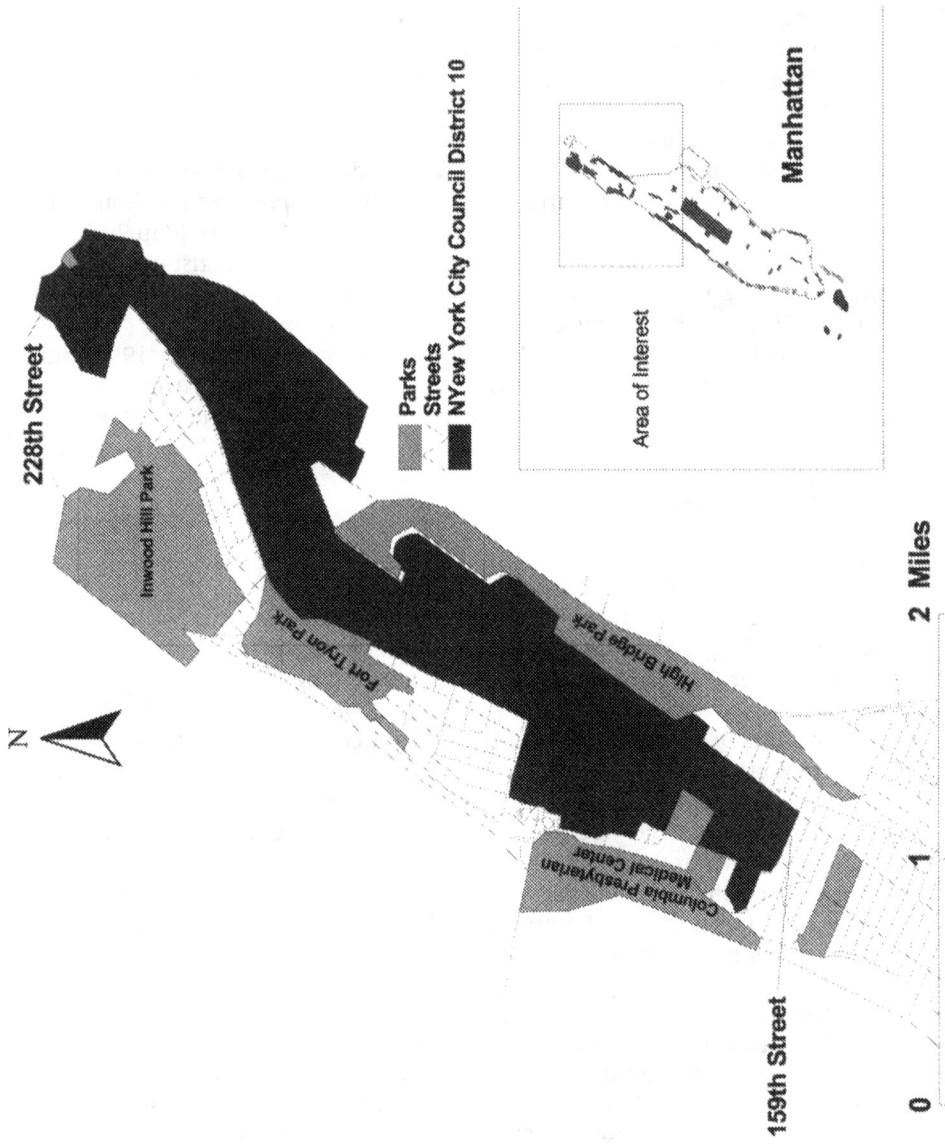

Map 2: Tenth (10) City Council District (New York City)

228th Street

Inwood Hill Park

Fort Tryon Park

High Bridge Park

Columbia Presbyterian Medical Center

159th Street

N

Parks
Streets
NYew York City Council District 10

Area of interest

Manhattan

0          1          2 Miles

**Map 3: 72nd New York State Assemby District**

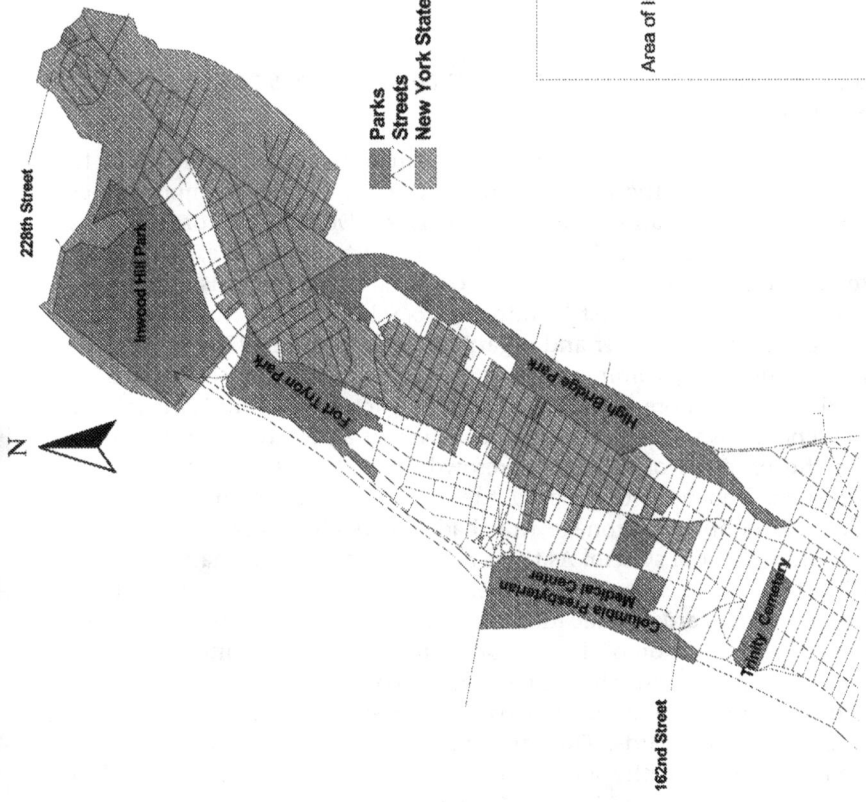

Parks
Streets
New York State Assembly District 72

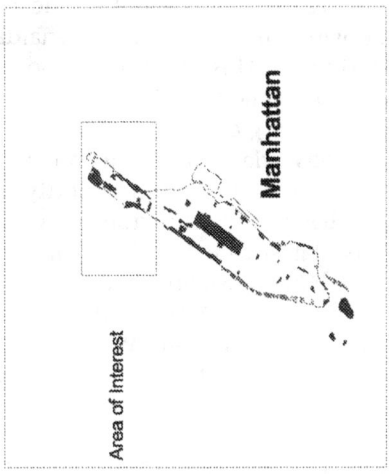

228th Street

Inwood Hill Park

Fort Tryon Park

High Bridge Park

Columbia Presbyterian
Medical Center

Trinity Cemetery

162nd Street

N

Area of Interest

Manhattan

0          1          2 Miles

Guillermo Linares successfully coordinated alliances with many other ethnic and racial groups in New York City. Other community leaders shared Linares's concerns about ethnic and racial coalitions. For example, the well-known community leader Zenaida Méndez, responsible for Hispanic affairs during Dinkins' administration and founder of the Dominican Women's Caucus, underlined the importance of establishing connections with other minorities groups in the city. Méndez stated that although efforts are made for networking, they are not sufficient when there are so many threats against immigrant and minority communities in the United States.

Beyond Washington Heights, both Guillermo Linares and Adriano Espaillat attracted multi-ethnic support. African-Americans supported them both. Congressman Charles Rangel was a strong supporter of these two candidates. David Dinkins, former mayor of New York City, was very influential in Linares' campaign. White progressives in New York City backed both candidates. Former Manhattan Borough President Ruth Messinger also endorsed the candidacy of Dominicans.

## FROM COMMUNITY BOARD TO THE NEW YORK STATE ASSEMBLY

By the late 1970s, Dominican leaders had already identified control of the community board and the school board as key components of empowerment and political incorporation (Lescaille 1994: 2). Dominicans or any other immigrant, regardless of their legal status can participate, vote, or be a candidate in both the school board and the community board. This initial phase led to the election of the first Dominican to School Board Number 6, Sixto Medina, a community leader and organizer from the late 1970s.

During the 1980s, community organizations linked themselves with parents and created a more expansive movement to elect Dominicans to community school boards. The boards were viewed as an electoral mechanism to address the problem of school overcrowding and substandard education. Organizations and parents exposed the educational mismanagement, corruption, and political patronage that had negatively impacted Dominican children in the school system. As these advocates pushed to change the local school system, a battle emerged between progressive Dominican educational activists and the Board of Education bureaucracy (Lescaille 1994: 3). The net result was the suspension of the school board in 1987 by Chancellor Nathan Quiñones, a Puerto Rican. The dismantling of community School Board 6 led to ongoing efforts by Dominican activists to elect Dominican parents to the community school boards. This movement led to the election of several Dominican activists to the school board, during the late 1980s and 1990s, among them Apolinar Trinidad and Guillermo Linares.

Since the late 1970s, the Dominican community has had a Dominican woman, María Luna, as district leader representing the inner circles of the Democratic machine in Washington Heights/Inwood and also as an active member of Community Planning Board 12. In 1985, Dominican activists, however, launched a movement challenging the political establishment in Washington Heights/Inwood. The grassroots character of this local empowerment movement led to the election of another Dominican district leader of the Democratic Party, Julio Hernández, a longtime community activist and co-founder of the Northern Manhattan Coalition, who defeated the incumbent, Dr. Albert Blumberg. Dominican Ivelisse Fairchild replaced María Gónzalez, of Spanish decent, as a district leader.

## THE 1990 NEW YORK CITY COUNCIL ELECTIONS AND DOMINICANS

The implementation of a new City Charter and the redistricting of electoral districts were essential to the election of the first Dominican to the New York City Council in 1990. That same year, three Dominican candidates ran in District 10 on the Democratic ticket, Guillermo Linares, María A. Luna, and Adriano Espaillat. Apolinar Trinidad, another Dominican, ran for the Conservative Party. The results of the primary races for New York City in District 10 were the following:

**Table 6: Results of the Democratic Party Primary, City Council District 10**

| | | |
|---|---|---|
| Guillermo Linares | 1,843 | 30% |
| María A. Luna | 1,585 | 26% |
| Adriano Espaillat | 1,550 | 25% |
| Harry C. Fotopoulos | 860 | 14% |
| Raymond Edwards | 294 | 5% |

Source: Fernando Lescaille, "Dominican Political Empowerment." Dominican Public Policy Project. New York: Dominican Public Policy. 1994: 4

Luna placed second, losing by 258 votes; and Espaillat was third, losing by 293 votes. The two non-Dominican candidates placed fourth and fifth respectively. Linares, capturing the Democratic Party nomination, later trounced Adriano Espaillat and Apolinar Trinidad on the liberal and conservative sides respectively. This was the first time that Dominicans participated in a United States party primary.

## GUILLERMO LINARES AND HIS POLITICAL CAMPAIGN

Linares is the first elected Dominican official in the United States and the leading elected official among new immigrants in the city.

Upon winning the Democratic Party primary, Linares attracted the support of white liberals, African-Americans, and Puerto Ricans. Although Linares
had the sympathies of parents who were with him when he was part of the
school board, he did not have a structure to organize his campaign in
Washington Heights. This was the first campaign of its kind in the
Dominican community. Were Dominicans ready to support a candidate of
their own? Dominicans were familiar with Dominican campaigns but not
with campaigning for a Dominican candidate for the United States system.
Linares and members of the Dominican Workers Party (Partido de los
Trabajadores Dominicanos-PTD) agreed to create the electoral apparatus for
the Linares campaign. Ramón Gutiérrez, Juan Villar and Radamés Pérez from
the PTD, Linares and Anthony Stevens, started a discussion process that led
two major agreements. First, they asked for a community agenda that included youth issues, community leadership, police brutality, and undocumented
immigrants. Second was the campaign's operative plan. This plan targeted
community voters through visits to apartments, street encounters, walks,
phone calls, direct visits to United States citizens in the community, and caravans. Dominicans responded positively. The following chart shows the
processes followed during the campaign.

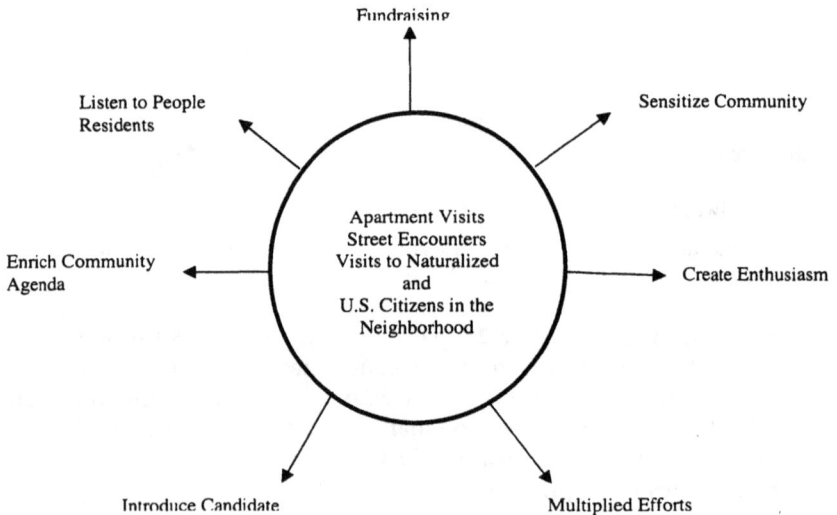

**Chart 6: Guillermo Linares' Electoral Campaign**

Through apartment visits and street encounters, Linares' campaign reached-
more people, created enthusiam, collected money, and multiplied efforts.

## EFFORTS TO WIN A SEAT IN THE NEW YORK STATE ASSEMBLY

The 1992 election provided a unique opportunity for the election of the first Dominican to the New York State Assembly. Redistricting of Assembly electoral districts had provided for the 72nd Assembly District to be composed of 78 percent Latinos, mostly Dominicans. The 72nd Assembly District encompasses Washington Heights, Inwood, and Marble Hill in Upper Manhattan. Three candidates ran for the seat in 1992: white incumbent Brian Murtaugh and two challengers. One of them was Julio Hernández, a Dominican activist, former district leader, and former deputy director of Mayor Dinkins' Office of Latino Affairs. The other, William Alicea, a Puerto Rican, was former district leader and a city government employee. Assemblyman John Brian Murtaugh emerged as the winner obtaining 3,196 votes. Julio Hernández, the Dominican challenger obtained 1,993 votes. William Alicea ran third place. Julio Hernández' campaign lacked unity among Dominicans. Moreover, alliances with other ethnic and racial groups were also poor. The first attempt to conquer a seat in the New York State Assembly failed.

The 1996 elections provided another opportunity for the election of a Dominican candidate. In 1996 the conditions were more favorable for the Dominican candidacy for several reasons: first, a great number of Dominicans as well as other immigrants had become U.S. citizens previously; social service agencies in Washington Heights made extraordinary efforts to register the maximum number of voters in the neighborhood; and a wide variety of alliances were possible at the community level, in the city and state to support the Dominican candidate. Adriano Espaillat, a longtime Dominican leader emerged as the winner against Brian Murtaugh.

## CONCLUSION

Dominicans are gaining increasing political representation in New York. Electoral victories are the result of a conscious process of community control in which many different factors converge to create favorable conditions. Dominican process of incorporation was a bottom-up process that involved grassroots politics to sensitize community residents.

For example school board elections became occasions in which Dominican parents learned about the American political process. They serve in the creation of a community political base by not only denouncing school overcrowding and low standards in education, but also gaining the support of parents in denouncing and voting to change the old leadership and old political structures in Washington Heights.

Besides the leadership built through school board elections and community agencies, many other factors were at play in the political success in the city council and state Assembly elections. First, two Dominican political parties (PRD and PTD) created a political base, gaining the favor of many newer immigrants. Dominican parties supported and even designed political strategies for one of the candidates during the city council campaign in 1990. The

Dominican Workers Party (Partido de los Trabajadores Dominicanos) claims that it was actively involved in the design and implementation of the Linares political campaign. These activities reflect a wide base of support at the community level for its candidates.

An important segment of the Dominican community of Washington Heights has, consciously and successfully, become involved in activities to create a political voice for Dominicans in New York City. Concomitantly with dual/transmigrant behaviors, another process is taking place within the Dominican community, a process that resembles what happened to earlier immigrant communities in New York City and other cities of the United States, such as Puerto Ricans and Mexicans and even white immigrant communities, which earlier during this century started to evolve as ethnic communities building political and economic niches. Like the Italian or Irish community in the United States, Dominicans are starting a process that might culminate in the construction of a firm Dominican ethnic political community in New York City.

Washington Heights' leadership has been successful in bringing people together, creating political citizens with a political voice, and generating social capital for the development of their community. Marginality pushed Dominicans to struggle to overcome social afflictions. Dominican leadership awareness of Dominican "otherness" pushed them to create organizations, to take control over the community political structure. Political gains, recognition, the creation of a political voice, and representation in the decision-making bodies in New York City and State are part of Dominican political success. However, it seems that when power was achieved, leaders forget about the reasons that originated the struggle. Leaders start to define themselves according to their own individuality and personal aspirations and the well being of the community is forgotten.

The process of community control and incorporation is also plagued with divisions, animosity, and competition between political leaders. The episode of the construction of a mega supermarket in East Harlem and other events illustrate my point. In 1995, the New York City Council had to vote for the construction of a Path mark supermarket in East Harlem. Dominican grocery store owners opposed the supermarket because it would harm their business. Dominican businessmen seek the support of the Dominican councilman Guillermo Linares, who committed himself to the plight of Dominican businessmen. The night of the elections, Guillermo Linares voted in favor of the construction of the Path mark solving a voting tide. The next morning many Washington Heights walls were graffiti with "Linares Traitor." Flyers circulated in the community denouncing Linares sell out. This episode brought divisions and animosity between community leaders and the community itself.

In 1997, a New York Times article claimed that there was not political unity in the Dominican community. The article referred to the battle between Guillermo Linares's candidate Victor Morrisetti and the incumbent

Adriano Espaillat in the Democratic Party primary for the candidacy to the New York State Assembly in Voting District 72nd. Guillermo Linares opposed Adriano Espaillat throughout the campaign, first supporting Victor Morrisetti and eventually supporting a Dominican woman against Espaillat. Eventually Espaillat won the primaries and re-elected. Linares and Espaillat remained enemies since then.

Politics of incorporation has also neglected the participation of women. For example, in 1999, the Dominican-American Roundtable took part in Providence, Rhode Island. Most women organizations and other women leaders were present. Workshops were held, discussing women political position in the Diaspora. During the general assembly meeting, women demanded to be part of the decision-making body, the directive committee of the Dominican-American Roundtable. The answers of Dominican male leaders were: "this is not the moment," "there are more important issues ahead to waste time with these women," "you have to wait a more proper time." No a single woman was elected to the directive.

Moreover, the Dominican community remains significantly isolated from other minority communities, such as the African-American, Asian, and other Latino communities in New York City. Consequently, the Dominican community has had little impact on major societal transformation.

# CHAPTER 7

# The Added Burden for Dominican Women

THE NUMERICAL IMPORTANCE AND THE VISIBILITY OF DOMINICANS CONTINUE TO grow in New York City. Dominicans are developing their own communities and at the same time incorporating themselves into American society. Dominicans work to "legalize" their status in the United States, to learn the English language, to naturalize, to exercise their voting rights, to participate in politics, and to mobilize their communities for social and economic gains. Dominican women incorporate into the United States faster than men. Women develop roots faster than men in the United States. Dominican women have higher levels of naturalization, college enrollment, and lower levels of return migration.

The success of Dominican women is a surprise. Dominican women have an added burden. They have to fight the ill effects of the decline of the manufacturing sector that left thousands of Dominicans unemployed. They also have to become their household breadwinners. For example, statistical data show that women head more than 49 percent of Dominican households. Women learn that adapting—learning the English language, pursuing an education, involving into politics—may be the key for success in a city that places them at its margins. Moreover, Dominican women encountered a society that in spite of its structural constraints offers more opportunities than what they left behind. I identify, through personal testimonies, the complex and compelling reasons for how women incorporate into the United States.

María Vasquez migrated from Santo Domingo, the capital city, to New York City in 1983. Now in her forties, María heads her households, supporting her three teenage sons. Her husband abandoned her a few years ago and she had to provide for her children. She had worked everywhere, in factories, selling clothing, and cleaning houses. When she first came to New York, she worked in a belt factory for three years. Then the factory closed and she remained unemployed. With the help of a friend, she got in contact with a man who sold stolen designers' suit at very cheap prices. She used to get $300 suits for less than $40 dollars, which she then sold for $100. But the supplier went to jail and she lost the business. Then she started to clean houses in Manhattan and Westchester. She saved some money and bought a car that she now uses as a taxi. Even though she always wanted to achieve an education, she could not attend college because she did not have anybody to help her with the children. She took ESL classes. But still, she feels she can do better than driving a taxi.

As illustrated by María's story, Dominican women have an added burden. They are both breadwinners and household caretakers. In spite of this added burden, María is incorporating faster than her male fellow workers. For example, Maria Vasquez speaks English, participates in their children's school PTA, and is working actively in the organization of a livery taxi union. She became a United States citizen some years ago and has voted in all subsequent elections. When I asked about her male, fellow workers' knowledge of English, union participation, and naturalization rates, she said:

> I always have to translate for them. Only the man helping us to put the union together speaks English, the rest of us with my exception do not speak the English language. In the group I believe I am the only one with American citizenship.

She feels different. While she aspires to buy a house in the suburbs someday, and help her children through college, many of her male counterparts "work as horses to save money and come back to the Dominican Republic eventually."

Many Dominican women's experiences are similar to María's. Many are unemployed, are head of households, make a living in the informal sector of the economy, but most of them also aspire to get a college education.

## DOMINICAN WOMEN STRATEGIES OF ECONOMIC SURVIVAL

My research also shows that Dominican women create alternative survival strategies. When the manufacturing sector shrank, leaving thousands of Dominican unemployed, Dominican women took refuge in the informal sector of the economy. During my research, I encountered numerous forms of this underground economy performed by women. My list of "off-the-books" activities includes itinerant beauticians, bakers, and clothing peddlers. There are many advantages in these jobs. Through these activities women support themselves and their children. They do not have to care about babysitting because they work at home. They work in their own schedule allowing them to schedule to take English as a Second Language classes and/or technical courses, and attend college.

## Itinerant Beauticians

Many Dominican women who do not have the money to rent space for their beauty parlors, offer their services to their clients in their own apartments. They travel in subways and buses with big bags full of cosmetics and other beauty aids. One Saturday morning in 1995, I was in the apartment of Nancy, a Dominican woman, married and with three children. Nancy invited me to her house so I could meet Altagracia, an itinerant beautician who was coming to her house to do her nails and hair. I wanted to meet Altagracia so I could ask her for an interview. Altagracia knocked at Nancy's door at about 11:15 A.M. We all sat in the kitchen. Altagracia asked Nancy if she still wanted to color her hair. Nancy said yes. Altagracia placed Nancy's head in the kitchen sink and, after she had placed a couple of bottles and boxes around the sink, shampooed her, applied the color, and then a plastic cap while, asking Nancy to sit next to the table to do her nails. When she finished Nancy's nails, she took Nancy to the sink to finish her shampoo. She blew-dry Nancy's hair, leaving a beautiful hairdo. Altagracia charged Nancy $35. She was done at 12:30 P.M. She spoke to me while working on Nancy. She gave me her phone number and asked me to call her on Monday, her free day.

When I talked to Altagracia, she told me that she had ten steady clients in different parts of the Bronx. She made between $200 and $400 every week depending on the number of clients and the service. She did not plan to get a location for her business because rents were very high and she was doing fine. Altagracia is single and lives by herself. She is taking evening GED and ESL classes in her neighborhood public school. She longs to get her High School diploma so she can go to college. She got her permanent residency card two months ago but is already making plans to become naturalized within five years when the legal waiting time is due.

Nora, another Dominican woman, separated and with two children seven and nine years old, whom I met through Altagracia, takes care of her clients in her own house. Nora gives morning appointments when her children are at school. She told me that she had an average of one or two clients a day. Now she is also taking care of clients on Saturdays. For Nora learning English has not been easy. She said that she will never learn the language. But her lack of English does not stop her from taking United States citizenship classes at a community center.

## The Dominican Cake Industry

During my research, I met several women who made their living baking birthday, Baptism, anniversary, and other special occasion cakes. Mary, a Dominican, married with three children, 3, 5, and 9 years old, said that the only way that her family can live in relative comfort is with what she contributes with her cake business. She bakes an average of six cakes a week of different sizes and weight. She charges $35 per pound making at least $400 weekly. Mary and I went shopping. We bought decorations, flour, sugar, butter, vanilla, syrups, eggs, liquor, and other ingredients to supply her baking business for two weeks. She spent $177. The following week she baked four cakes. One of the cakes weighed one pound, the other two pounds, and the other two, three pounds each, making $315. She had plenty of material for the following week. Mary's major ambition is to see their children grow and become professionals. She joined a program at her children's school to learn English and learn skills to help her children with home works.

Minerva is another Dominican woman who makes a living baking cakes. Minerva's specialty is decoration. She makes the best *suspiro* (merengue) and also the most attractive ornaments for children's birthdays and weddings. When I first came into her house, the first thing I spotted was the kitchen. Even though it looked small with all the utensils and decorations hanging from the ceiling, the living room was a workshop. Her teenage daughter was sitting in a corner in the living room away from all the pots full of *suspiro* and the cakes waiting for Minerva's artistic hands. Within two hours, Miverva transformed four layers of plain cakes into the most beautiful wedding cake with water fountains, sugar flowers, and sophisticated layers of *suspiro*. Immediately she took two big layers of cake and put one on top of the other, after spreading a guava paste between the two. She covered the whole thing with blue *suspiro*, which she decorated with yellow and green layers of *suspiro* in different shapes and artistic forms. On top of this work of art, she placed a huge Barney toy decorated with blue, yellow, and green ribbons. Barney was holding a flag reading Happy Birthday. For both cakes, Miverva made $800.

Minerva separated from her husband when her daughter was three years old. At the beginning she was devastated. She did not know what to do. She was feeling so depressed she wanted to kill herself. But soon she learned that life had to go, mostly because her daughter depended only on her. She took a job in a factory and hired a babysitter for her daughter. She realized that working in a factory was not very promising. She went on welfare and started her business baking cakes. At the same time, she finished an associated degree at Hostos Community College and managed to communicate in English. "That was very beneficial for me and my daughter. I could help her with homework and I could communicate with her teachers." She also said: "even though I have an associated degree I decided to keep my home business because I can stay home and keep an eye on my daughter. Maybe when she is gone to college I might come back to get a bachelor degree."

## Clothing Peddlers

"Selling clothes and underwear is the best business of all," Mercedes told me. Mercedes and Elena were in the business of selling clothes and underwear for many years. They buy clothes and underwear in New Jersey and Pennsylvania and sell each piece of clothing for twice the price it cost them. This price is still competitive in New York City. On many occasions when they *fian* (give credit) people, they raise the price three times more. Maria sells bags. She buys them in downtown Manhattan at the warehouse a 28th Street and 6th Avenue. Juana sells perfumes and Avon deodorants in the street along St. Nicholas Avenue. Nieves organizes credit-rotating associations in which her clients get towels, bathroom sets, bedspreads and sheets, pots, and other household appliances on credit.

These ethnographic narratives call attention to a growing economic sector in New York City. These off-books activities deserve further research and many more questions should be explained, such as the sheer numbers, the range of survival strategies, and the gendering of income-generating activities. However, I conclude the following. First, women in my sample have found alternative ways to make a living and provide for their families. Some of them combine welfare benefits with informal income generating activities, making their lives more livable. Second, these women can make a living and take care of their children while working at home. Third, they also find the time to take ESL classes, technical courses, United States citizen classes, and participate in their children's school activities such as PTAs, and parent skills development workshops.

## DOMINICAN WOMEN HEAD OF HOUSEHOLDS

The Dominican diaspora exhibits high numbers of female-headed households. Other Hispanic populations in the United States such as Colombians, female-headed households result from widowhood, while for Dominicans as well as Puerto Ricans, the higher percentages of female-headed families fall into the divorced, separated, or never-married categories (Bean and Tienda 1987: 191–192 and Gilbertson and Gurak 1992: 23). These female-headed households are considered to be the poorest in the nation.

The economic situation of Dominican women heading households in the United States is worsened by several factors: first, the constraints imposed by policy makers and politicians, embedded in an ideology that favors nuclear families and neglects single parent households; second, as has been the case with Puerto Ricans (and especially women), their poor labor-market standing is explained partly by their geographic concentration in the Northeast, where employment opportunities in the garment and textile industries declined sharply (Bean and Tienda 1987: 286). Similarly, employment transformations in New York City accelerated poverty and welfare dependency among Dominican women. New York City is part of a society planned and organized for nuclear families. What are the advancement opportunities for women heading households in this society? When one deals with immigrant women, the picture gets more obscure. Immigrant women, and specifically Dominican women, confront the problem of language, immigration status, and discrimination, among other obstacles such as sexism and structural constraints. Women struggle every day against such adversities. They share their lives in the following pages.

The case of Ana Lara, shows the struggles of a divorce woman to raise her children and get an education. Her husband abandoned her and later on divorced her when her two children were still small. They had properties in the United States, a supermarket in Washington Heights and money in the bank. When he left her, he sold the business and took all the money with him back to the Dominican Republic. She kept a house in Jackson Heights. With no job, not knowing the English language and with only enough skills to work in the garment industry, Ana took ESL classes, took a nursing course, got involved in community issues, and raised her children. Ana organized her block to ban a bus that, when turning on her corner, drove inside the sidewalk every morning while her children were going to school. She called neighbors to tell them about the danger. She and other neighbors went to the community district, to politicians, and to city transit until the bus route was changed. During the 1980s, Ana and other friends organized a social service agency in Queens.

Carmen came from the Dominican Republic in 1988. She had several jobs until she earned her green card and got a more stable job as a home attendant. She met a man who promised he would marry her. She became pregnant and discovered that the man was married. She quit her job when she was seven months pregnant and went on welfare. When the baby was five months old, she got a home attendant job off books and found somebody to take care of her baby. Two years later, the old lady she was taking care of died, and almost immediately social services reduced her food stamps. She then made the decision to go back to school. She wanted to go to college to study nursing. When she communicated that to her social worker at the social services department, she learned that she was not going to get babysitting allowances if she went to a four-year college. That discouraged her, so she enrolled in the job-training program held by the social services administration, although she knew that after she finished she would not be able to make enough to support herself and her son. She knew that with the skills she was learning in that program she would not be able to compete in the labor market. I met Carmen again in May 2000. She was still on welfare and taking care of old people.

Fela came to the United States in 1991. She came with her three daughters. Back in the Dominican Republic, her husband had left her for a younger woman. After the divorce, she went to school and became an accountant. But job opportunities were scarce and she decided to migrate, looking for a better life in the United States. She moved with a relative and soon got a job with a cleaner company. She wanted to learn English and take a job as an accountant. But she was working twelve hours a day and did not have the time to take English classes. She still longs to go to school but her reality is that she has to support her three daughters, pay rent, buy groceries and clothing, leaving her with no time or energy to go to school.

Luz came to the United States in 1972 with her father and her two brothers. Her mother came first and later on filled out INS family reunification papers. She was 9 years old and had never gone to school in the Dominican Republic. Here she went to elementary school, junior high and high school and dropped out of school in the ninth grade. At that time their parents wanted to go back to the Dominican Republic, but she wanted to stay here. She left school and got a job in a clothing store. When she was 17 she got pregnant by a man 9 years older than her and who was married and with other children. Eventually, the older man abandoned her and she moved in with her sister.

While living with her sister she dreamed of becoming somebody, getting an education. She started to study to become a secretary but she never finished. She met a man and she moved in with him. She had two other children. But the guy liked to drink and abused her emotionally and physically. He was a very good breadwinner, and her relative did not want her to leave him. She got very depressed. She lost a lot of weight and lost her self-esteem. After ten years of abuse, she abandoned him.

Life was hard after the separation. She worked in a grocery store as a cashier. One day her social worker advised her to go to school. She went and earned her GED at Boricua College. At Boricua College she felt special. She liked people. She liked the social environment. She spent six months preparing for the GED. She went to school from 9 A.M. to 2 P.M. Her sister used to take care of her children, and after school she went to work in the grocery store. After finishing the GED she stayed and completed her bachelors'. When she entered Boricua College she met a man and she fell in love with him. They moved in together. The story of abuse started again. He interrogated her when she smiled or when the phone rang, or when she said hello to somebody in the street. He abused her physically and emotionally. She separated from him and got an order of protection. After the order of protection he got worse. One day he took her in his car near the Hudson River and tried to strangle her. Fortunately, there was a police car coming by and he ran away. Today she is still afraid to walk in the streets. After graduation, she continued to work in the grocery store and took training in a senior citizens center. She found out about a position in Alianza Dominicana and sent her resume. They called her for an interview and she got the job. Since 1996, she is facilitating mandatory court workshops about domestic violence for abused women.

These testimonies are eloquent. In spite of adverse social conditions, women in my sample strive to obtain an education to improve their lives. Ana Lara's story tells about a woman that in spite of her husband abandonment and economic limitations became a community activists. Carmen was limited by institutional policies to pursue an education but learned the English language, became naturalized and exercises her voting rights as a hope of influencing changes that might benefit her. Fela's added burden limited her to pursue her career objectives but also became a United States citizen. Luz used her experience as a battered woman to counsel other women in her community. In summary, women's education is limited by the lack of daycare services, low self-esteem, spouse abuse, and lack of programs sensitive to the reality of these women. Through the testimony we learned that women who received institutional support such as women benefiting from the job placement program of Alianza Dominicana and the Dominican Women's Development Center, and women with mentors prosper in their aspirations.

## CONCLUSION

The data presented above have different readings. Working-class Dominican women evolved different strategies of survival that help them and their families to improve their quality of life. In the midst of their struggles and added burdens women strive to get an education. Many of them are limited by welfare and school policies. But the majority of them are naturalized, and the rest are in the process of becoming United States citizens. All of them strive to learn the English language. The majority of them are involved in community issues such as PTAs, block associations, and social service agencies.

Economic and social burdens are a limitation for these women aspirations. But in spite of all these economic constraints, Dominican women are better represented than Dominican men in higher education. Moreover, Dominican women have much higher rates of naturalization than Dominican men. According to United States Immigration and Naturalization Services and the New York City Department of City Planning, Dominican women have had much higher rates of naturalization than men historically. For example, in 1997, 21,092 Dominicans naturalized, 60 percent were women. Similarly, the number of Dominican women in college is higher than Dominican men. For example, in Lehman College, City University of New York, 77 percent of all Dominican nationals were female during 1993 and 1999. Table 7 shows the rate of graduation, male versus female with their respective graduation dates.

Table 7: Dominican Women, Men, and Graduation Rates, Lehman College (1997-1999)

|        | 1999 | 1998 | 1997 | Total |
|--------|------|------|------|-------|
| Female | 83.3 | 76.7 | 71.4 | 77.9  |
| Male   | 16.7 | 23.3 | 28.6 | 22.1  |

Source: Lehman College, City University of New York, Office of Institutional Research.

Women's added burden, providing for their families financially and emotionally as well as taking care of their households, push them to better themselves. In so doing, they learned ways to adapt to the United States, learning the language, becoming United States citizens, pursuing an education, voting, and becoming community activists.

# CHAPTER 8

# Gender and Dominican Political Incorporation

W OMEN HAVE BEEN ESSENTIAL TO THE DEVELOPMENT OF THE DOMINICAN community of New York City. Women are the foundation of their communities protesting, organizing, bringing resources, and raising consciousness. But few people look at the building of foundations. When one looks at the Dominican community of New York City, the base of that community is also neglected. This chapter examines the role of women in the political incorporation of Dominicans in the United States. I have previously argued that Dominican men dominated mainstream politics, both social service politics and electoral politics, leaving women out of the picture. Dominican women, however, are present, both building and leading the community grassroots politics. While men are the mainstream leaders, running for office, directing the "powerful" social service agencies, being the media spoke-persons, women politicize the grassroots of their communities. The following event descriptions illustrate my argument.

On July 6, 1992, Washington Heights witnessed an uprising characterized by its spontaneity and by its anger at the death of a young Dominican at the hands of a white American police officer. Women were in the spotlight, organizing the protest and negotiating with individuals who wanted to react violently. Women Against Violence, a Dominican organization seeking to stop violence in the community, ran to the place where the first protest was being conducted. These women lighted candles and shouted slogans. Soon thereafter some of the male community organizers found out about the women's organization and started to take control and compete with each other to dominate and lead the movement. These were members of the Dominican left, community-based organizations, and official sectors of the political system of New York City. None of the women organizers were ever recognized as the initial organizers of this movement.

The morning of September 15, 1995, Miriam Méjia, an Alianza Dominicana program officer, on her way to work, passed by the place where María Rivas was murdered the night before by a police officer. Rivas was caught in the middle of a fight between a Dominican man and a police officer in a restaurant in Washington Heights. The police officer shot at the Dominican man, but the shot killed Rivas. Mejía went to her office and met Milagros Batista, the organizer of Dominican Women Against Violence. They called several other women to protest in front of police precinct 34. They gathered more than 300 women and brought the issue into the spotlight. The evening news showed Guillermo Linares defending the case of Rivas against police brutality in Washington Heights. Once again, women were left out. These women, however, continued their struggle until the police officer was sentenced for the death of María Rivas.

These stories show Dominican women creating the political foundations of their communities. Women politicize their communities and also create their organizations. Prior to the 1980s, women's activism remained invisible and in some cases was limited to their roles as secretaries and fundraisers officers of the many Dominican political parties and social clubs. In the 1980s, emerges a consciousness process of creating women's own organizations. This process was characterized by the tension between here and there. Where is the focus of women's struggle? Is it the Dominican Republic? Is it the Dominican community in New York City? Is it both locations?

## HISTORY OF DOMINICAN WOMEN'S ORGANIZATION

With one exception all Dominican women organizations emerging in New York City during the 1980s were politically torn between the Dominican Republic and the United States. Both the Association of Dominican Women and the Women's Collective lived and died to this contradiction. However, there were attempts to create a Dominican women's organization by second-generation Dominican women in the 1980s. This organization focused on the United States and made alliances with other Latina women in New York. A chronicle of Dominican women's organizations looks as follows.

One of the first attempts to create a Dominican women's voice was in 1982 with the creation of the Association of Dominican Women. In this organization converged both women representing different Dominican leftist political parties and independent women. Their first activities focused both on the problems of the Dominican community in the United States while seeking solidarity with issues in the Dominican Republic. Chart 7 on the following page shows these activities.

Two different factions emerged within the Association of Dominican Women. One group of women wanted to focus on local community issues, affecting Dominican women in New York City, such as health, domestic violence, school overcrowding, drugs, housing, and employment. Most of these women did not respond to the political interest of any of the leftist parties influencing the organization. Another group of women were militant leftists. Each represented a different leftist party and each responded to that party's line. Their objective was to gain sympathies for the revolutionary struggle in the Dominican Republic.

**Chart 7: Activities Developed by the Association of Dominican Women 1982-1984**

| ADDRESSING PROBLEMS IN THE UNITED STATES | ADDRESSING PROBLEMS IN THE D.R. |
| --- | --- |
| Community rally to protest against rapists 50 people marched along St. Nicholas Ave. chanting slogans against rapists and calling for immediate police action | Talks about political situation in the D.R. representatives of the Dominican left seeking to gain women sympathies for revolutionary struggle in the D.R. |
| Protest against a sweatshop located at 184th Street between Audubon and Amsterdam. They picketed in front of the sweatshop until authorities closed the illegal factory | More activities oriented toward solidarity in the D.R. |
| Organized the first health fair in Washington Heights at the Juan Pablo Duarte Public School in 1983 | More activities to bring the revolutionary struggle from there (D.R.) to here (U.S.) |

Contradictions based on the focus and nature of Dominican women's struggles arose between party-independent and affiliated women. Contradictions also arose within the affiliated, due to the contradictions between the different political parties behind them. In 1984, these contradictions emerged in a heated and violent discussion that ended up in the organization's rupture.

Many independent and affiliated women disbanded. But also in 1984, some independent women as well as a group of militant created the Dominican Women's Collective. But this organization also succumbed to the same contradictions disbanding the Association of Dominican Women. After many fights, both affiliated and independent women claimed the Collective's name and two organizations with the same name Dominican Women's Collective emerged in 1986. Independent women kept the name until 1988.

A parallel Dominican women's movement was also emerging in New York City during the 1980s. Second-generation Dominican women were organizing themselves with a pragmatic and feminist approach. In late 1980s, these second-generation Dominicans merged their political views with women from the independent Women's Collective and both groups founded the Dominican Women's Development Center, a social service agency.

Affiliated women, basically members of the Dominican Workers' Party (PTD), kept the name for a few months and then disbanded. Another group of both affiliated and independent women who disbanded in 1984 after the rupture of the Association of Dominican Women, created the Dominican

Women's Caucus in 1991. That same year the Caucus divided and a group created a new organization with the name of Dominican Women United. Another organization emerged in the 1990s. The Association of Progressive Women (La Asociación de Mujeres Progresistas), directed by Donis Sánchez, has worked to create a feminist voice in the Dominican community of Washington Heights.

The following chart illustrates the development of the Dominican women's movement in New York City from 1982 to 1999.

**Chart 8: Chronology of Dominican Women Organizations in New York City**

**1982**
Association of Dominican Women
**1984**
Rupture of the Association of Dominican Women
**1984**
Dominican Women's Collective (converged both independent and
dependent  political parties)
**1986**
The same contradictions that ended the association also ended the Dominican
Women's Collective and two organizations with the same name emerged.

| (Independent) | (Dependent) |
|---|---|
| Dominican Women's Collective | The Dominican Women's Collective |
| This organization was renamed | disappeared. |
| "Dominican Women in Action" | |

**1991**
Efforts to re-structure the Association of Dominican Women led to the Dominican
Women's Caucus. Almost immediately the caucus was divided and a new group
emerged called Dominican Women United.

Organizing efforts of second- generation Dominican women in NYC
**1980s**

| Organizing efforts only toward | Efforts to Dominican/Latina |
|---|---|
| Dominican women | Became part of Dominican Women's |
| Dominican Women Against Violence | Development Center |

At present most of these organizations define themselves in relation to their permanent status in this country. Most women organizers and activists define themselves as Dominican-Americans.

## MODELS OF DOMINICAN WOMEN'S ORGANIZATIONS IN THE 1990S

Already in the 1990s, the focus of women's organizations was rooted in the United States. There was not tension between here and there. Instead, the women's movement developed different objectives. Organizations emerged seeking to solve problems affecting the security of sons, husbands, and bothers threatened by police brutality, crime, and street violence. Other organizations emerged seeking to empower women through education and the provision of social services. While other organizations were seeking to create intellectual spaces to discuss women's position in society and bring concrete solutions to Dominican women in the diaspora.

One organization that emerged to care about the safety of sons and husbands was the Dominican Women Against Violence. Women in this organization, protested against street violence in Washington Heights.[1] It was very common in this neighborhood to witness the discovery of dead bodies in parks, dark corners, basements, and other hidden places in Washington Heights and adjacent neighborhoods. Frequently people were caught in the middle of shootings.

Milagros Batista, the founder of Dominican Women Against Violence, said in an interview that women often had to frantically flee the police precinct to the court seeking justice because a son, husband or relative was killed. One woman told me that her son had been killed while buying a soda in a *bodega,* when robbers entered the store and started to shoot their guns. Another woman said that she was once cleaning her house, when she told her husband to go out and not to bother her with the cleaning. Her husband was out in front of the building smoking a cigarette, when he was caught in the middle of gunfire and was killed. Another mother complained that her son was paralyzed from his waist down because he was the victim of a violent act.

Mothers started to make connections among themselves in police precincts, courts, and lawyers' offices. While requesting the same information and going through the same anguish, they shared common experiences. Milagros Batista, a mother, also witnessed violence. She once had to turn away while walking along Amsterdam Avenue because a bloody, dead body was in her way. She was not a direct victim of violence, but she cared for her children, herself, and her community as a whole. She went to the police precinct asking for answers. There she met other mothers. Later on, in Alianza Dominicana, she met more. They organized a meeting and formed their organization. They lobbied for justice. They marched. They gathered in front of City Hall. On one of the gatherings, an illiterate, middle-age woman spoke into the microphone, and as she was speaking sounded like the most fervent political orator. When Batista asked this woman, "Where did you learn to speak like that?" the woman answered, "I always listened to my father, who was a peasant organizer in the Dominican Republic." Many other women also became fervent orator while seeking justice for the death of their sons. Moreover they worked to organized hundred of people to support their struggle, politicizing an entire community. Although, police brutality and crime is still an issue in Washington Heights, these women's struggles brought fruits. Today, Washington Heights is safer. Workshops to sensitize police members about the community have been organized in the neighborhood's police precincts. More Dominican, Latino, and African American policemen and policewomen have been sent to patrol the neighborhood. Entire neighborhood blocks are working together with the police to fight drugs.

From a different perspective, the Dominican Women's Development Center grew out of a pragmatic feminist approach, seeking to empower women and bring solutions to their economic, health, educational needs. Different from a feminist organization in which women get together to analyze and bring intellectual solutions to women's issues of subordination, the Dominican Women's Development Center is a service agency oriented to provide social services to Dominican women as a means of empowering them.

The Center was born on October 6, 1988. The idea of creating the center emerged after a trip to Mexico. Mireya Cruz went to Mexico for a women's conference in 1987, and visited different *colonias* (neighborhoods), and saw women's projects. When she came back, she started to make connections with other Dominican women about the creation of a center similar to those observed in Mexico. According to Rosita Romero, "That was a very interesting period of time. Many women were dispersed and others were disappointed, with so many divisions in the women's groups due to the influence of political parties. There was a lot of apathy about working with women and getting organized." Mireya Cruz added the following:

The center came about as part of the division of the Dominican Women's Collective. Many of the women in the collective took part in the formation of the center. But there was also something very interesting. Other women who had not participated in the women's movement but did participate in parents' and tenants' association in the United States, other women who were second generation Dominicans and have created their own organizations, as well as other Dominican women who participated in international solidarity movements, especially in Nicaragua, became part of this project. The center emerged with a very interesting combination of women of different backgrounds.

The center has undergone many different phases since its foundation. Mireya Cruz provides a chronology of the Center:

> We met for the first time in my house. Later on we decided not to meet anymore in houses and asked permission to hold our meetings in public places. After that we met in Broadway Temple.[2] There were

thirty women present that night. Nine of these women became part of the board of directors. They were Amalia Peña, Rosa Lavern, Rosita Romero, Sonia Gonhorn, Franchesca, myself and more women that I don't remember. What is important is that the center was created in that meeting. I and Rosa Lavern became the co-chairs, Rosita was the treasurer, Amalia was the secretary, and that night all officers were elected among ourselves. Later on we met to create the bylaws. Rosa and myself were working on the bylaws. Rosa was pregnant in her last month. We were talking when she said that she was having contractions. We stopped and amazingly after three hours she called me from the hospital and she told me that she had the baby one hour ago. We continued the meeting by phone. This is impregnated in my mind for the type of engagement, that after a delivery one can keep working about the organization. We were all Dominicans and we continue to work in Broadway Temple. They lent us the place twice a week. I was working part-time and when I left work I stayed working at Broadway Temple until 9 P.M. I was the Center coordinator. We did not have any money, only $30 that we collected in a hat the day the center was created.

The center survived few years without a budget, after Ruth Messinger gave the center $1,500. With this money they started to buy materials for ESL classes. That was the first center's program. For three years everybody worked as volunteer. In 1991, the center got its first grant with the New York Women Foundation for $30,000. After that they hired Rosita as the center executive director. That same year, Rosa Lavern, a second generation Dominican and member of the board of directors, sublet her apartment to become the center's location, when she and her family moved to New Jersey.

The center has grown gradually. After the women's foundation grant, they got funds for the Gift Foundation. After that came the Healthy Hearts program of Columbia Presbyterian Hospital, and after that they received funds from the Community Development Agency in 1992. At present, the center is funded by both private and government institutions. Rosita Romero, executive director of the Dominican Women's Development Center, believes that several Washington Heights groups are succeeding in empowering the community through the provision of services. Romero told me that the main objective of her organization was to unite Dominican women and look for solutions to problems affecting their lives health issues, education, day care, immigration, and male/female relations. In their programs, they use a grassroots curriculum to integrate issues such as women's role in society and assertiveness training, teaching skills such as filling out forms, and dealing with city agencies. Women, participating in the center's programs, can bring their children with them. According to Romero, that way the children feel proud of their mothers, who learn how to help their children with homework and other issues. Furthermore, women's self-esteem is improved.

One of the most important and popular programs at the center is the training and job placement program aimed at community women. In that program, women are taught practical occupational skills such as typing, data entry, and file organizing. The program aims to place these women in jobs at the end of the training. Hundreds of community women have benefited from this program.

In 1998, the Dominican Women's Development Center created an off-site domestic violence program, *Nuevo Amanecer* (New Dawn). This program offers a 24-hour hotline, support groups, individual counseling, and advocacy. Mireya Cruz, the program director, told me that she became involved in domestic violence programs in 1987, when she worked as a volunteer at the Violence Intervention Program in El Barrio and then became the board of director's chairperson. She said, "I always advocated for a domestic violence program in Washington Heights and specifically in the center. We wrote proposals for many years but we never received the funds. But we kept insisting because is a real need to have a program about domestic violence in the community. Finally in 1997, the Crime Victim Board approved the Center's first program on domestic violence. Almost immediately the Division of Criminal Justice also approved another proposal on domestic violence."

Cruz's and the center's insistence on opening a domestic violence program in the Dominican community of Washington Heights responded to the absence of a domestic violence program directed by Dominican women in the community. Most of the programs were located outside the neighborhood, making it even more difficult for women to mobilize to get the benefits of the program. Now women, mostly Dominicans, are referred from the community police precinct, Manhattan's District Attorney Office, and available shelters. Other women travel from Brooklyn and Queens seeking help from women of their own nationality. Some have come to the center's program through its hotline. More significantly, women participating in the center's ESL, training, and other programs have also requested counseling. Cruz told me that she participated in a radio program one Sunday at 6 A.M. On Monday, they received fifty calls from women requesting counseling and information.

The program offers women individual counseling and support groups. Cruz and other women at the center take victims to court and to the hospital as well as place them in refuges. One of Cruz's ambitions is to have a refuge center. She says:

> We help them to get the order of protection and we explain to them what the order means. This is a very frustrating process especially for our women that are not accustomed with dealing in a court and in another language. I wish we could also offer a place where women take refuge, communicate in their own language, and are counseled by other Dominican women.

Other women's organizations in Washington Heights are feminist oriented and instead of providing services provide intellectual spaces for women. Dominican Women United serves as a healing, bonding, and reflection resource. A group of women of different social sectors started to get together in 1991 to talk, study women's issues, and socialize. Dominican Women United—Union de Mujeres Dominicanas (UMD)—is supported by contributions made by its members every month.

During the summer of 1994 the UMD offered space and time for discussion and relaxation for women of different social classes and academic backgrounds every Friday evening. Women gathered in a location that the organization rented at Audubon Avenue and 183rd Street, just across from the well-known Dominican *Liberato* supermarket. I was invited to attend a workshop at UMD's office one Friday afternoon. I arrived half-hour early and found two women waiting outside the building, sitting on the stairs. Antonia Urbaez, UMD's president, arrived at 7:30 P.M.

On the second floor where the women's space is located was a large room attractively decorated with purple pillows and purple curtains. For many feminist organizations in the Dominican Republic and in other countries, the color purple symbolizes the feminist movement. Several posters from different Dominican women's organizations back on the island decorated the walls.

The room started to fill with women. The workshop that evening was about women and power. By 8 P.M., twenty-five women were sitting on the floor, forming a circle. The facilitator distributed a set of cards to the five groups that had been formed previously. Each group studied the pictures on the card, and developed a story that suggested the sequence of pictures. Each of these stories was related to situations dealing with different power relations between women and men. Next the facilitator asked the group to ponder the different stories. The women started to talk about their own experiences and about power situations in their own families. There was a man in the group who wanted to talk about his own definition of power. The man asked the women to first define the concept of power because he found that the discussion was very chaotic.

The facilitator asked him to remain silent and try to understand the dynamic established by the group. She also explained to him that women's meetings were "not rigidly structured and organized as men's." Another woman said that this was a feminist meeting and that the man was imposing his point of view, not allowing the women to express themselves. He was asked to leave. He tried to divide the group by asking several women if they wanted a ride home. Two women left with him. After they left, a discussion started about the disruption of allowing men to come to the meetings. The facilitator argued that men should not be allowed in these meetings, but she added, "We have to question ourselves if we are doing the right thing." Discussion continued, and women discussed other power relationships between men and women in both the domestic and public spheres and how men always wanted to impose their points of view. They also talked about different types of power. A lawyer and the director of Alianza's immigration program said that when "we women" talked about power related to men's world, women were left out. She added, "There is another kind of power that women have, and sometimes they do not use it, and that power comes from within, it is given to anybody." Other women agreed, and one cited the French thinker Foucault to explain power relations in society. Other woman reflected on power relations within the community of Washington Heights and the role of women in shaping a Dominican-American community. Women contributed their ideas but the discussion never came to any conclusion. Women took their own reflections and insight with them. After the discussion we all enjoyed beers, wine, cheese, Dominican crackers, and salami.

Informal meetings are vital in bonding women together, healing them from work alienation and the isolation of migration. More important, they contribute to consciousness-raising, understanding women's position in the process of community, and identity construction as far as their relation to men.

These organizations namely Dominican Women Against Violence, the Dominican Women's Development Center, and Dominican United have different points of departure for their struggles. For example, the Dominican Women Against Violence started their protests because somebody in their household and their community was killed or hurt. The household, which is considered women's realm, was threatened by police brutality and street violence. Women's sons, husbands, nephews, and other relatives were the victims. They went out and protested. As Temma Kaplan (1982) argues, the sexual division of labor assigns women the roles of take careers and protectors of their households and neighborhoods. As a continuation of this role, women develop a "female consciousness" driving them to protest against the dangers affecting women's loved ones. In so doing, Dominican women politicized themselves and their communities around issues of household and neighborhood safety, and brought solutions to the problem affecting them.

The point of departure of women at the Dominican Women's Development Center was more centered around a feminist pragmatic ideology. By pragmatic feminism, I mean the struggle to achieve material needs, for example, education, health, job, housing, and human rights. It is also an awareness of the need to connect these struggles to the strategic struggle for women's rights (Schirmer 1993: 60). Many of the programs developed by the Dominican Women's Center reflect this feminist pragmatic approach. More importantly, the center's leaders identify themselves as feminists. Mireya Cruz expresses her own self-perception as a pragmatic feminist. "I consider myself a feminist. I walk with my feminist banner and when I have to show it, I do to defend my rights as a woman and as a Dominican in the United States." The center has integrated this ideology into the organization endeavors.

The Dominican Women United group defines itself as a feminist group. Miriam Mejía, a member in 1994, said:

> Yes, I am a feminist. And I was feminist before I could understand the concept. When still a girl I was very critical of my position in the household. Why did I have to do the dishes and not my brother? But then I did not have the theory, the concept of feminism.

This organization seeks intellectualize the concept of feminism through conferences, talks, encounters, and workshops.

## CONCLUSION

As Maria Pardo argues, women usually disappear in the sociology of urban politics (Pardo 1998: 244). Similarly, Dominican women disappear in most Dominican Diaspora studies. There are exceptions, such as the work of Grasmuck and Pessar (1991), which focuses on labor market and household dynamics and provide an analysis of the position of Dominican women in the U.S. labor market. During the course of this chapter, I moved beyond statistical figures and looked at the contribution of women to community development. The data presented here relate to previous studies about women's consciousness and community activism.

According to these studies, women of all ethnic and racial groups create the foundations of their communities. Karen Stack (1974), in her well-known study of the African-American community, shows the importance of women as community builders. Terry Haywoode (1994) portrays white working-class women also as community builders. Hondagneu-Sotelo (1994) analyzes the role of Mexican immigrant women also as community builders. Virginia Sanchez-Korrol (1983) points to the central role of women in building the Puerto Rican community in New York City.

My research in New York City corroborates early findings on the role of women as community builders with a Dominican-American identity permeate by both a female and a feminist consciousness. Women activism encountered the opposition of their husbands and male community leaders. Women had to work twice as hard as men to gain a leadership role in the community of Washington Heights. While taking care of their children, husbands, and households, women also managed to find time to work for the improvement of their communities.

## NOTES

1. During the 1980s, Washington Heights was a major center of drug trafficking. Violence erupted among drug dealers and among drug dealers and the police. In some cases, the police use the excuse of drugs selling to brutalize ordinary residents in Dominican neighborhoods.

2. Broadway Temple is a United Methodist Church located in the heart of Washington Heights (Broadway and 175th Street). This church has been very much involved in the Dominican community political developments.

# CHAPTER 9

# Dominicans in a Multiethnic Neighborhood

W HAT DOES HAPPEN WHEN DOMINICANS SHARE RESIDENTIAL SPACE WITH VARI- ous national Latin American groups? How does ethnic mingle affect the incorporation of Dominicans? My research in Corona, Queens, New York City suggests that the answer to this important question is that in this particular community an additional identity emerges-that of "Latino" or "Hispanic." Indeed, pan ethnicity affects the incorporation of Dominicans. Different from Washington Heights a basically Dominican neighborhood, in Corona, Dominicans create pan ethnic organizations and develop a pan ethnic discourse to include other Latino groups in the community.

I argue that geographic concentration of different Latino national groups produce commonalities being the Spanish language the medium for that interaction. Corona is also a neighborhood with unique characteristics that allow macro variables such as geographic concentration and the Spanish language to be more effective in the ethnic cohesion of people with different nationalities. The uniqueness of Corona lies in three major factors. First, almost all Latin Americans came to Corona around the same period of time. Second, none of them is numerically larger. Third, none of these groups hold political power. In such a setting residents do not have to fight over resources namely power, and recognition. These factors promote trust rather than competition among Latinos in Corona, creating a viable atmosphere for positive interethnic interactions.

This ethnic blending occurs at the grassroots of the community through everyday life interactions. Through daily life interactions, people in Corona create the experiential dimension of pan ethnicity in apartment buildings, stores, parks, and churches. When politicians and other activists look at the community of Corona they commonly see an ethnically diverse community where no ethnic group is dominant. Latino leaders appropriate a pan-Latino discourse to reach not only one single ethnic group but also the entire Latino community. Latino leaders forge the organizational dimension of pan ethnicity providing social services, mobilizing the community for political reasons, and creating a political voice borough and city wide. Thus, local politics tends to reinforce what is being built at the community level—a new Latino identity.

My objectives in this chapter are three folded. First, I present a discussion of the impact of geographic concentration and Latino Studies in New York City. Second, I analyze the literature on Latino ethnicity in the light of Corona experience. Third, I study the activities of both Dominican social service agencies and political organizations, concluding that Dominican politics of incorporation in Corona is also pan-Latino incorporation.

## GEOGRAPHIC CONCENTRATION

In 1980 over half of the nation's Hispanic lived in two states alone—California and Texas—an additional 17 percent resided in New York and Florida (Bean and Tienda (1987:78). More recent data show that Latinos live in every state, but their population is still concentrated in nine states: California, Texas, New York, Florida, Illinois, New Jersey, Arizona, New Mexico, and Colorado. About 85 percent of Hispanics live in these states in late1990s (Population Reference Bureau, 1997: 2).

National groups from the Spanish-speaking Caribbean, Central and South America converged in New York City and became concentrated in specific neighborhoods of Manhattan, Queens, Bronx, and Brooklyn. Corona is the best example of Latino diversity residing in a single neighborhood. Colombians (23.8), Dominicans (20.9), Ecuadorian (11.9), Puerto Ricans (11.3), Cubans (5.0), Mexicans (4.7), Peruvians (4.7), Salvadorians (2.0) and other nationalities in smaller numbers share apartment buildings, streets, workplaces, churches, supermarkets, Laundromats, in one word they share their lives—*convivencia diaria*— in the same geographical space.

Demographic changes in Corona have been dramatic during the last fifty years. While in 1950 the population census did not count any Latin American people in Corona, in 1960, the census counted 1,007 Puerto Ricans in the area. Beginning in 1970, the population census started to count people of Spanish-speaking origins or "Hispanics" under the same label. The Latin American population grew from 15,515 in 1970 to 40,821 in 1990. These Latin Americans comprise people from every single country in Central and South America, as well as the Spanish-speaking Caribbean.

Even though Latin American national groups are becoming concentrated in specific neighborhoods, Latino studies on New York City are related to a single national group, namely Puerto Rican, Dominican, Colombian, and Mexican groups. Few studies offer a comparative analysis of two or more groups. No study so far looks at the social interaction of different Latino groups sharing residential and/or occupational settings.

For example, academic studies on Puerto Ricans include issues such as labor market characteristics (Rodríguez 1989); labor market characteristics in comparison to African-Americans (Torres 1995); political participation (Falcón 1985); community formation (Sánchez Korrol 1983); culture (Flores 1987, 1994, 1996).

Mexicans, whose presence in New York City although significant was never large, started to grow rapidly during the 1980s. Mexicans in the United States Southwest have been the focus of tremendous research and studies. One study, however, stands for Mexicans in New York City (Smith 1996). Drawing from his ethnographic fieldwork in New York City, Smith (1996) show the following: first, numbers of Mexicans have an annual growth of 10.5 percent (62); second, Mexicans in New York lack concentration in one particular area (63); and most Mexicans work as service workers (75).

In the case of Colombians, one study points to the fact that most Colombians (85.4 per cent) came here during the 1960s, and settled in Queens (Cruz 1980: 49). In her study about Colombian women, Garcia Castro (1985:24) estimated that the Colombian population in Queens was between 32,000 and 42,000. Elsa Chaney (1976: 87–88) identified a section of Jackson Heights, a neighborhood adjacent to Corona, as "chapinero," a neighborhood of Colombia Capital City, Bogota, because many of the residents came originally from that area of Bogota.

In terms of Latin American immigrants' occupational and family patterns, there is a significant amount of literature comparing Colombians and Dominicans. In 1987, Douglas Gurak and Mary Kritz analyzed the social and economic situation of Dominican and Colombian women in New York City. This study concluded that Colombian and Dominican women in New York City show significant differences in terms of household structure and employment patterns. "Compared to their Dominican counterparts, Colombian women tend to migrate at an older age, be more urban in background, and have more employment experience prior migration (. . .) Colombian women are more likely to be part of a nuclear family household (20)." More recently, Greta Gilbertson (1995) while analyzing ethnic enclaves in the Dominican and Colombian communities concluded that in both communities women do not benefit from ethnic enclaves as much as men. In terms of household composition and headship for both Dominican and Colombian immigrants, Gilbertson and Gurak (1992) concluded that Dominican women headed more households than Colombians (1992: 23).

Latino scholarly literature in New York City has been ample and have brought important element into the discussion of each of the national groups that form the Latino population in the city. None of these studies, however, look at the processes of community interaction between Latinos—Puerto Ricans, Dominicans, Colombians, Cubans, Ecuadorians and so on—residing in the same geographical space. None of these studies attempt to explain the forces uniting or dividing Latinos in the City.

## SOCIAL FORCES UNITING OR DIVIDING LATIN AMERICANS IN THE UNITED STATES

I present four sets of Latino studies that offer a suitable background for the ensuing theoretical discussion on pan Latinism.

First, one of the issues much discussed about Latin Americans in the United States is the fragmentation of the Latino community (Gilbertson 1995, Hagan 1998, Hondagneu-Sotelo 1994, Portes and Stepick 1994, Mahler 1995). Each of these authors has focused on factors present in the Latino community that hamper unity. Greta Gilbertson, for instance, argues that ethnic enclaves, in the case of Dominicans and Colombians, limit the possibilities of women's economic advancement. Along the same line, Hondagneu-Sotelo, also focusing on Mexican networks, finds that their older Mexican immigrants exploit newcomers. Portes and Stepick portray Miami as a city divided by ethnicity and race. Jacqueline Hagan shows how social networks have disparate effects on the incorporation for men and women immigrants from Central America. Sara Mahler's study presents a community of immigrants in Long Island, New York, infected with competition, jealousy, and egotism regardless of their country of origin, aspirations, or class background.

My study shows the opposite. In Corona there is an experience of cooperation, trust, and unity among Latin Americans of different nationalities. How Corona is different from the above experiences? What social factors are at play in Corona reducing competence and influencing solidarity?

Second, other studies acknowledge diversity but question the validity of inclusive ethnic labels such as Latino or Hispanic (Oboler 1995, Nelson and Tienda 1985, Bean and Tienda 1987, de la Garza et al. 1987, Portes and Truelove 1987, Anzaldúa 1987, Anzaldúa and Moraga, eds. 1983, Moore and Pachon 1985, Sullivan 1985, Bacca Zinn 1980). These studies acknowledge the complexities and differences among Latinos in the United States. These differences include great socioeconomic, racial, immigration, historical, and cultural diversity, as well as different patterns of entry and settlement in the United States (Portes and Truelove 1987: 360). It is also argued that the label, "Hispanic," categorizes a diverse group that does not share social, national, racial, gender or historical background (Oboler 1995: 1).

Corona's experience shows a community where "imposed" ethnic labels such as Hispanic or Latino acquire significance. What factors do trigger the significance of pan ethnic labels in Corona? Here we found a set of social interactions portrayed in both kinship and intra-ethnic networks. These interactions promote affinities and commonalities that are translated into a new identity. An identity already named or labeled by outsiders as Hispanics or Latinos. But the label acquires significance when Latin Americans start using it to identify themselves.

Third, other scholars admit that Hispanic/Latinos might come together for political reasons. For example, Portes and Truelove (1987: 379) understand that Latino groups might unite when dealing with problems such as the defense of bilingualism, although they conclude that there is an absence of a firm, collective self-identity among Latinos. The work of Felix Padilla, on the other hand, provides an analysis of the process of Latino/Hispanic ethnic group formation within specific situational contexts that he calls pan Latinism. The experience of inequality in areas such as education and employment was shared by Spanish-speaking ethnic groups (Mexicans and Puerto Ricans) from different geographical communities in Chicago. The struggle for employment and better education provided the overall structural framework linking these groups.

Padilla (1985) acknowledges unity among Latinos in Chicago. However, I see two difficulties with Padilla's study in respect to my work. First, Padilla focuses on only two national groups—Puerto Ricans and Mexicans, living in two geographically separated neighborhoods. Second, Padilla shows politics as an essential element homogenizing the Spanish-speaking community. My analysis is different from Padilla's work. My analysis looks at the results of everyday life interaction in a residentially concentrated neighborhood, and the Spanish language shaping unity. What does happen at the grassroots that affect politics and identity in Corona? How do the grassroots affect political alliances, political mobilization or political pan-ethnic discourse?

Fourth, recent studies suggest that state policies, geographical concentration, and the Spanish language are essential uniting Latin Americans in the United States (Jones-Correa 1998, DeSipio 1996, Zentella 1997). For example, Jones-Correa (1998: 111) argues that the State offered incentive and self-interested mobilization of various Latin American origins have encouraged, at the very least, the formation of a kind of Latino identity constructed around ethnic labels. Also an important factor uniting diverse Latin American groups is the Spanish language. The variety of Spanish that each group speaks is the most distinctive marker of its individuality, but the Spanish language also is their most powerful unifier (Zentella 1997: 168). DeSipio, on the other hand, argues that there are foundations for a pan-Latino identity such as common culture, a common language, and geographic concentration (DeSipio 1996: 177 and 186).

In conclusion and according to this review, the dilemmas of a pan-Latino identity lie on three different approaches. First, there is a focus on instrumentalist paradigms emphasizing competition rather than solidarity among Latin American immigrants. Second, pan Latino labels such as Hispanics or Latinos are labels imposed by external forces that have no meaning to a diverse population. Third, Latin American groups commonly come together for political reasons or pushed by external factors.

On the contrary, the dilemmas of Pan Latinism in Corona lie in the uniqueness of Corona. Residential concentration, the Spanish language, and lack of competition over power and prestige, create trust and solidarity between and among the different Latino groups in Corona. These factors facilitate cultural blending and the creation of a new identity. The uniqueness of Corona gives prevalence to a primordial context of ethnicity such as language; religion, customs, and food and so on to unite instead of divide.

In the case of Corona it is not possible to study each Latin American national group separately, without looking at their interactions. Looking at these interactions, I discovered a story of cooperation and solidarity in the daily life setting of residence, neighborhood, and workplace; here diverse Latinos interact with each other using the medium of Spanish, and establish a variety of new cross-nationality ties with each other. Also, categorical panethnicity emerges in these settings as persons view and speak of each other as *hispanos* or *latinoamericanos*. Third, institutional panethnicity emerges when social and cultural organizations are created by leaders to attract and serve all Latinos in Corona. Consequently, ideological panethncity is voiced by these leaders of what they usually identify as "Latino" or "Hispanic" social service, cultural, and political organizations. Each of these dimensions are examined in the following pages.

## CREATING IDENTITY IN CORONA

But how does this new pan-Latino identity affect national boundaries? I argue that ethnicity is a social construction. In this social process individuals recreate what they left behind and what they found in the United States. It is also permeated by levels of acceptance by the larger society and social conditions encountered in their residential and work environments. In Corona, each individual national group goes through their own ethnic construction. Individual ethnic construction, however, enter in contact with other Latinos also sharing their residential and workspaces and speaking the same language. The result is the emergence of many ethnic identities that change according to the situation or the audience. One individual can hold many different and shifting identities. Among these identities are her/his own ethnic identity, Hispanic or Latino, and a hyphenated identity such as Dominican-American. One identity does not substitute or replace other identities. These many ethnic identities have been illustrated by other social scientists (Nagel 1994, Espiritu 1992, Cornell 1988). According to Nagel, the content of identity is culture. Nagel uses the image of the shopping cart that individual use picking here and there elements that shape their identities. In the case of Corona, individuals of many Latin American nationalities exchange cultural traits. This cultural exchange fosters an additional identity, Hispanic or Latino.

The cases of Martha, Aida Gónzalez, Haydee Zambrana, and Rev. Dilca Lebrón-Mazariego illustrate the portfolio of identities of Latinos in Corona.

Martha is a working class woman who came from Guatemala in 1980 and married a Dominican in 1984. While interviewing her she referred proudly to her Guatemalan heritage. When I asked her, where are you from, Martha? She said: "I am from Guatemala." She invited me to eat *taquitos* that she prepared while answering questions. She said that Guatemalan food has many similarities with Mexican and other Central American foods. I asked her to describe her neighborhood. She told me that her street was, Hispana. She said: "Hay gentes de todas partes, Dominicanos, Colombianos, Ecuatorianos, mi vecina de arriba es Ecuatoriana y la del piso de más arriba es Colombiana—There are people from everywhere Dominicans, Colombians, Ecuadoreans, my neighbor above is from Ecuador and the other is from Colombia." When she referred to an incident that happened in the factory she was working in Long Island where INS police raided the place and caught many undocumented immigrants she referred to herself as Hispanos being attacked by la migra/INS police.

Another case is Aida Gonzalez, an appointed official for Claire Shulman, Queens Borough President. Gonzalez, is a middle-class woman who came From Ecuador in early 1970s. During an interview, I asked her, who are you ethnically? She showed me an Ecuadorian clay pot with a U.S. flag and said, "I am Ecuadorian-American working and serving a Latin-American community. I am also Latino-Americana." She spoke about the importance of Latino unity in Queens. She said, "Here in Queens we are of many nationalities and numbers are almost equal, in order to gain political recognition we need to have a united voice." Dominican leaders in Queens have supported Aida Gonzalez's candidacy to the New York City Council's elections.

Reverend Lebrón-Mazariego, Puerto Rican, leads an ethnically diverse Methodist church that includes a significant number of Dominicans. Rev. Lebrón's discourse recognizes both differences and commonalities among church members in order to have a successful Latin American church community. She acknowledges differences to build unity.

## EMERGENCE OF PAN-LATINISM AND DOMINICAN SOCIAL SERVICE AGENCIES

Dominican Americans have built social service organizations of the same nature of social service agencies in Washington Heights. However, both organizations are different. Corona's Dominican organizations appropriate a pan ethnic discourse.

An examination of two Dominican social service agencies in Corona revealed both of them serving a multi-ethnic community. These two organizations are the Father Billini Association and the Dominico-American Society of Queens. Both organizations were created by Dominicans to serve a Dominican community. Both organizations, however within few years of their creation started to serve a diverse community and integrated to their boards persons of other Latino nationalities.

For example, Ana López, Dominican, created the Father Billini Association in 1978. The initial goal of the organization was to teach and propagate Dominican culture in the United States and to help Dominican children coming from divorced or separated homes. The site of its operation is Our Lady of Sorrows Roman Catholic church in North Corona. They started in 1978 with only Dominican dances, but the organization soon expanded to teach Ecuadorean, Mexican, and Colombian dances. In an interview Ana López commented that this change was seen as essential to building a wider Latin American base of support, taking into account that the community was Dominican but also Colombian, Ecuadorian, Mexican, among others. From eight children in 1978, the association had expanded during the period of my fieldwork, in 1988, to 140 children of many nationalities. Father Billini Association's board of directors used to be entirely Dominican. This ethnic composition changed over the time. In 1999 the board was composed of Dominicans, Colombians, Ecuadorians, and Haitians.

The Dominico-American Society of Queens was created in 1993 by a Dominican married couple. The purpose of the organization was to address the educational, social and cultural issues affecting Dominicans in Corona, Queens. This purpose, however, changed to serve not only Dominicans but also other Latinos in the community. In 1998 Genaro Herrera, the organization co-founder, reported: "Approximately 45 percent of them [beneficiaries] are Dominicans; 35 percent South Americans (within this percentage, 40 percent are Colombians, 40 percent Ecuadorians, and 20 percent Peruvians); 4 percent Mexican; 4 percent Central Americans (within this proportion, 50 percent are Salvadorians, 40 percent Nicaraguans, and 10 percent Hondurans); 4 percent U.S. born; 1 percent Puerto Ricans and 7 percent others." In 1998, the executive director of the organization was from Venezuela. The other two staff members were from Ecuador and from El Salvador.

Genaro Herrera, in his president's message, during the Second Annual Dinner Dance in 1998, said: "We are pleased with the diversity of our student/client population." When talking about the mission of the organization, he said: "Our mission is to enhance the self-esteem of the Hispanic community by meeting the goals and aspirations of this population."

In the year 2000, Genaro Herrera, run against the incumbent Lafaffete for the New York State Assembly in the Democratic primary. During the campaign, Mr. Herrera presented himself as a Latino and appropriated a pan Latino discourse.

## CONCLUSION

Corona is a dynamic community that has forged a panethnic identity. Dominicans socialized in a diverse environment where a sense of belonging and unity emerges at the root of the community with daily life interactions. Moreover Dominican social service agencies and political leaders started to appropriate a pan-Latino discourse.

This study presents a unique view of the Latino community in the United States—the creation of an identifiable pan ethnic community. This account derives from the ethnographic recollection and experiences of those who lives in Latino multi-ethnic neighborhoods not available in earlier studies. It also paves the way for future intensive studies in this direction, for comparisons with other multi-ethnic communities in the United States, taking into account the unifying role of the Spanish language, and residential concentration of Hispanics.

# CHAPTER 10

# Conclusion

N EW YORK CITY IS A CULTURAL SET OF SIGHTS, SOUNDS, AND AROMAS, WHICH vary according to the creativity of the diverse ethnic and racial groups that are its contemporary inhabitants. In New York City each ethnic group, for example, has erected store signs, which reflect places and meanings left behind in their countries of origin. Other signs reflect a melted identity that evokes both what was left behind and what was found here. Each individual will associate with these signs a different cultural framework, depending on their national and cultural background. New York City politics also reflects its diversity. New York City experiences a continuous process of ethnic and political incorporation. The Irish, Italians, Jews, and Poles, among others, played their ethnic political roles decades ago. Puerto Ricans and African Americans engaged the New York political machinery in the 1960s and 1970s. Today new immigrants also contribute to New York City politics with their own way of practicing politics.

Dominicans in New York City are a visible population. Their numbers grow and they concentrate in specific city neighborhoods. In these neighborhoods, Dominicans develop their own businesses. For example, *bodegas*, the quintessential Dominican business, proliferate throughout the New York City. Many of the store names have a meaning reflecting historical accounts, place-names, saints, or virgins. These names are typical ("La Altagracia," the Dominican virgin; *El Cibaeño*, a person from El Cibao, the northern central region of the Dominican Republic) stamping a Dominican seal throughout the city. Dozens of Dominican restaurants bearing the same name—Caridad or Malecón—make Dominican roast chicken, white rice, beans, and watercress salad a familiar meal for many New Yorkers. Dominican merengue music blasts in a record store at 86th Street and Lexington Avenue. The Dominican parade kidnaps Sixth Avenue every August 16, commemorating the Dominican separation from Spain in 1864. More recently, Washington Heights celebrates a street festival to commemorate the renaming of Saint Nicholas Avenue for Juan Pablo Duarte, the father of Dominican independence from Haiti in 1844. Washington Heights has become a Dominican city with nicknames such as *Quisqueya Heights* or *Platano City*.

Accompanying visibility and cultural presence in the city, Dominicans also develop their communities and incorporate themselves into city and state politics. I have argued throughout this study that Dominicans are at the margins of New York City society. Dominicans suffered the decline of the manufacturing that left thousands of Dominicans unemployed and pushed many to alternative income generating activities in the informal economy. Dominicans have not participated in any significant extent in the well remunerated "service" industries, such as finance, advertising, and law. Moreover, Dominicans were lumped together in poor inner city neighborhoods afflicted with decaying infrastructure and inadequate social services. These economic constraints are important in shaping Dominican identities in the diaspora. Indeed, the interplay of these socioeconomic forces have shaped Dominican ethnicity. An awareness of "otherness" emerges when immigrants learn about the hardships of American society. Many Dominicans have learned that by "assimilating"—learning the English language, pursuing an education, getting involved in politics—may be the key to success in the United States. Others are skeptical.

The continuous and increasing migration of Dominicans to the United States creates a wide continuum in the level of incorporation of Dominicans in the United States. While new Dominican immigrants have more loyalties to the Dominican Republic, established and second-generation Dominican immigrants develop a "mobilizationist ethnicity" and seek their position and rights in the United States. Ethnicity becomes a weapon Dominicans use to mobilize their community for resources and political empowerment. In this task, Dominicans create associations and organizations to empower the community. Social capital is generated through ethnic associations, groups, and organizations in Washington Heights and elsewhere. The social capital generated is translated into political participation, civic involvement, community control, and electoral politics. The result is a vibrant community that, in spite of many constraints has achieved a political presence in New York.

In spite of the relative successes of Dominican incorporation, I see several obstacles in the political development of Dominican New Yorkers. First, gender bias brings a major limitation. Women are essential in the political construction of Dominicans in New York. But the constant neglect women endure overburdens them with responsibilities, often in the family, and their energy for politics. A recognition of women's contribution to the development of the Dominican community may be an important boost to the fortunes of Dominican politics in New York and nationwide.

Second, Dominican electoral politics has been characterized by a lack of unity between leaders. The first electoral efforts that took Guillermo Linares to the City Council was characterized by the unifying efforts of the different sectors in the Dominican community and counted with the support of other ethnic groups throughout New York City. However, subsequent electoral campaigns were shadowed by riffs among the main political leaders in the Dominican community. The political fragmentation between Guillermo Linares and Adriano Espaillat hamper the advancement of Dominicans in New York City.

Moreover, the Dominican community needs political leaders who are committed to the community. Otherwise, electoral politics instead of being a medium to obtain collective power translated in the advancement of the immigrant community would be a medium to pursue individual power. At times, Dominican elected officers have obtained their piece of the pie and forgot about the community. An emerging community cannot afford the division of forces, such as the electorate and key supporters of Dominican candidates

Third, the Dominican community remains significantly isolated from other minorities. Current political strategies treat the Dominican community as a minority enclave and do not present a project of coalition building with other minority communities to expand the locally-generated social capital into the whole city, and even nationwide. The collective activism of minority communities is vital, first, to obstruct the process of "ghettoization" of minority communities, such as cuts on education, social services, housing, lack of job opportunities, and the increase in crime, and second, to develop a strong activism to bring resources into these communities and develop alternative strategies to economic stagnation.

During the first half of the twentieth Century, the challenges of European immigrants consisted of assimilating to the American mainstream. In the contemporary era, and in the specific case of Dominicans, the options are less clear. Nonwhite immigrants may not have the opportunity to gain access to the advantages of whites, no matter how acculturated they became. Preserving their ethnicity and taking advantages of the political vindications of the civil rights movement may be the best chance to achieve power and capitalize on otherwise unavailable opportunities. Yet the successful implementation of this strategy also depends on the characteristics of the community and the social context that surrounds it.

# Bibliography

Abramson, Harold. 1973. *Ethnic Diversity in Catholic America*. New York: John Wiley.

Alba, Richard, Nancy Denton, Shu-Yin Leung, and John Logan. 1995. "Neighborhood Change Under Conditions of Mass Immigration: The New York City Region, 1970–1990". *International Migration Review*, 29 (3): 625–32.

Anzaldúa, Gloria. 1987. *Borderlands/La Frontera*. San Francisco: Spinters/Aunt Lute.

Anzaldúa, Gloria, and Cherrie Moraga, eds. 1981. *This Bridge Called my Back: Writings by Radical Women of Color*. Watertown: Persephone.

Appadurai, Arjun. 1996. *Modernity at Large: Cultural Dimensions of Globalization*. Minneapolis: University of Minnesota Press.

———. 1991. "Global Ethnoscapes: Notes and Queries for a Transnational Anthropology." In Richard Fox, ed. *Recapturing Anthropology: Working in the Present*. Santa Fe: School of American Research Press. 191–210.

Bacca Zinn, Maxine. 1980. "Gender and Ethnic Identity among Chicanos." *Frontiers: A Journal of Women Studies*, 5 (2): 18–24.

Banton, Michael P. 1983. *Racial and Ethnic Competition*. New York: Cambridge University Press.

Basch, Linda, Nina Glick Schiller, and Cristina Szanton. 1994. *Nations Unbound: Transnational Projects, Post Colonial Predicaments, and the Deterritorialized Nation-State*. New York: Gordon and Breach Publishers.

Bath, Fredrik. 1969. "Introduction." In Fredrik Barth, ed. *Ethnic Groups and Boundaries*. Boston: Little Brown and Company.

Bean, Frank, and Marta Tienda. 1987. *The Hispanic Population of the United States*. New York: Russel Sage Foundation.

Blauner, Bob. 1972. *Racial Oppression in America*. New York: Harpher & Row.

Bluestone, Barry, and Bennett Harrison. 1986. *The Great U-Turn: Corporate Restructuring and the Polarizing of America*. New York: Basic Books.

———. 1982. *The Deindustrialization of America: Plant Closings, Community Abandonment, and the Dismantling of Basic Industry*. New York: Basic Books.

Bonacich, Edna, and John Modell. 1980. *The Economic Basis of Ethnic Solidarity: Small Business in the Japanese American Community*. Berkeley: University of California Press.

Bray, David. 1984. "The Economic Development: The Middle-Class and International Migration in the Dominican Republic." *International Migration Review*, 18(2): 217–36.

Chaney, Elsa. 1976. "Colombian Migration to the United States." *Dynamics of Migration*, Washington, D.C.: Smithsonian Institution, Interdisciplinary Communication Program.

Chen, Hsiang-shui.1992. *Chinatown No More: Taiwan Immigrants in Contemporary New York*. Ithaca: Cornell University Press.

———. 1990. *Chinatown No More: Changing Patterns of Chinese Organization in Queens, New York City*. Ph.D. dissertation. New York: City University of New York.

Coleman, James S. 1990. *Foundations of Social Theory*. Harvard: The Belknap Press of Harvard University.

Committee for Economic Development. 1995. *Rebuilding Inner City Communities: A New Approach to the Nation's Urban Crisis*. New York: Committee for Economic Development.

Cornell, Stephen. 1988. *The Return of the Native: American Indian Political Resurgence*. New York: Oxford University Press.

Cruz, Carmen I. 1980. "The Migration Process in Colombia: Some Considerations about its Causes and Consequences." In Roy Simon Bryce Laporte, ed. *Source Book of the New Immigration*. Brunswick: Transaction Books. 85–97.

Cruz, José E. 1998. *Identity and Power: Puerto Rican Politics and the Challenge of Ethnicity*. Philadelphia: Temple University Press.

Danta, Rosalia. 1989a. *Conversion and Denominational Mobility: A Study of Latin American Protestants in Queens, New York*. MA thesis, New York: Queens College, City University of New York.

———. 1989b. "Latin American in Protestant Churches: Reaffirmation of Culture, or Acculturation?" Roger Sanjek, ed. *Worship and Community: Christianity and Hinduism in Contemporary Queens*. Flushing: Asian American Center, Queens College, City University of New York. 30–40.

Davis, Mike. 2000. *Magical Urbanism: Latinos Reinvent the US City*. New York:Verso.

de la Garza, Rodolfo O., Louis DeSipio, F. Chris Garcia, John Garcia, and Angelo Falcón. 1992. *Latino Voices: Mexican, Puerto Rican, and Cuban Perspectives on American Politics*. Boulder: Westview Press.

Denton, Nancy, and Douglas Massey.1991. "Patterns of Neighborhood Transition in a Multiethnic World: U.S. Metropolitan Areas, 1970–1980". *Demography*, 28 (1): 41–63.

DeSipio, Louis. 1996. "More the Sum of Its Parts: The Building Blocks of Pan-Ethnic Latino Identity." In Wilbur Rich, ed. *The Politics of Minority Coalitions: Race, Ethnicity, and Shared Uncertainties*. Westport: Praeger. 177–189.

Duany, Jorge. 1994. *Quisqueya on the Hudson: The Transnational Identity of Dominicans in Washington Heights*. New York: Dominican Institute, The City University of New York.

El Diario/La Prensa. 2000. "Los Dominicanos Ausentes y la Elecciones." *El Diario/La Prensa*. May 16, 2000. New York City.

Espiritu, Yen L. 1992. *Asian American Panethnicity*. Philadelphia: Temple University Press.

Falcón, Angelo. 1985. "Black and Latino Politics in New York City: Race and Ethnicity in a Changing Urban Context." *Institute for Puerto Rican Policy*. New York: Institute for Puerto Rican Policy.

Fernández-Kelly, María P. 1983. *For We are Sold, I and My People: Women and Industry in Mexico Frontier*. Albany: State University of New York Press.

Flores, Juan. 1996. "Puerto Rican and Latino Culture." In Gabriel Haslip-Viera and Sherri L. Baver, eds. *Latinos in New York: Communities in Transition*. Notre Dame: University of Notre Dame Press. 331–338.

———. 1994. "Puerto Rican and Proud, Boyee! Rap, Roots and Amnesia." In Andrew Rose and Tricia Rose, eds. *Microphone Friends: Youth Music and Culture*. New York: Routledge. 89–98.

———. 1987. "Rappin', Writin' and Breakin': Black and Puerto Rican Street Culture in New York." *Dissent*, Fall: 580–84.

Gans, Hebert J. 1962. *The Urban Villagers: Group and Class in the Life of Italian-Americans*. New York: Free Press of Glencoe.

Garcia-Castro, M. 1985. "Women in Migration: Colombian Voices in the Big Apple." *Migration Today*, 10 (3/4): 22–31.

Georges, Eugenia.1984. "New Immigrants and the Political Process: Dominicans in New York." *Occasional Papers*, 45. New York: Center for Latin American and Caribbean Studies, University of New York.

Gilbertson, Greta. 1995. "Women's Labor and Enclave Employment: The Case of Dominican and Colombian Women in New York City." *International Migration Review*, (29): 657–70.

Gilbertson, Greta, and Douglas Gurak. 1992. "Household Transition in the Migrations of Dominicans and Colombians to New York." *International Migration Review*, 26 (1): 22–45.

Glazer, Nathan. 1981. "The United States." In Robert G. Wirsing, ed. *Protection of Ethnic Minorities: Comparative Perspectives*. New York: Pergamus Press: 21–41.

Glazer, Nathan, and Daniel. P. Moynihan. 1968. *Beyond the Melting Pot*. Cambridge: MIT Press.

Glick Schiller, Nina, Linda Basch, and Cristina Szanton Blanc. 1992. "Transnationalism: A New Analytical Framework for Understanding Migration." In Nina Glick Schiller, et al., eds. *Toward a Transnational Perspective on Migration: Race, Class, Ethnicity and Nationalism Reconsidered*. New York: New York Academy of Science.

Gordon, Milton.1964. *Assimilation in American Life*. New York: Oxford University Press.

Graham, Pamela. 1998. "The Politics of Incorporation: Dominicans in New York City." *Latino Studies Journal*, 9 (3): 39–64.

Grasmuck, Sherri. 1983. "Immigration, Ethnic Stratification, and Native Working-Class Discipline: Comparisons of Documented and Undocumented Dominicans." *International Migration Review*, 18 (3): 692–713.

Grasmuck, Sherri, and Patricia Pessar. 1991. *Between Two Islands: Dominican International Migration*. Berkeley: University of California Press.

Gregory, Stevens. 1992. "The Changing Significance of Race and Class in an African American Community." *American Ethnologist*, 19: 255–74.

———. 1993. "Race, Rubbish and Resistance: Empowering Difference in Community Politics." *Cultural Anthropology*, 8: 24–48.

Greely, Andrew.1976. *Ethnicity in the United States: A Preliminary Reconnaissance*. New York: John Wiley.

Guarnizo, Luis E. 1997. "Los Dominicanyorks: The Making of a Binational Society." In Mary Romero, Pierrette Hondagneu-Sotelo, and Vilma Ortiz, eds. *Challeging Fronteras: Structuring Latina and Latino Lives in the U.S.* New York: Routledge. 161–174.

Gurak, Douglas, and Mary Kritz. 1987. "Dominicans and Colombians in New York." *Migration Today*, 10 (3/4): 16–21.

Hagan, Jacqueline M. 1998. "Social Networks, Gender, and Immigrant Incorporation: Resources and Constraints." *American Sociological Review*, 63: 55–67.

Haywoode, Terry. 1994. "Working Class Feminism: Creating a Politics of Community Connection and Concern." Paper presented at the American Sociological Association Meeting, August.

Hendricks, Glenn. 1974. *The Dominican Diaspora: From the Dominican Republic to New York City—Villagers in Transition*. New York: Teachers College Press.

Hernández, Ramona, Francisco Rivera-Batiz, and Roberto Agodini. 1995. *Dominican New Yorkers: Socio-Economic Profile.* New York: Dominican Institute, City University of New York.

Hernández, Ramona, and Silvio Torres-Saillant. 1996. "Dominicans in New York: Men, Women, and Prospects." In Gabriel Haslip-Viera and Sherrie L. Baver, eds. *Latinos in New York: Communities in Transition.* Notre Dame: University of Notre Dame Press: 30–57

Hondagneu-Sotelo, Pierrette. 1994. *Gendered Transitions: Mexican Experiences of Immigration.* Berkeley: University of California Press.

Jones-Correa, Michael. 1998. *Between two Nations: The Political Predicaments of Latinos in New York City.* Ithaca: Cornell University Press.

Kamel, Rachael. 1990. *The Global Factory: Analysis and Action for a New Economic Era.* Philadelphia: American Friends Service Committee.

Katznelson, Ira. 1981. *City Trenches: Urban Politics and the Patterning of Class in the United States.* Chicago: University of Chicago Press.

Kaplan, Temma. 1982. "Female Consciousness and Collective Action: The Case of Barcelona, 1910–1918." *Signs,* 7: 545–566.

Kennedy, John F. 1964. *A Nations of Immigrants.* New York: Harper and Row, Publishers.

Kornblum, William. 1974. *Blue Collar Community.* Chicago: University of Chicago Press.

Lankevich, George. 1998. *American Metropolis: A History of New York City.* New York: New York University Press.

Larson, Eric M. and Teresa A. Sullivan. 1987. "Conventional Numbers in Immigration Research: The Case of the Missing Dominicans." *International Migration Review,* 21 (4): 1474–97.

Lescaille, Fernando. 1994. "Dominican Political Empowerment." *Dominican Public Policy Project.* New York: Dominican Public Policy Project.

Levitt, Peggy. 1998. "Social Remittances: Migration Driven Local-Level Forms of Cultural Diffusion." *International Migration Review,* 32 (4): 926–948.

Lieberson, Stanley. 1980. *A Piece of the Pie: Black and White Immigrants since 1880.* Berkeley: University of California Press.

Logan, John. 2000. *Immigrants Enclaves in the America Metropolis, 1990–2000.* Albany: Lewis Munford Center

López, Nancy. 1998. "The Structural Origins of High School Drop Out Among Second Generation Dominicans In New York City." *Latino Studies Journal,* 9 (3): 85–105.

Loury, Glenn C. 1987. "Why Should We Care About Group Inequality?" *Social Philosophy and Policy,* 843–867.

Lowenstein, Steven. 1989. *Frankfurt on the Hudson.* Detroit: Wayne State University Press.

Mahler, Sarah. 1995. *American Dreaming: Immigrant Life on the Margins.* Princeton: Princeton University Press.

———. 1989. "La Dinámica de la Legalización en Nueva York: Un Enfoque hacia los Dominicanos." In Eugenia Georges, ed. *Dominicanos Ausentes: Cifras, Políticas, Condiciones Sociales.* Santo Domingo: Fondo para el Avance de las Ciencias Sociales/ Fundacion Friedrich Ebert, 139–181.

Massey, Douglas, and Nancy Denton.1993. *American Apartheid: Segregation and the Making of the Underclass.* Boston: Harvard University Press.

Mollenkopf, John, and Manuel Castells. 1991. *Dual City: Restructuring New York.* New York: Russell Sage Foundation.

Moore, Joanne, and Harry Pachon. 1985. *Hispanics in the United States.* Englewood Cliffs: Prentice-Hall.

Moore, Joanne, and Raquel Pinderhughes. 1993. "Introduction." In Joanne Moore and Raquel Pinderhughes, eds. *In the Barrios: Latinos and the Underclass Debate.* New York: Russell Sage.

Muller, Thomas. 1993. *Immigrants and the America City.* New York: New York University Press.

Nagel, Joanne. 1994. "Constructing Ethnicity: Creating and Recreating Ethnic Identity and Culture." *Social Problems,* 41 (1): 152–176

Navarro, Armando. 1998. *The Cristal Experiment: A Chicano Struggle for Community Control.* Madison: University of Wisconsin Press.

Nelson, Candence, and Marta Tienda. 1985. "The Structuring of Hispanic Identity." *Ethnic and Racial Studies.* 8 (1): 49–74.

New York City Department of City Planning. 1999. "The Newest New Yorkers, 1995–1996: An Update of Immigration to NYC in the mid 90's." New York City Department of City Planning.

———. 1996. "The Newest New Yorkers, 1990–1994: An Analysis of Immigration to NYC in the early 1990s." New York City Department of City Planning.

———. 1993. "Socioeconomic Profiles." New York City Department of City Planning.

———. 1992. "The Newest New Yorkers: An Analysis of Immigration into New York City During the 1980s." New York City Department of City Planning.

New York Times. 1998a. "Rivalry for Leadership Shadows Assembly Race." *The New York Times.* August 2, Section 1.

———. 1998b. "Rivals Renew Contest for Dominican Vote." *The New York Times.* April 6, Section B.

———. 1997. "Dominicans, Scrabbling for Hope; As Poverty Rises, More Women Head the Households." *The New York Times.* December 16, Section B.

———. 1995 "Council Overrides Giuliani On Veto of Pathmark." *The New York Times*. August 25, Section B.

Oboler, Suzanne.1995. *Ethnic Labels, Latino Lives: Identity and the Politics of Representation in the United States*. Minneapolis: University of Minnesota Press.

Olzak, Susan, and Joanne Nagel. 1986. "Introduction." In Susan Olzak and Joanne Nagel, eds. *Competitive Ethnic Relations*. New York: Academic Press.

Padilla, Felix. 1985. *The Latino Ethnic Consciousness: The Case of Mexican Americans and Puerto Ricans in Chicago*. Notre Dame: University Of Notre Dame Press.

Pardo, Mary. 1998. *Mexican American Women Activists: Identity and Resistance in Two Los Angeles Communities*. Philadelphia: Temple University Press.

Park, Kyeyoung. 1997. *The Korean American Dream: Immigrants and Small Business in Queens, New York City*. Ithaca: Cornell University Press.

———. 1990. *The Korean American Dream: Ideology and Small Business in Queens, New York*. Ph.D. dissertation. New York: City University of New York.

Paxton, Pamela. 1999. "Is Social Capital Declining in the United States? A Multiple Indicator Assessment." *American Journal of Sociology,* 105 (1) :88–127.

Pessar, Patricia. 1982 "The Role of Households in International Migration." *International Migration Review,* 16:342–364.

———. 1987. "The Dominicans: Women in the Household and the Garment Industry." In June Nash and Helen Safa, eds. *Women and Change in Latin America*. South Hadley: Bergin and Garvey.273–294.

Piore, Michael. 1979. *Birds of Passage: Migrant Labor and Industrial Society*. New York: Cambridge University Press,

Population Reference Bureau. 1997. "Generation of Diversity: Latinos in the United States." *Population Bulletin*, 52 (3).

Portes, Alejandro. 1996. "Global Villagers: The Rise of Transnational Communities." *The American Prospect*, 2: 74–77.

Portes, Alejandro, and Alex Stepick.1994. *City on the Edge: The Transformation of Miami*. Berkeley: University of California Press.

Portes, Alejandro, and Luis Guarnizo.1991. *"Capitalistas del Trópico: La Inmigración de los Estados Unidos y el Desarrollo de la Empresa Pequeña en la República Dominicana."* Santo Domingo: Facultad Latinoamericana de Ciencias Sociales, Proyecto República Dominicana.

Portes, Alejandro, and Ruben G. Rumbaut. 1990. *Immigrant America: A Portrait*. Berkeley: University of California Press.

Portes, Alejandro, and Cynthia Truelove. 1987. "Making Sense of Diversity: The Recent Research on Hispanic Minorities in the United States." *Annual Review of Sociology*, 13:359–395.

Portes, Alejandro, and Robert Bach. 1985. *The Latin Journey: Cuban and Mexican Immigrants in the United States.* Berkeley: University of California Press.

Putman, Robert D. 1998. "Bowling Alone: America Declining Social Capital." *Journal of Democracy*, 65–78.

———. 1993. "The Prosperous Community: Social Capital and Public Life." *The American Prospect*, Spring: 35–42.

Ricourt, Milagros. 1998. "Patterns of Dominican Demography and Community." *Latino Studies Journal*, 9 (3): 11–38.

———. 1994. *The Creation of a Pan-Latino Ethnicity: Gender, Class, and Politics in Corona, Queens.* Ph.D. dissertation. New York: City University of New York.

———. 1989. "Latin American Protestant Women and Community Needs in Corona." In Roger Sanjek, ed. *Worship and Community: Christianity and Hinduism in Contemporary Queens.* Flushing: Asian American Center, Queens College.

Rodríguez, Clara. 1989. *Puerto Ricans: Born in the U. S.* Boston: Unwin Hyman.

Rodríguez, de León Francisco. 1998. *El furioso merengue del norte: una historia de la comunidad dominicana en los Estados Unidos.* New York.

Rosen, Ellen I. 1987. *Bitter Choices: Blue Collar Women in and out of Work.* Chicago: University of Chicago Press.

Sainz, Rudy A. 1990. *Dominican Ethnic Associations: Classification and Service Delivery Roles in Washington Heights.* Ph.D. dissertation. New York: Columbia University.

Sánchez-Korrol, Virginia. 1983. *From Colonia to Community: The History of Puerto Ricans in New York City.* Westport: Greenwood Press.

Sanjek, Roger. 1998. *The Future of Us All: Race and Neighborhood Politics in New York City.* Ithaca: Cornell University Press.

———. 1992. "The Organization of Festivals and Ceremonies among Americans and Immigrants in Queens, New York." In Åke Duan, Billy Ehn, and Barbro Klein, eds. *To Make the World Safe for Diversity: Towards an Understanding of Multi-Cultural Societies.* Stockholm: The Swedish Immigration Institute and Museum and the Ethnology Institute, Stockholm University: 123–43.

———. 1988. *The People of Queens from Now to Then.* Flushing: Asian American Center, Queens College, City University of New York.

Sassen-Koob, Saskia.1979. "Formal and Informal Associations: Dominicans and Colombians in New York City." *International Migration Review*, 13 (2): 314–332.

Sassen, Saskia. 1992. "Why Migration?" *Report on The Americas*, NACLA 26 (1): 14–19.

Schirmer, Jennifer. 1993. "The Seeking of Truth and the Gendering of

Consciousness: The COMADRES of El Salvador and the CONAVIGUA Widows of Guatemala." In Sara Radcliffe and A. Sallie Westwood, eds. *Viva: Women and Popular Protest in Latin America.* New York: Routledge, 30–64.

Smith, Michael P., and Luis E. Guarnizo. 1999. *Transnationalism from Below.* New Brunswick: Transaction Publishers.

Smith, Robert. 1996. "Mexicans in New York: Memberships and Incorporation in a New Immigrant Community." In Gabriel Haslip-Viera and Sherri L. Baver, eds. *Latinos in New York: Communities in Transition.* Notre Dame: University of Notre Dame Press. 57–103.

Stack, Carol B. 1974. *All Our Kin: Strategies of Survival in a Black Community.* New York: Harper & Row Publishers.

Sullivan, Teresa. 1985. "A Demographic Portrait." In Pastora Cafferty and William C. McCraedy, eds. *Hispanics in the United States: A New Social Agenda.* New Brunswick: Transaction Books: 7–32.

Suttles, Gerald D. 1968. *The Social Order of the Slum: Ethnic Territory in the Inner City.* Chicago: University Press of Chicago.

Sutton, Constance R.1987. "The Caribbeanization of New York City and the Emergenceof a Transnational Sociocultural System." In Constance R. Sutton and Elsa M.Chaney, eds. *Caribbean Life in New York City: Sociocultural Dimensions.* New York: Center for Migration Studies of New York. 15–30.

Tabb, William. 1982. *The Long Default: New York City and the Urban Fiscal Crisis.* New York: Monthly Review Press.

Torres, Andrés. 1995. *Between Melting Pot and Mosaic: African Americans and Puerto Ricans in the New York Political Economy.* Philadelphia: Temple University Press.

Torres-Saillant, Silvio, and Ramona Hernández. 1998. *The Dominican Americans.* Westport: Greenwood Press.

Ugalde, Antonio, Frank Bean, and Gilberto Cardenas. 1979. "International Migration from the Dominican Republic: Findings from a National Survey." *International Migration Review,* 13 (2): 235–54.

United States Immigration and Naturalization Service. 1999a. "Statistical Yearbook of the Immigration and Naturalization Service. U.S." Washington, D.C.: Government Printing Office.

———. 1999b. "Annual Report." Washington D.C.: U.S. Government Printing Office.

———. 1995. "Annual Report." Washington D.C.:U.S. Government Printing Office.

Velez-Ibañez, Carlos. 1993. "U.S. Mexicans in the Borderlands: Being Poor without the Underclass." In Joanne Moore and Raquel Pinderhughes, eds. *The Barrios: Latinos and the Underclass Debate.* New York: Russel Sage Foundation.

Walton, John. 1993. *Sociology and Critical Inquiry: The Work, Traditions, and Purpose.* Belmont: Wadsworth Pub. Co.

Wilson, William J. 1990. *The Truly Disadvantaged: The Inner City, the Underclass, and Public Policy.* Chicago: University of Chicago Press.

Whyte, William. 1943. *Street Corner Society.* Chicago: University of Chicago Press.

Yancey, William, Eugene Ericksen, and Richard Juliani. 1976. "Emergent Ethnicity: A Review and Reformulation." *American Sociological Review,* 76: 391–403.

Yang, Philip Q. 1995. *Post-1965 Immigration to the United States: Structural Determinants.* London: Praeger.

Yinger, Milton. 1985. "Ethnicity." *Annual Review of Sociology* 11: 151–180.

Zentella, Ana C. 1997. *Growing Up Bilingual.* Malden: Blackwell Publishers Inc.

Zimmerman, Joseph F. 1992. "Fair Representation for Minorities and Women." In Wilma Rule and Joseph F. Zimmerman, eds. *United States Electoral System: Impact on Women and Minorities.* New York: Greenwood Press: 1–12.

# Index

For Product Safety Concerns and Information please contact our EU
representative  GPSR@taylorandfrancis.com
Taylor & Francis Verlag GmbH, Kaufingerstraße 24, 80331 München, Germany